The Atonement
In Modern Evangelical Thought

The Atonement
In Modern Evangelical Thought

George M. Ella

Go *publications*

Go Publications
Gibb Hill Farm, Ponsonby, Cumbria, CA20 1BX, ENGLAND.

Cover photograph: Helvellyn from Nethermost Pike by David L. Birks

ISBN 978-1-908475-21-3

This book is dedicated to all those who faithfully proclaim the atoning mercies of God to a dead and lost generation. May it help them to set their eyes upon Jesus, the Author and Finisher of their faith, who endured the cross for the joy of reconciling them with God and making them partakers of His Divine nature. May they see the strength of Christ made manifest in their weakness.

Table of Contents

Appendices

Indices

Foreword

In a previous work[1] Dr George Ella referred to John Durie and his view of Systematic Theology as 'the dissecting of the bird into feathers, beak, sinews and bones rather than a contemplation of the whole Bird of Paradise, which would reveal its full beauty and wonder'.[2] The present work is not about the Covenant of Grace, and yet the Covenant plays a significant role. This is because one cannot—or ought not—to treat any one doctrine separately from the whole fabric and display of Holy Scripture. There is no covenant of grace without the atonement, and there can be no atonement without grace covenanted by God and displayed in his eternal and unchangeable word.

The inseparable nature of the one from the other is well illustrated in the work of John Ball (1585–1640), *A Treatise of the Covenant of Grace*. He wrote,

> The Covenant of Grace is either promised or promulgated and established. Promised to the Fathers, first to Adam, and afterwards to the Patriarchs, and lastly to the people of Israel, and that before their coming into the Land of Canaan, and after their returne from the Babylonish captivity. Promulgated, after the fulnesse of time came. And hence the Covenant of Grace is distributed into the Covenant of Promise, or the New Covenant, so called by way of excellency. For the Foundation and Mediatour of the Covenant of Grace is our Lord Jesus Christ, but

---

[1] *The Covenant of Grace and the People of God*, Go Publications, 2019.
[2] Quoted in *The Gospel Magazine*, September–October 2020, p. 146.

either to be incarnate, crucified, and raised from the dead, or as already incarnate, crucified, and truly raised from the dead, and ascended into Heaven. For there was never sin forgiven but in him alone, who is *the same yesterday, and to day, and for ever.* Therefore although before the Incarnation, Christ was only God, he was our Mediatour, yet not simply as God, but as the divine person, who should take our flesh, and in it should finish all the Mysterie of our Redemption, and therefore he is called the Lambe of God slaine from the beginning of the world, and the Fathers by his grace were saved, even as we. In the acts of Mediation three things may be considered. Reconciliation, by which we are accepted of God. Patronage, by which we have accesse unto the Father. Doctrine, whereby God hath made himself known unto men by a Mediatour. This third act might be done before he assumed our flesh, and indeed was done: but the two first did require his coming in the flesh, although the fruit of them was communicated to the Fathers under the Old Testament, by the force of the divine Promise, and certainty of the thing to come with God.[3]

Ball, among a number of other writers, saw the centrality of the Atonement, and placed it in its rightful place. The Atonement is an event in history, to which the whole of divine revelation ran before the event, and from which the subsequent revelation flows.

The whole history of divine revelation ran towards the Atonement as an historical event. From the moment of Adam's sin the grace, mercy and love of God towards his creation moved the revelation of salvation through the seed of the woman. I do not say that it moved the creation of the covenant of grace, for that was in existence already. But the moment of sin was the moment at which the covenant, with the central act of the Atonement, was made known. That revelation gave the hope of redemption to Adam as the federal head of the human race. His disobedience brought the creation under the curse. Hope would have been lost for ever had not the Lord God, in his infinite love, mercy, grace and faithfulness, shown that he had already prepared the sacrifice for sin. The seed of the woman should shed his blood to save sinners.

---

[3] *A Treatise of the Covenant of Grace*, John Ball. London, 1645, p. 27 ff.

As we read on in the Old Testament we see how this hope, where had, strengthened faith in those who believed the promise. The testimony of Scripture to the faith of Enoch and Lamech only makes sense within this framework, for otherwise we may be tempted to think that Enoch, for instance, was translated because his works justified him: they did not, but his faith in the promise—and in the God who promises—worked itself out in obedience and love, and it was for this that he was translated. The life of Abraham is well known, and his role as the father of the faithful (Romans 4 and Galatians 3) is the paradigm through which we understand our connection to the covenant, although we are not Israel after the flesh.

The problem, for many, comes with the giving of the law. We have a tendency to fall into either of two errors. On the one hand, the law seems to be an aberration, unconnected to the covenant of grace. It can appear to us that the Israelites were lifted out of the covenant, and placed into a covenant of works. The reason for this can be hard to fathom, unless we misunderstand Paul's teaching in Galatians 3:24 ff. and assume that Israel was relegated to a lesser place in the outworking of redemption—a conclusion that is so far from Scripture as to be utterly untenable. On the other hand, the passing of the law can seem to be an aberration, and the gospel can be viewed as only being comprehensible when set within a law context. Thus man is still required to observe rites and ceremonies, and to endure special regulations regarding diet and clothing, and so on, in order to obtain the reward of eternal life. Had there been no law, one might be tempted to think, the course of revelation in the matter of redemption would have been unambiguous. If so, why did Christ come in the flesh?

And yet, in the wisdom of God, the law was given. It was given to Israel through Moses. Disobedience, in many cases, resulted in the death of the law breaker. The law was a serious matter, and the burden it laid on the faithful was heavy indeed. Yet we find David continually rejoicing in the law, and delighting in God's precepts, testimonies, commandments and statutes, as Psalm 119 affirms over and over again. Why is this? Because in the law of the Lord David discovered Christ. David knew he was to be the father of the promised seed, as the covenant recorded in 2 Samuel 7 shows. But what manner of promised seed would come from David? A king, whose reign would be eternal, and whose dynasty would be without end. Unlike every other king, this one would be punished for his offences and yet not lose his kingdom. David knew from his own experience that he was responsible for certain national sins, as the judgment of God on Israel when David numbered the people shows (2 Samuel 24). David suffered the rebellion of his son Absalom, and the consequent shame brought on the nation by his having to flee. Examples could be multiplied, showing that David, more than any other king in Israel or Judah, represented the nation before the Lord. He was their type in many things, and his sufferings were all for the sake of the people.

In the generations that came after David the same hope is evident. It is found in the words of the prophets, from Elijah to Malachi. Yes, the prophets all called the nation and her kings back to the law, and to the standard of holiness required by the Lord. But they also pointed forward to the day of grace, in which atonement would be made for sin. Zechariah's visions, and his description of the temple, speak to this truth. The final words of the Old Testament are a dire curse unless they are read in the context of the work of salvation. That work is of course fully revealed in the New Testament, beginning with the announcement of the Incarnation. The life and ministry of our blessed Saviour Jesus Christ prepare us for the cross, and for that gracious and promised Atonement. Of course, if the giving of the law had been capable of giving life to any, then why was it necessary that Jesus Christ should come into the world, and suffer for our sins? A right reading of the Sermon on the Mount, paying attention to the similarities with the giving of the law on Sinai as well as the differences in the way Christ addresses those who are blessed in receiving his word aright, helps us to see why Christ must come. Given that we cannot hope to find life through the law we are cast back on the promise made in Eden, concerning the seed of the woman. Given that the faithful never lost sight of that promise, it comes as no surprise that the fulfilment of the promise is the hope of sinners. Christ died for the ungodly. This is our ground of rejoicing. The whole course of divine revelation has been leading up to this point, and we cannot comprehend aright the purpose of God in any part of history unless we have our eyes fixed on coming Atonement.

And what of those things that proceed from the Atonement? The whole ministry of the apostles, and the history of the Church, is the consequence of the Atonement. Take away the cross, and what have the apostles left to preach? Who is Christ to us, unless he is first and foremost the Lamb of God, which taketh away the sins of the world? Where is the good news of a crucified Christ, unless he is also risen, ascended and glorified? And if the crucified Christ is even now at the right hand of the Father, does this not show that all our hope of happiness is centred on him? To what end is he in heaven, unless it is to reign over his people, and to be their Keeper and Redeemer, as well as Judge and Advocate? And how can any have hope in a crucified Saviour unless he has made atonement for their sins? What gospel have we to preach unless we can say that there is a fountain opened in the house of David, a place where sin is washed away, and where all our spiritual diseases are healed?

The reader who has followed me this far may be asking, what has this to do with modern evangelical thought? Why has Dr Ella written about the Atonement in such a context? The answer is that, while all Evangelicals, and all the Reformed, confess the centrality of the Atonement, not all have always a full theology of it. The *fact* of the atonement is freely and rightly acknowledged: the *effects and consequences* are not always given their place. The Atonement must be set within the whole context and framework of the divine revelation of redemption. This can only be done when the Covenant of Grace is rightly understood, and its implications rightly applied to the whole of our theology. The views examined and critiqued in this book by its author are not those of heretics or fools, but are for the most part of men who have not always retained the doctrine in its rightful setting within a whole theology. The absence of that whole theology goes a long way to explain many of the controversies that have arisen over the centuries. The separation of theology into systematic themes serves a purpose for the scholar, but tends to lead to a distorted theology which reflects the particular interest of the student. The only safeguard against such distortion is to be able to set our theology in a proper frame, and the only proper frame is Scripture. And if we would know the shape of that frame, look to the Covenant of Grace. See Christ, and him crucified, within that frame, and the word of God will speak afresh. Look to the blood of Christ as it was promised from the beginning, and the grace, mercy, faithfulness and love of God will fill your heart and mind with joy and understanding. See the Atonement in the context of the whole of Scripture, and many theological conundrums will be solved. The Arminian's elevation of free will, the Universalist's attempt to apply the Atonement to all will fade and fall, and the confusion of the Amyraldian will be cleared. The attempts at works-righteousness, and trust in rites and ceremonies, will both be replaced by the grace of God with trust in the shed blood of Christ. And the more we see our dependence on Christ and him crucified, the greater and deeper our love for him will be. May this be the fruit found in all who read this book, that love to Christ may increase in all of us, as we give thanks for his wonderful love and condescending grace towards lost sinners who are the special objects of that saving work.

Edward Malcolm
Presiding Bishop,
The Church of England (Continuing)

Chapter 1

Neo-Evangelicalism and the Atonement

Theological fashions harmful to the gospel
There have always been those professing to be Christians who yet have developed their theories of the Word of God according to the general rules, philosophies and fashions of their contemporaries. They understood their Christian culture as adapting the Scriptures to the needs of the time or to the 'contextualisation' of their day and age. Now Bible translators tell us how vital it is to translate God's Word 'cross-culturally' and even campaign for 'inter-faith' translations. Philosophers are often more honest than theologians and call these theories 'moving with the Zeitgeist'.[1] We cannot call them 'moving with the times' as time seems to have stood still in the Liberal and Rational camps. There is nothing new under the sun in those quarters. The Christian Gospel as Moses, David, Isaiah, Jeremiah, the Lesser Prophets and our New Testament authors teach it through the Holy Spirit is 'ever fresh'. This Biblical sense of being 'ever fresh' is what the term 'new' conveys in God's 'New Covenant' which has been there for all time.

---

[1] Zeitgeist = The spirit of the age.

Looking back, we see the wheel of fallen human fantasy turning round and round, introducing the follies of a Godless religion from generation to generation. One age choses to challenge the Sonship of Christ as in the days of J. C. Philpot (1802-1869).[2] Another generation comes round with the idea of giving us an Arian Bible.[3] Another generation strives for a 'politically correct' Bible. There have been generations producing Presbyterian, Arminian or Baptist Bibles as also a number of ages which presented and still present us with supposed Pentecostal pneumatological translations where the Godhead is reduced to a spiritual agency only and the Personalities of the Father and the Son are faded off. People are constantly coming up with 'ecumenical' Bibles which seemingly include everything but the kitchen sink!

Spiritualising the Scriptures
The 'Pentecostal' view of the Scriptures seems to be very strong today, especially in Asia and South America. On studying the development of the Serampore College in India from its founding as Denmark's third university after Copenhagen and Kiel with the cooperation of the Danish King, William Carey and the Marshman family, it appears that 'Pneumatology' now ranks high on their curriculum. Unlike some modern interpretations of the Newbigin Commission of 1969-70 concerning the Serampore College, the college was actually founded for secular studies amongst students from all religious bodies. It was not intended as a training college for native Christians to prepare them for evangelistic activities.[4] Reading the latest publications of today's Serampore staff members on The Pneumatological Theology of Religions one fears the worse for the spreading of the true gospel in such a secular framework. Arguing that theocentric and Christocentric Bible interpretations have failed, we are told we must interpret the Bible in a pneumatological sense which includes being enriched by the teaching of the Spirit in other religions. As a theological student of 'Comparative Religion' for very many years and one who has taught

[2] See the Earthen Vessel controversy of 1860 when the newspaper challenged the Eternal Sonship of Christ. J.C. Philpot defended the doctrine in the Gospel Standard Magazine.
[3] See Ram Mohan Roy's and William Adam's translation work.
[4] See Brian Stanley's article 'The Vision of a Christian Higher Education for India: 200 Years of Serampore College History' BQ, No. 1, Vol. 51, Jan. 2020. Obviously the writer had not looked beyond the Newbigin Report or considered the true history of the Serampore College.

the subject for almost as many, I have found no Holy Spirit outside of the Christian Bible but I am judged old-fashioned and biased. Much is made of Clark Pinnock's Inter Varsity Press work *Flame of Love: A Theology of the Holy Spirit* which was chosen as Christianity Today's Book of the Year, 1997 and much is done to bring Roman Catholic Karl Rahner into this 'spiritual' fold but I find references to Rahner more hearsay than factual. Otherwise most of the writing on the subject seems to be done by Asians trained by dubious Western missionaries. However, if we cut the Father and the Son out of our Christian faith and look for the 'spiritual' in a Father and Son-less 'Theology of Religions' we have a hard task ahead.

Demythologising one's own myths
From the Marcionites of old to the New Covenant Theology (NCT) of today there have been cut-up and pasted Bible versions which cannot be beaten for their ignorance of the true Biblical faith which Christ gives freely to those who trust in Him. Since earliest times thinkers such as Rudolf Bultmann of Marburg (1884-1976) have come up with the idea of demythologising the Scriptures according to their own myopic view and restricted thinking. In order to 'demythologise' the Scriptures, Bultmann first read into the Bible 'myths and legends' and then 'demythologised' them out. Nevertheless, Bultmann had a large fan club in his day. This writer was thus happy to find through his doctoral studies at Marburg, Bultmann's old university, that the only trace left of Bultmann there was a bust in the Quad donated by some Norwegian ex-students. This is rather looked upon as a mischievous students' prank.

A Bible for Feminists
'Gender Theology' which plagued Commonwealth times has now hit back at us. In our home church in Germany, we had a once most Bible-loving pastor who, at the last Bible study, told us that in view of politically active women we must reconsider and even re-write the Bible for the use of 'modern people'. On my desk, I have a new translation of the Old and New Testaments in 'equitable language'. There are some very accurate translations in this work but it is terribly

17

spoilt by so-called 'gender theology' and 'macho feminism'. Even many 'evangelical' churches today in this country are 'manned' by ministers who address all their flock as though all were 'women', using new feministic endings for formerly 'neutral' nouns. Sadly, the language I have loved so much since my early teens, Swedish, has become riddled with feministic grammar and an acute dumbing down of the language. Just the other day I was sent a tract by post inviting me to believe in Jesus. I read it eagerly but to my dismay, I soon found it referred to a Bible inspired by a female angel called Gabrielle who had de-masculinised and dehumanised all that was in the real Bible. The writers were obviously influenced by the Muslim story of Gabriel and the Koran but had turned the Angel into a female gender-carrier. Anyway, as far as I understand the real Bible, angels are genderless but Zoroastrianism has female angels such as Anaita. I believe if we stick to the real Bible we shall not go wrong on human relationships.

Attempts to separate the theological from the historical
Alleged evangelicals are telling us nowadays that we need translations which distinguish between the historical background of the Bible and the modern theological interpretation which relieves Christianity from its historical basis. It is surprising how many evangelicals nowadays believe in a most unscientific form of evolution, each book which I read on this subject contradicts the assumed dates of the other as they make the world's age now older now younger in order to fit in their theories. They remind me of the Dispensationalists with all their contradictory dating of the future of which we do not know more than the ancient past. What we do not know allows for much speculation which one can hardly call 'scientific', 'academic' or 'scholarly'. We humans tend to forget that our faith is built on facts and not fallen man's fancies. 'If Christ is not risen, then is our preaching vain and your faith is also vain'[5] needs to be preached more than ever today. History and the gospel stand together and it is as senseless to try and re-write history as it is to re-write the gospel. Our faith stands on a theological and historical fact. I was reading Darwin's *The Decent of Man* and his *Origin of the Species* at the age of ten and gave an illustrated lecture on these works as an elementary school project. It thus amuses me when

---

[5] 1 Corinthians 15:14.

modern pseudo-academics tell me that Darwin was right when modern scientists have altered so much of his teaching since those years in the late forties. Now we are told there are no races and no species, the two terms being foreign to modern social and political thinking. However, social politics and lack of knowledge of the God-Only-Wise have always been behind evolutionary ideas of a 'superior being' whether animal, vegetable, mineral or divine. As ancient Heraclitus is thought to have said, 'Everything is in a state of flux', but nobody seems to wonder in what direction this flux is flowing. I find Darwin's ideas amongst the ancients which prove to me that the flux sadly means 'ever learning and never able to come to the knowledge of the truth'[6]. Our wise Bible, however, tells us to fix our gaze on the 'love of Christ which passeth all knowledge, that we might be filled with the fulness of God'[7]. We Christian educators have this as our goal.

Faulty understanding of God's one will
Equally erroneous is the modern trend deep within alleged evangelical 'Reformed' circles to attribute three separate and contradicting wills to the Godhead. This hardly believable stance is presently claimed to be orthodox, evangelical and Reformed teaching, though it is completely foreign to God's Word. We see in this dumbing down of God's Word how one age looked to the verbatim Word of Scripture as their vade-mecum or handbook of life and yet another used it as a book of aphorisms for general guidance. In one age it was fashionable to be social-minded in theology, presenting us with a 'Social Gospel' void of Biblical doctrine but yet another age chose to be ascetic and turn its back on the world with all its responsibilities, and hide in a cloister. As one Christian wit said, it is no use being good if you are good for nothing! Happily such voluntary prisons are dying out for both men and women but our minds are being imprisoned by modern 'Reformed' preachers. God's 'will' is now reduced by our 'Reformed teachers' to God's indefinite 'wish' in salvation as will be discussed in the Appendices to this book.

---

[6] 2 Timothy 3:7.
[7] Ephesians 3:19.

The permanency of God's grace-bringing law challenged

Throughout the ages from the time of Marcion (c.85-c.160),[8] God's Law has been challenged by some as God's revelation of His own eternal character, and denied by others as being everlasting as Himself. Yet others such as Andrew Fuller (1754-1815)[9] and the modern so-called New Covenant theologians see that same revealed law as arbitrary and temporary and subordinate to what they call 'Natural Law'. They forget we only know God through His gracious revelation and the only 'Natural Law' we had fell with Adam when sin marred all.

Liberal Tillich's ideas have now become 'evangelical'

Now at the core of evangelical and Reformed thinking there are those who claim Christianity is a religion of imagery, symbolism and the figurative so that evangelicals have joined hands with the old Liberals such as Paul Tillich, who always looked for the symbol behind the symbol thus ever learning but never coming to know the 'God above God' or the 'Christ behind Christ' for whom he searched.

The influence of Babel Christianity on world missions

As hinted above, when one studies closely the history of Christian Missions in countries such as India, Africa and South America, one finds that the 'evangelised' were often taught by misguided missionaries to accept all the Babel-like diversions mentioned above as balanced Biblical Christianity, so hindering the spread of the gospel. The full Deity of Christ was severely challenged in the early nineteenth century in India as Arianism and Socinianism arose through the misguided teaching of such as Ram Mohan Roy (1772-1833), theological contributor to a Baptist Mission newspaper, in association with William Adam (1796-1881) of the Baptist Missionary Society trained at the Baptist Bristol College and John Nicol Farquhar (1861-1929)[10] of the London Missionary Society and was spread throughout

---

[8] Marcion taught that the God of the New Testament was different to the God of the Old. He also propagated the discontinuity of the New with the Old as taught by modern Dispensationalists and so-called NCT followers. Marcion was condemned as a heretic in 144. Modern Liberalism allows them to pollute the churches anew.

[9] See Fuller's teaching on Moral Law, Positive Law, Revealed Law and Natural Law in his *Works*, Banner of Truth, 2001 with its Introduction by Michael A. G. Haykin. See also my *Law and Gospel in the Theology of Andrew Fuller*, 2nd edition, 2011.

[10] Farquhar sought to popularise the so-called 'Fulfilment Theology' of his age.

India eventually merging Arian Christianity with Hinduism. Baptist Adam and 'over-denominational' Roy founded the Calcutta Unitarian Society. Carey called the work of his co-Baptist missionary 'the second fall of Adam' but even Carey merged much of his translation with Hindu thought causing the Hindus to claim that Christ was a good Hindu!

Political Churchmanship
Then there was the idea of Christianity according to the colonial principles of the British raj as propagated by Joshua Marshman (1768-1837) in his political manifesto *The Advantage of Christianity in Promoting the Establishment and Prosperity of the British Empire in India* published in Calcutta in 1813. This work, backed by absentee bishop Fuller, made the Indians highly suspicious of foreign missionary influence and almost put an end to Western missionary liberty under British, French and Portuguese control. This suspicion was also fostered by some most dubious Scripture translations of 19th century missionaries who mixed their translations with terms and expressions culled from other religions. All these philosophico-political break-offs and break-ups from the true Vine with their multi-cultist flair, as always, challenge the fundamentals of Biblical Atonement Theology. We do not gain anything with a gospel that uses Hindu or Muslim names for the Trinity. To many Asian Christians Christ has become a mere guru or avatar. However, all these features of Babel are also present in today's Neo-Evangelical churches. Modern Evangelicals seem hell-bent on outdoing the old Liberals.

A myopic focus on Christ's Atonement
Now many modern Christians are claiming we must focus our gaze on the very centre of our faith and salvation which is the work of the Lord Jesus Christ on the cross, otherwise known as the Atonement. This sounds like sound advice until one realises how numerous are the various interpretations of what the Atonement signifies presented by our Christian authors and church leaders and how great is the lack of consensus amongst them.

Each has established a favourite word for the work of Christ on the cross such as 'expiation', 'covering', 'propitiation', 'reconciliation', 'redemption', 'ransom', 'cleansing from sin' and a 'sacrifice', and each term has produced a different understanding of what Christ did for the sinner. In God's covenant of grace with His Son there is only one Atonement and that is the only way into the divine covenant for us.

Few works on the Atonement present a united Biblical concept
Having read theological and devotional works on the subject of the Atonement since the late fifties, I have come across a host of authors, evangelical and otherwise, who appear to have done their level best to complicate the Biblical story of the Atonement for ordinary readers of the Scriptures by analysing the Atonement into parts which they have then turned into 'wholes' for further analysis. It does not matter whether we read a Denney, a Headlam, a Dale, a Dalzell, a Dillistone, a Pink, a Ryder Smith, a Smeaton, a Morris, a Murray, an Owen, a Packer, a Piper, a Stott, a Hodge, a Warfield or a Remensnyder,[11] to limit our reading to those who write in English, we are left with the feeling that only the half has been told and much has been told which was far better unsaid. So, too, little synergising is attempted though the gospel is a united whole and not merely a sum of favourite parts.

I have thus grown weary of these 'analytical' and 'systematic' works on the Atonement which purport to examine first 'Paul's doctrine' then the 'Synoptic doctrine', then 'Luke's doctrine', then that of the Book of Hebrews as if our one Bible describes different views which are up for choice so that we might pick out either the one or the other which we think best provides our individual needs. They merely strive to rend the robe of Christ in their ignorance of how Christ rent the temple curtain. Our view of the Atonement determines our view of the Church.

Heresy has become orthodoxy
The consequence of this splitting up of the one Christian gospel of the Atonement into different 'theories' of interpretations of the gospel has led to bad theology, wrong ecclesiology, and misleading eschatology being taught in our denominations and churches. So, too, they break up the solid, singular unity of God's covenant with Christ on behalf of

---

[11] Part of my reading before writing this book.

man. This has made a united witness by Christians to those in need of an Atonement impossible as the maze of denominational offshoots preach separate gospels. All are like the curate's egg which is good in parts but stinks in others. I had often misunderstood the teaching of 1 Peter 4:18 'And if the righteous scarcely be saved, where shall the ungodly and the sinner appear?' Now I understand how this is the mark of modern times.

Contrary views of the Atonement prevent gospel evangelism

After studying the evangelisation of India from the first century to our time, I have seen how it was the different views of the Atonement leading to different views of the Lord's people which broke the back of the united Protestant missionary movement in the early nineteenth century from which it has not yet recovered. Seventeenth and eighteenth century missionary evangelism knew better. This different understanding of the very ground of Christianity led to different Bible translations of the Indian languages which caused further rifts. Nowadays, there is a Bible-Babel in India, Pakistan and Bangladesh because of supposed translations which mix up the Christian with Hindu, Arian and Muslim features. These religions are a challenge enough without our mixing our religion with theirs. We do not preach 'faiths' but faith in the Atonement of Christ which faith none of the other 'faiths' have. I have recently received an academic paper from Serampore College extolling inter-faith translations. Is this our Western dowry for India?

In Chapter 2, it will be shown how various more or less influential figures in history have challenged the Biblical doctrine of the Atonement and how their erroneous views are having repercussions in modern Neo-evangelical preaching today. It is vital for the well-being of our faith that we know the enemy and the truths that put him to flight. After sweeping away the cobwebs and cleaning out the stables, I can then go on to examine the unified and synergised Biblical doctrine of the Atonement.

Chapter 2

Answers to the 'Modern Question'

A theoretical Atonement

Today such rifts between the brethren are growing deeper as modern highly influential Neo-evangelicals maintain that he alone preaches the atoning blood of Christ who teaches it as a mere provision of God which gains its efficacy through reception. In other words, God's provision in the Atonement does not secure salvation but it is the appropriation of it by the human agent which renders it effective. This idea arose and was fortified in the United States and Britain by enthusiasts who wished for a new Christianity based on natural reason and natural law and was propagated by most of the former evangelical denominations. It appears to have started in English Latitudinarianism, moved over to Congregationalism, then to North American Presbyterian New Divinity and then back to England nesting in those rebel Baptists who were interested in adopting a more Arian theology in rebellion against such balanced pioneer Baptists as Jessey, Bunyan, Ryland Sen., Gill and Brine. They called it the 'Modern Question' then but its ideas were as old-fashioned as the beginning of time when Adam was led by Satan to feel he could be his own saviour.

Error becomes orthodox

Proponents of this pseudo-evangelism and their theories will be dealt with throughout this book and their errors compared with the gospel of the Atonement found in the Scriptures from Genesis to Revelation. The tragic situation has arisen in which those who were once rightly considered heretics in the churches are now usurping the mantel of orthodoxy and proclaiming that holders of traditional views of the Atonement are Hyper-Calvinists and Antinomians and thus criminals in God's eyes and unworthy of being given the right hand of fellowship. It is thus of the utmost importance that we consider this fundamental doctrine of our faith, the Atonement, in order to see if our feet really stand on the Rock of Ages who is faith's only safe and sure foundation. In my youth we were pestered with the fantasies of the Three Bs, alias Brunner, Barth and Bultmann but now the rot is within evangelicalism and so-called Reformed Churches.

Cleaning up error first
It was John Gill's practice to refute error before he began to expound the truth to avoid misunderstanding and he has thus been criticised by many, even Spurgeon, for dwelling so long on what needs to be rejected. However, this was the way our fathers in the faith dealt wisely with heresy. Wrong thinking must be rejected before a better way can be understood. We must thus examine the many perversions of the general understanding of the Atonement within evangelical theology before examining the Biblical evidence showing how the fundamental act of the Atonement secures for the elect a total blotting out of their sins and a total covering with Christ's righteousness which is secured for them in Christ who was chosen from eternity to unite them with Himself through His ransoming, vicarious suffering, obedience, death and resurrection. This is the faith once delivered to the saints according to the wisdom of God, which is sadly proclaimed to be foolishness by those who are wise in their own esteem. We shall see how a rational, moral and political religion has striven to force out all that is Biblical, theological and historical.

Abelard's alternative atonement of moral achievement
Although there has been nothing under the sun in new heresies since Satan's rebellion and man first wished to become as the gods, the main break away from the Biblical doctrine of the Atonement was made by Pierre de Palais (1079-1142) better-known by his assumed name, Abelard. He maintained that the doctrine was immoral. Not too saintly

to father the child of the woman he refused to marry, Abelard told the world that God could not have been so immoral as to plan the death of His Son as the grounds for His forgiving sin. God is love, Abelard maintained, and demands no satisfaction to help Him forgive penitent sinners. Christ's aim, he believed vainly, was to assert a sound moral influence on man, proving divine love by assuming our nature and living an exemplary life even to the point of death. It is a contemplation of this great love that awakens love in our heart and it is this love given back to God which is the basis for forgiveness of sins. As a result of this act, the saint can live freely in obedience to God, motivated by the love in his heart. He forgot that sinful man is at enmity with God and cannot conjure up love for God in his heart.

As an enquirer in my teens, I was fascinated by the teaching of following Christ via Moral Encouragement, walking in Christ's footsteps behind Him and striving to love the Son as did the Father. This 'sweet nonsense' soon left me. I realised as I entered into my conversion experience that Christ's footsteps were far, far too big for me and though I longed for God, I had no personal faith to love Him. Through good pastoral care and a growing interest in New Testament Greek, I found that followers of Christ were those with whom Christ walked and not those who were Christ-imitators. An examination of the Greek text when I sat soon after my conversion at the feet of Henry Oakley, then at the London Bible College, showed me that the texts involved spoke of going with Christ and not going after Christ. That made all the difference to my young theology and Christian hope.

True religion dropped for a moral philosophy
Abelard brought into theology an entire new picture of God, a God who is so lost in His attributes, that His Personality disappears and He becomes a mere moral philosophy. This is one of the major reasons why I am so suspicious of so-called systematic theologies. They usually deal with the attributes of God as seen by this and that theologian and thus never find the whole and wholesome God. They deal with lop-sided part-truths concerning God's Character.

Abelard's god is a god so motivated by love that he pays neither attention to his own justice nor his own holiness and completely fails to answer the question posed by Anselm, 'Why did God become man?'[1] Rather than it being a cruel thing for God to reconcile sinners to Himself through the vicarious, voluntary death of Christ, Abelard's theory of a God who allows His Son to suffer and die the death of a criminal when he could have morally influenced the sinner in a thousand other, safer, ways, seems cruel indeed. Abelard, too, must have had a very imperfect view of the grip sin has on man if he thought that an example alone, no matter how good, might cause and enable him to live a life pleasing to God.

The Socinians follow suit
The followers of Faustus Socinus (1539-1604), were delighted with the views of Abelard which helped support their own brand of heresy. They too, had no real teaching of the Trinity, believing that the Holy Spirit was a mere divine influence and that Christ was a man born in time. They, as Abelard, denied outright the need for justice in God's dealing with sin. In their view, God is not limited in His forgiveness of sins by the need to do it for the sake of Christ who bore them. He forgives freely, His love and mercy alone determining who is to be forgiven. This display of love and mercy is granted to all who repent and obey. This example is given by Christ who shows us how to obey. The Socinians do not seem to have been in need of an example of how to repent. There is, therefore, no direct link between the death of Christ and redemption, indeed, redemption in the sense of ransom is rejected by the Socinians just as fervently as by Abelard.

However, the Socinians did connect salvation in some way with Christ's death as they taught that after the Lord Jesus Christ died, God raised Him from the dead and gave Him the power to grant eternal life to those who accepted and followed His example. Socinianism has affected all our churches yet it is rarely viewed as the insidious inner-denominational problem it still is but is always examined as a theory afar off.

---

[1] The title of *Cur deus homo* is often translated 'Why the God-Man?' but this does not tally with the internal testimony of the work. See Chapter 1 entitled *The Question on Which the Whole Work Depends*. At the commencement of Chapter 2, Boso poses the question, 'By what necessity and for what reason hath God, being omnipotent, assumed, in order to its restoration, the humiliations and weakness of human nature'.

The atonement as a political, governmental hypothesis

As both Abelard and Socinus had been declared heretics by various church councils, those in public office thought it prudent to declare their opposition to their teaching, however they might sympathise with it. One Dutch dignitary and statesman who protested in this way was Hugo Grotius. This highly gifted man was born on 10th April, 1583 and became a pupil of Johannes Uytenbogaert (1557-1644) the Remonstrant leader and friend of Jacobus Arminius (1560-1609). Viewed by all who encountered him as a child genius, he was sent to Leyden University at the age of 12 and made rapid progress, reaping all the academic honours available.

By the time he was 14, he was known as the 'Boy without an equal' and it is said that his professors were ashamed to debate with him as his knowledge was far superior to theirs. By the time he was 20, he was looked upon as one of the leading intellects of the Dutch Provinces and was entrusted with writing the official history of the Dutch struggles with Spain besides being given high government posts, representing the Dutch in international diplomacy as, for instance, in the fishery disputes with the British.

The doctrine of grace forbidden in church preaching

Grotius, alongside Johan van Oldenbarnevelt (1547-1619), strove to put into politics the Five Points of the Remonstrants (or Arminians) drawn up by Uytenbogaert and forty-six other ministers in 1610, a year after Arminius' death. Grotius' power was so great that in 1614 he influenced the Dutch Provinces in passing a bill forbidding any exegesis of the doctrines of grace from the pulpit, a move which pleased neither Reformed believers nor Arminians. Grotius' policy became to seek peace by using political power to ban controversy. It was a most ineffectual way of exercising political reason. Inevitably, there was a tremendous outcry from both the Reformed and Arminian camps and soon the religious and political tables were turned drastically against Grotius' party. Oldenbarnevelt was put to death as a traitor and Grotius was imprisoned for life.

A dramatic escape

Grotius' escape, after being in prison for two years, was as dramatic as his whole life. Grotius' wife received permission to provide her imprisoned husband with a trunk of books. The trunk was duly carried into Grotius' cell, emptied of its contents and returned to Mrs Grotius' quarters. Little did the guards know that on the return journey Grotius was tucked up safely inside the trunk. Grotius then fled his country, never more to be accepted by its governing bodies. He had, however, obtained a name for himself abroad as a great statesman and it was not long before the Swedish powers chose him as their Ambassador to the Court of France, an office he carried out for a period of ten years. Grotius died at Rostock in 1645 whilst on his way to Stockholm to hand in his resignation.

Theological error popularised through pop songs and shanties

Grotius views, which were to challenge the work of the 18th century revivals, were first published in a popular verse form and were eagerly taken up by the people and became the favourite shanties of many a ship's crew. They became the pop songs of the age. These ditties were then worked out into a more academic form by Grotius in 1627 and were published in Latin rather than the mother tongue and appeared under the presumptuous title *de Veritate Religionis Christianae* (*The True Christian Religion*). The most marked feature of the work is not a trust in the revealed religion of the Bible but in the validity and demonstrability of natural reason and the supremacy of Christian ethics as understood merely by the human mind. As a reading of my book *The Covenant of Grace and the People of God*[2] will show in detail, this so-called Enlightenment view became also current in contemporary England where Grotius gained much lasting influence. The three main thrusts of Grotius' argument were the high ideals of the Christian religion, the excellence of its rules of duty and the pre-eminence of Christ seen in His demonstrated ability to work miracles. The doctrines of the Trinity and the Atonement, are entirely absent from this work. They are superseded by the emphasis on the reasonableness of living the Christian life according to Christ's teaching. Where such reason

---

[2] Go Publications, 2019.

apparently triumphs in man, there is no need of an Atonement. The very idea rejects the Biblical doctrines of both God and man.

Atonement by token

Grotius' political theory of the Atonement is taken up in his *Defensio Fidei Catholicae de Satisfactione Christi* in which he strives to distance himself from Socinianism. His view of Christ's substitutionary, propitiating death is, however, far nearer the Socinian view than the Biblical doctrine of redemption in Christ. He rejects, as did the Socinians, any idea that Christ could take over the debts of another and provide payment for them in suffering as a ransom to settle the debtor's account regarding the broken law. God, he argues, is not to be viewed as a creditor but as an administrator, rector or benign governor. This divine administrator admittedly rules by laws but these laws are mere guides to right living and not absolute chains. As God does not demand that the law be obeyed in every particular, there is no need for a full satisfaction as if He did. Sin is always viewed by Grotians in a non-theological way as that which is contrary to 'the nature and fitness of things'. The Grotian idea of punishment need not fit the crime as God's statute book is not absolute, laws and punishments being entirely at his benevolent discretion.

Christ as a Probation Officer

Rather than view Christ as the One who bore our exact penalty for breaking an absolute law, Grotius sees Him as a Probation Officer who gives God an opportunity of displaying benevolence to His Adam-like probationers. Christ's defence on behalf of the probationers is not what He has done to settle the score for them in the vicarious penal and judicial sense of ransom and remission. It is a plea for a removal of man's obligations through God's benevolent discretion. God, on His part, does not demand that the whole law, spirit and letter, be kept in any way by anyone but especially not His Son. He simply requires that some symbolic act or token should be performed in order to demonstrate that man's obligations have been cancelled. This token demonstration is claimed by Grotius as being a true satisfaction. He sees no point in Christ's putting Himself under the Law on our behalf, thus both fulfilling and establishing the law. Indeed, he lifts the entire doctrine of the Atonement out of its spiritual, theological and historical background and places it in the airy-fairy world of moral philosophy and governmental speculation, shunning the revealed Word. Grotius can thus sum up the Atonement by saying, 'There is no unconditional absolute; there is no payment of the exact debt; there is no substitution of a new obligation; but there is a remission in consequence of a precedent satisfaction'. This satisfaction was merely a nominal or token one, in Grotius' view, though he is quick to add that there was no inherent necessity for God to supply this, but He thought it was the best way to make sure His administration was shown to be unquestionable. The main thrust of Grotius' theology is, however, that remission of sin comes via relaxing the law. Thus Christ's death was in no way retributive but, in accordance with Socinianism, merely exemplary.

Christ's death seen as a mere moral deterrent
Throughout all this teaching, which is claimed to be a metaphor explaining the common sense of Natural Law, the Persons of the Godhead, especially those of the Lord Jesus Christ and the Holy Spirit are almost phased out. The role of Christ as in Socinianism, is reduced to that of a hero who is prepared to suffer in order to act as a deterrent for others so that they might shun evil. The truth expressed by the words of the well-known hymn, 'There was no other good enough to pay the price of sin', is entirely absent from Grotian thinking. Jesus, in Grotius' eyes, was merely a person of incomparable dignity who was used as a symbolic means of demonstrating God's displeasure (the nearest the Governmentalists come to speaking of the wrath of God) and a moral deterrent and a demonstration of God's benevolence to man. In no way do we see Christ as providing a full and perfect compensation for man's wrongs as a result of his fallen nature. Though emphasising Christ's death as a moral deterrent against man's future sins and an establishment of God's administration of the world as a result of Christ's example, there is no back-working in Grotius' theory and one wonders what happened to the world's sinners before Christ's deterrent death and how did God administer His rule of benevolence then?

Though Grotius constantly speaks of man's reason and logical powers, there is no reason or logic whatsoever in his Governmental politico-theology. The whole system is a mere dupe to frighten man off from doing wrong and to convince him that his sins do not really cut him off from God; they do not really need to be atoned for by a redemptive act which removes the deadly penalties under which he is eternally damned. Grotius' Christ never reaches even the dignity of the Socinian hero. He pictures Christ as performing an act to save sinners which was merely arbitrary and in no way compelling. Worse still, Christ is actually lowered to God's dupe as He suffered untold agonies where there was no judicial or redemptive necessity to do so.

An attempt to popularise religion through dumbing it down
In presenting his view of salvation, Grotius' major mistake was in believing he could make religion popular by drawing it into the realms of political and philosophic thought, redefining the theological terms of the Bible and traditional theology to make them appeal to natural reason. Even here, Grotius failed as his vocabulary, apart from his seamen's yarns and pop songs, is more reminiscent of the ancient Greeks than the language of the party he sided with in his time as Advocate General of the Dutch Provinces. For a statesman, Grotius is surprisingly unconcerned with law and order as he portrays God as not being so much concerned with a broken law and a reign of justice as in demonstrating benign benevolence. His naive belief is that a God who does not want to be taken seriously must be a good God.

An Atonement at discount prices
Grotius, in wishing to demonstrate the loving nature of God, nowhere reaches the expression of love found in Christ's act of redemption. There is no union of Christ with His people in Grotius' theology and no absolute identification. Christ did not go the whole way to save the otherwise unredeemable. He did not stand where we stood in having our sins imputed to Him and we cannot stand where He stands by having Christ's righteousness placed on us. Indeed the Biblical doctrine of imputation is as foreign to Grotius as that of ransom. The Biblical account of the 'greater love' of Christ in redemption is seen by Grotius as a pictorial metaphor. Against this, he taught that Christ's demonstration of suffering to deter man from sinning was not by placing the onus of fulfilling the law on Christ on our behalf as Christ

was above the law all along and could not, because of His innocence, have ever really taken our place. This led him to deny that Christ paid the price demanded by God out of love to His people in order to balance the scales of God's just claims against them. He thus rejects the deep divine benevolence of Christ's vicarious act of loving grace for His Church and substitutes it for a veritable charade of a mocked-up, benignant token sacrifice which gives spectators no real clue whatsoever to the great and crucial act it is supposed to signify.

Sola scriptura rejected

Though Grotius was prepared to accept the Bible as a true record of Jewish and Christian traditions, and, indeed, made a name for himself as a Bible expositor, he refused to come down on the Reformed side regarding verbal inspiration. This is chiefly because he believed that man can attain to a perfect knowledge of the nature and fitness of things through understanding the law which is within his own nature which Grotius called the conscience. The canonical authors would thus have no reason for lying. The Dutchman, in fact, seemed to think that the nearer the saints of the post-apostolic period were to New Testament times, the more perfect was their understanding of the inner law. This caused him to develop his doctrine of *pia antiquitas*, lean heavily on the teaching of some more radical early Church Fathers and reject the entire idea of *sola scriptura*.

Natural Law versus Divine Will

Grotius distinguishes between the Divine Will and Natural Law. The latter is ever fixed and unchangeable but this is not the case with the divine will. God, unlike Natural Law, does not will a thing to be because it is just but decrees that a thing is just because He wills it. Though Natural Law is permanent, revealed law, which reflects the divine will (Governmentalists insist on spelling Natural Law with capitals but the divine law in small letters) is only as permanent as God wishes it to be and is, in fact, merely a metaphorical demonstration and illustration of Natural Law, requiring human reason to interpret it, in this way removing the kernel or spirit of a law from its outer shell or letter.

True to his desire to combine theology with theories of statesmanship, Grotius outlined his views concerning divine revelation and the Word of God in his Latin treatise on war and peace, *de Jure*

Belli et Pacis, written in 1625. The Laws of Nature, he argues, are so infinite, unalterable and fixed that even God could not change them as He is subject to them Himself. All God's creation reflect these laws as God has no other alternative but to work according to them. Rational man is able to comprehend these laws by means of *a priori* and *a posteriori* reasoning. The laws can be deduced *a priori* from the conception of human nature itself. Though Grotius wrote at a time of acute political and religious unrest, his optimism concerning the perfections of human nature were boundless and he really thought that human reason could accept and understand the underlying nature and fitness of the universe as the best of all possible creations. Grotius found this basic conviction in man – one could almost call it instinct – strengthened *a posteriori* as what he called 'the more civilised nations' were unanimous in their respect for and adherence to Natural Law.

This has its relevance, Grotius believed, in interpreting the Scriptures, which often seem to contradict human reason. Grotius even went further by affirming that every man has not only an awareness of these eternal laws but has a natural feeling of duty towards them. Here we see the seeds sown which have produced the duty-faith weeds of modern evangelism and very much of Grotianism is present in modern Fullerism. Man's eyes, we are to believe, are naturally open to his predicament and the way of salvation is clear before him, all he needs is the encouragement from the gospel to change his moral disposition.

A gospel that ignores sin and the grace of God to deal with it
Such a view is to confuse law with gospel and the work of Moses with that of Christ. In his great work *Christ Alone Exalted*, Tobias Crisp (1600-1643), that great winner of souls, tackles Grotius-like Christian Pharisees and explains to them the difference between a blind sinner and one whose eyes have been open:

> The first of all these kinds of the grace of God, that he doth ever bestow upon a person, is, The opening his eyes to see himself filthy, and to see what he is: here begins a closing with Christ, to see a need of him, and to see the usefulness of him being received. Now mark this great business, of the opening of

the eyes of a person, and you shall see he is a way unto it, Isaiah 42:6. There the Father doth treat with Christ, and in his treaty he speaks thus to him, 'I will give thee for a covenant to the people, to open the blind eyes'. You see this, it is Christ that must open the blind eyes of men. Beloved, men are mistaken that think that the law makes them to see their own vileness; for a gracious sight of our vileness is the only work of Christ. The law is a looking-glass, able to represent the filthiness of a person; but the law gives not eyes to see that filthiness: bring a looking-glass and set it before a blind man, he seeth no more spots in his face than if he had none at all; though the glass be a good glass, yet the glass cannot give eyes; yet, if he had eyes, the glass might represent his filthiness. The apostle James compares the law to a looking-glass, and that is all the law can do, to have a faculty to represent; but it doth not give a faculty to see what it doth represent: it is Christ alone that doth open the eyes of men, to behold their own vileness and filthiness; and when Christ will open the eyes, then a man shall see himself what he is.[3]

Chapter 3 will show how Grotianism was fought in England by John Gill and in America by Benjamin Warfield and how their arguments form a firm basis for tackling modern Governmentalist theories which are masquerading under the name of 'Evangelical Calvinism'.

---

[3] See Tobias Crisp Series, Issue 1, *Christ the Only Way*, Christian Bookshop, 21 Queen Street, Ossett, West Yorkshire, WF5 8AS, 1995, p. 29.

Chapter 3

Revealed Law versus Natural Law

A faulty view of law leads to a faulty view of Atonement
Church history plainly shows that where a faulty view of the law is maintained, an erroneous view of the Atonement always follows with its corollary, a mistaken view of sin and the entire gospel of salvation. Where the symptoms are wrongly diagnosed, the medicine prescribed can hardly be effective. This is well-illustrated in the views of Hugo Grotius who sees Natural Law or the law of nature as being superior to the revealed laws of God in Scripture. Such revealed laws, which Grotius and later Andrew Fuller called 'positive laws' are seen as being neither universal, as they were only given to the Jews, nor as eternal because the new dispensation in Christ shows a progression from the Old Testament understanding of law. Readers of Grotius may be puzzled by this strange usage of the word 'positive' as, when applied to the Scriptures, it can only be judged by evangelicals as having a very 'negative' connotation. So, too, this division of Scriptural truths into what is 'natural' and what is 'positive', leaves us with a Bible in tatters. 'Positive laws' are thus, by definition, artificial or arbitrary laws as opposed to Natural Laws, which are thought to be real, eternal laws. This is in stark contrast to the 17th and 18th century evangelical practice of using the term 'positive law' to describe absolute, authoritative, binding and peremptory commands of God. For Andrew Fuller, who

took over much of Grotius' rationalism and added more, 'positive laws' are of a temporary nature only until God decides to go back to placing Himself under Natural Law.[1] However, just as 'positive law' was now used by the Grotians, followed by the Fullerites, with a new connotation, so also were many other traditional theological terms emptied of their meanings and filled with new connotations creating a Christian Babel. I believe that the most condemning part of Babel is not so much the human chaos caused by different languages but the sinful chaos caused by using the same words with entirely different meanings. This becomes most evident when reading articles and books by modern Fullerites. Most of these new meanings given to old terms, especially when dealing with what we Christians call 'the language of Sion', interpret the old terms metaphorically or as mere imagery depicting no one knows what. It is here that Fuller, building on Grotius via the Latitudinarians, Cambridge Neo-Platonists and New Divinity teaching, is in grave error as he believes that revealed Law is arbitrary and temporary but Natural Law is permanent, indeed, eternal. Naturally, however, according to the Bible, it is the other way around. The Bible clearly shows that God will never stop revealing Himself to his loved-ones according to His revealed nature but Natural Law will be wound up in the New Creation where only God's revelations endure. Why must natural law end? Why must revealed Law as God intended it triumph? The reason is found in the very corrupt nature of natural law. All nature fell with man and the whole creation was marred by man's sin. Romans 8:22 shows clearly that fallen nature longs for delivery from man's sin. Natural Law as we know it until resurrection times is the work of man not God. Because of man's sin the whole creation is marred. We can thus understand why those who praise man's agency in salvation also praise natural law but in doing so they merely praise man's Fall. Their gospel is a fallen gospel; good news made bad.

God's revealed will is allegedly arbitrary
Borrowing from Anaxarchus via Plutarch, Grotius argues that God's own law is not Natural Law but a law which merely reflects His will

---

[1] See Fuller's *On Moral and Positive Obedience* and my comments on this aspect of Fuller's theology in my *Law and Gospel in Andrew Fuller*, p. 102 ff.. See also pages 111, 113, 116, 121, 145, 297 in this work and especially my comments on Haykin's handling of Fuller's doctrines.

and that God does not will anything because it is just but regards it as just because He wills it. In other words, God's revealed will is arbitrary. Grotius leaves the impression that a Christian who trains himself in the use of his natural faculties is able to view the temporal 'positive' revelations of the Scriptures and through their metaphorical language and imagery find the Natural Law. Governmentalists call this looking for the spirit of the law hidden in its letters. This whole exercise of getting behind the 'positive' to find the eternal and interpreting the artificial to grasp the natural, must appear highly irrational to any person exercising a little common sense. Why bother about finding the Natural Law behind the positive law if reason can approach Natural Law directly? It would thus seem that Grotius' religion gets in the way of his philosophy. In any case, Grotius often presents man as living closer to Natural Law than God Himself.

Grotian influence worldwide
Opinions concerning Grotius have always been greatly varied. These range from calling him a noble dilettante (W. Philipp), to viewing him as the great originator of the Enlightenment (Hans v. Voltelini and Erik Wolf). No one can deny that he identified himself closely with the philosophy of the scholastics. Grotius sought to unify the most rational in all denominations although he tended mostly towards Rome himself. His ecumenical work however was mostly unsuccessful. The Lutherans called him Grotius Papista, the Pope placed a ban on all his theological works and the Calvinists denounced him as being a mixture of Arminianism, Socinianism, Arianism and Atheism. In the opinion of this writer, the Calvinistic criticism sums up Grotius' theology perfectly just as it sums up his modern perpetrators who hide under the 'evangelical Reformed' mantle and even call themselves 'Calvinists'. However, Grotius' governmental theory was quickly exported to other countries being adopted in England by the Latitudinarians and Neo-Platonists of the Anglican Church. Grotius had told the Anglican hierarchy that he wished to live and die according to the rites and ordinances of the Church of England but his loyalty to the Swedish

Government hindered him from openly admitting this.[2] Grotianism, however, did not remain within the Church of England but spread his views throughout the Chandlerites, Presbyterians and what we call today Fullerite Baptists. In America, after the influence of Whitefield and Jonathan Edwards had declined, Grotianism was adopted and further liberalised by the New Divinity School of Jonathan Edwards Jun., Joseph Bellamy, Samuel Hopkins and Nathaniel W. Taylor. These were men who paved the way for a thorough-going rejection of the Biblical doctrine of the Atonement. The latter school, according to modern writers such as Professor Michael Haykin, was influential in winning Andrew Fuller over to Grotianism as I have demonstrated in various works published by Go Publications and the Christian magazines New Focus and Evangelical Times. Indeed Fuller's works reflect this Grotian teaching perhaps more than any other writer who yet claimed allegiance to Calvinism and the 'gospel worthy of all acceptation', Fuller's 'gospel' being no gospel at all.

Upholders of the truth against Grotianism
John Gill, the great Baptist preacher of the righteousness of Christ amply dealt with Samuel Chandler's rationalism and no less than Benjamin B. Warfield revealed the fallacies of New England Divinity. Fullerism was combated in England by such stalwarts as John Stevens, J. A. Jones, William Gadsby and J. C. Philpot and the bulk of the Christian press with the Gospel Magazine to the fore. George Wright's most accurate condemnation of Fullerism point for point ought to be studied carefully by such modern proponents of Fullerism as Michael Haykin, Chris Chun and Curt Daniel.[3] Chandlerism and the New Divinity School have ceased to play their individual parts in perverting the truth but in recent years there has been a resurgence of Fullerism, combining both the European and North American aberrations, and this fatal error (as it perverts the Biblical doctrine of the Atonement), is once more attacking the true Church of Jesus Christ and threatening to overrun evangelical and Reformed Christianity.

---

[2] See Dr John Clerc's 1729 edition of Grotius' *The Truth of the Christian Religion* in which the editor introduces both Grotius and his wife as 'Anglicans', and explains why.
[3] *Gospel Magazine*, Vol. XII, 1877, p. 343.

Samuel Chandler's fitness campaign unfit for a Christian
In combating the rationalism of Chandler,[4] presented under the guise of 'Moderate Calvinism', Gill claims that all talk of 'Natural Law' and 'the nature and fitness of things' were meaningless phrases coined to serve as a retreat from the superior force and evidence of divine revelation. He asked vendors of Chandler's Grotianism which nature they were talking about and in what way was it fit and how this pointed to rational perfection in man, only to find that his questions caused them embarrassment. Gill wonders why those Christians who profess to believe in the necessary existence of Natural Law, in its eternity, independence, supreme power and authority over all reasonable things, do not worship Natural Law as God, especially seeing that God Himself is judged to be merely a provider of metaphors, camouflaging Natural Law more than revealing it. Before Gill's readers, however, prostrate themselves before Natural Law and worship it, he asks them to bear a few points in mind.

Natural Law cannot be of the character of God
First, if the Natural Law of the rationalists is quite independent of God and not His revealed will, then it cannot possibly be of the character of God, nor can it provide the high ideals of eternal holiness which God requires as:

> Every good gift and every perfect gift is from above, and cometh down from the Father of lights, with whom is no variableness, neither shadow of turning.[5]

What is fit or unfit in this world, must be measured alongside what is God's eternal and providential will or not. What is not of His will is evil because what is of His will is the fulness of goodness and Godliness.

---

[4] *Sermons and Tracts*, Vol. 3, p. 463 ff..
[5] James 1:17.

The 'fitness of things' is found in God's own character
Secondly, Gill argues that good and evil can neither be as old, nor older, than God Himself as all standards of good and bad must be measured according to His eternal standards before whom nothing ever was as He is the creator of all things. The evil that has come into creation was not there as a separate entity before creation so must have come as a rebellion against the goodness of God. If there is thus any such thing as the fitness of things, that fitness must be found in God's own character.

God's Law is not arbitrary, nor His revelation
In Gill's third point, he meets the Grotian and Fullerite maxim that God does not make a law because it is just but declares a law just because He has arbitrarily made it thus. Gill points out that we should expect God who is holy to make laws which are fit and proper but, we must add, these laws are not solely fit and proper because He commands them arbitrarily. God is unchangeable and cannot lie, therefore He only commands that which is in keeping with His own eternal character and nature. Any nature and fitness of things, worthy of the name must reflect the very nature of God. Hence God commands laws for the very reason that they are fit and proper because they reflect the fit and proper nature of God. There is not a spark or shadow of the arbitrary in God, thus there is no spark or shadow of caprice in His laws as God cannot deny Himself and does not change.

There is no outside law which determines God's will
The fourth point in Gill's criticism of an outside law, i.e. the Law of Nature, that determines God's will, is that nothing could be more contrary to divine revelation which explicitly and in no uncertain terms, denies such a fallacy. God indeed, does as He pleases (Psalm 115:3), He 'works all things after the council of his own will' (Ephesians 1:11), and 'he does according to his will in the army of heavens, and among the inhabitants of the earth' (Daniel 4:35). However, that will is good and as eternal as God Himself. Gill points out that Chandler is confusing Stoic philosophy with Christian exegesis as the ancient Stoics believed in a Law of Fate that determined the nature of things and compelled both the gods and men to act according to it. Nothing, however, can be a rule to God but His own nature and moral perfections within Himself which express His will and conduct.

Those who exchange God's revealed law for Natural Law have no God

Fifthly, Gill argues that those who propagate a Natural Law as opposed to God's law have already dropped God out of their system. Who wants an arbitrary and metaphorical presentation of a law if they have the real thing without having to worry their brains about interpreting it? Such a rejection must be accompanied by a complete reinterpretation of the concept of sin as, according to Scripture, sin is the transgression of the law (1 John 3:4). This is expressed in the Westminster Catechism as, 'Sin is any want of conformity unto, or transgression of any law of God given as a rule to the reasonable creature'. If God's revelation to man is merely of secondary purpose and highly metaphorical to boot, then the Christian concept of sin has no absolute relevance. Sinning itself becomes a mere metaphorical breech of an arbitrary law. If, too, all men have the perfect rule of Nature to guide their reason, then all human laws of whatever make must be seen as superfluous. Each individual, as a natural creature must be the measure of all things, reflecting the great Law of Nature.

Man's moral capacity allows for no law-keeping

In Gill's sixth point, he shows how the moral capacities of fallen man are just not fitted to aspire to law-keeping in any way. In alienating himself from God, man is in moral darkness and ought not to be viewed as Chandler does, as if he were still in his pre-fallen state. Mankind in general, as Hosea emphatically and truthfully states (11:7) of the Jews, is bent on backsliding. Thus Gill takes away the *a priori* argument of Grotianism that man has the perfect law (the Law of Nature) in his very being. Man is an anarchist at heart. Dealing with the *a posteriori* argument, Gill shows that even so-called 'civilised' nations are at sixes and sevens concerning what the moral law of nature is. One nation condones suicide, another condemns it. Polygamy is accepted by some and rejected by others. Fornication is accepted and permitted by one civilisation and frowned on by another. Gambling is seen as sociably respectful even by some Christians and others find it criminal. Thus where is the international and inter-cultural agreement as to the Law of Nature?

I remember almost with amusement the writings of an editor of a Christian magazine with the name 'Reformation' in its title. This brother usually started his preaching or writing by quoting a part of Matthew 5:45 out of context which reads:

> For he maketh his sun to rise on the evil and on the good, and sendeth rain on the just and on the unjust.

From this point of view, our 'Reformed' editor went on to talk about a 'common' grace revealed by nature which brought with it a common appeal to duty-faith in man. There were several leading Reformed men at that time who agreed to this sunny or rainy start to a life in Christ. It always reminded me of that adage:

> The rain it raineth on the just
> And also on the unjust fella;
> But chiefly on the just, because
> The unjust hath the just's umbrella.

Obviously it can rain and rain and rain on anyone but rain gives natural man no claim to the washing away of sin. Furthermore, the Scripture passage in question speaks of the just and unjust as states which have already happened whatever the weather.

God's law is older than Nature
Whilst dealing with this point, Gill takes up the Scriptural references which Chandler gives to show that the Law of Nature antedates the revealed law and is the true, perfect and eternal law. He quotes such passages as Psalm 119:142, 160, 'Thy righteousness is an everlasting righteousness', and 'Thy word is true from the beginning'. Gill accepts these verses as indicating 'the perpetuity of moral law, its immutable obligation upon us, the veracity and justice of God; which appear in it and will abide by it, and continue with it, to defend the rights, and secure the honours of it'. He then goes on to ask, 'What is all this to the nature and fitness of things? or, How do these passages prove the eternal and immutable obligations of moral virtue, as prior to and independent of the Word of God? When the Psalmist is only speaking of the will of

God as revealed in his law and testimonies; from whence, and not from the nature and fitness of things, he had learned of old, many years ago, the truth, righteousness, and continuance of them'. Gill also quotes Chandler's only 'proof' of Natural Law which he gives from the New Testament, i.e. Philippians 4:8:

> Whatsoever things are true, whatsoever things are pure, whatsoever things are lovely, whatsoever things are of good report; if there be any virtue, and if there be any praise, think on these things.

Gill comments:

> That these expressions necessarily suppose and infer, that truth, honesty, justice, and purity, are essentially different from their contrary vices, are lovely in their nature, praiseworthy in their practice, and which both God and man will approve and commend, will be easily granted; but still the question returns, what is all this to the nature and fitness of things? To the immutable and eternal obligations of moral virtue, as prior to, and independent of the will of God? Does the apostle make moral fitness, in this sense, the rule of action, or of judgment, with respect to truth, honesty, justice, and purity, and not rather the revealed will and law of God? The latter seems to be manifestly his sense, since he adds, 'those things which ye have both learned and received, and heard, and seen in me, do, and the God of peace shall be with you'. Whence it appears that the things he advises them were such as he had taught them, according to the will of God, and which they had received upon that foot, and had been practised by himself, in obedience to it. Gill goes on to show how the Natural Law theory explained by the 'nature and fitness of things' leads 'logically' to polytheism and at least has a tendency to introduce Deism and Libertinism. Worst of all, Gill sees the idea of rule by the nature and fitness of things as encouraging absolute Antinomianism as 'to set aside, and disregard the law of

45

God, as a rule of life and conversation or action, is strictly and properly Antinomianism.[6]

This could not be a more condemning verdict on modern Fullerism which puts the imagined 'nature and fitness of things' above God's revealed nature. In the light of such revelation, I cannot imagine why such Fullerites as Haykin, Chun and Daniel can claim to teach the Christian gospel of divine, saving revelation to perishing sinners.

Grotianism and the metaphorizing of Scripture

Though in England, the influence of the moral government theory was mainly centred about problems concerning law, atonement and revelation, this inevitably raised the question of the inspiration of the Scriptures. As it became philosophically acceptable to challenge Biblical revelation, the orthodox view of Scriptures as the venue of revelation was also challenged. Thus we find the Cambridge Platonists with their New Philosophy, arguing that the rational mind should use his knowledge of the nature and fitness of things to discern what is the essential message of the Scriptures, hidden in the inessentials which have accumulated during the formation of the canon. It was in the new republic formed out of the American colonies after the great awakening of the first three-quarters of the 18th century that the New Divinity, or New England, School was founded, built four square on the moral government theory of God's supposed rectoral administration of the world. This brought with it a metaphorical use of Scripture which paid lip service to orthodox terminology such as total depravity, atonement, satisfaction, substitution, redemption, imputation and righteousness but completely changed its meaning and paved the way for an upsurge of Pelagianism and the start of the modern Liberal Movement. Indeed, it was Andrew Fuller's Baptist Association which left traditional Baptist paths and denied the inerrancy and infallibility of the Word of God.

---

[6] See Gill's *The Moral Nature and Fitness of Things Considered Occasioned by Some Passages in the Rev. Mr. Samuel Chandler's Sermon*, Gill's commentaries on Deuteronomy 27 and Romans 3:19. It is a great perversity indeed when modern Fullerites claim that Gill was an Antinomian when they themselves have such a lawless theology at heart.

Benjamin Warfield refutes New Divinity error
As John Gill was God's choice in combating Grotianism in Britain, so He used Benjamin B. Warfield towards the end of the following century to point out the fallacies of the New Divinity School. Warfield, however, argued rightly that such views had disappeared from Reformed thought and become the standard Arminian doctrine. He would be amazed today, to find the same rank heresies now sporting under the name of Moderate Calvinism and being taught as if it were the true gospel worthy of all acceptation. Indeed, Grotian New Divinity and Fullerite teaching is being praised today by former Reformed men as the doctrinally purest form of Evangelical Calvinism! Warfield's voice, therefore, still serves as a warning to Reformed men against the present re-appearance of these Antinomian and Anti-Reformed views under the cloak of Reformed orthodoxy. Christians beware! The Counter-Reformation is not only still with us – it has its fifth column within us.

Warfield sees Grotianism as entering North America after the golden age of the Puritans culminating in Jonathan Edwards' death. Until then, it would appear, the Reformed faith was secure in America and the evangelical outreach of such as Whitefield, Brainerd and Edwards had been spiritually profitable to Native Americans and European immigrants and their offspring alike. In his essay 'Edwards and the New England Theology', Warfield points out that the rot set in with Jonathan Edwards Jun. reassessing his father's doctrines and publishing what he called 'Improvements in Theology' which he had allegedly inherited from his father. These 'improvements', as Warfield emphasises, were clearly the very opposite to the teaching of Edwards Sen..

The Satisfaction doctrine of the atonement is replaced by Grotian Governmental teaching and the doctrine of the imputation of sin is rejected by an 'each responsible for his own sins' teaching. The latter might not seem heretical at first sight as each sinner is obviously, according to God's word, responsible for his own sins. The idea behind this Grotian view, however, is that mankind was not represented in Adam as far as responsibility goes but actually suffered innocently under the death penalty due to Adam's initial transgression, thus giving God more cause to exert benevolence instead of justice.

The new 'evangelical Calvinism'

This view became the common belief in later so-called 'evangelical Calvinism' in which condemnation through being in Adam was virtually ignored and condemnation and salvation were seen merely as a result of each individual either rejecting or accepting Christ on hearing the Gospel. The third cardinal break with Edwards Sen. was the emphasis on man's supposedly intact natural abilities, including his reason (but not necessarily his reasoning), and moral powers which opened the doors to American Pelagianism. Another new teaching of this school which was not ashamed to openly declare that it had produced a New Divinity, was a shift of emphasis from the atonement to repentance as the means of securing salvation. This did away with the Reformed teaching of the objectivity of the atonement which secured the salvation of the elect. The New Divinity set up a half-way house in which the atonement opened up the possibility of salvation for all but it became valid to the elect on their demonstration of repentance and faith. In other words, they taught that the atonement was not the finished work on the cross traditional Christianity had taken it to be. Again, this new doctrine may not seem particularly dangerous as it accepts that the elect will be saved one way or another. The Bible, however, teaches that there is only one way of salvation and this is through the real vicarious, penal and redemptive sufferings of Christ on the cross. This one-way doctrine was dropped gradually from New Divinity teaching along with the Biblical doctrines of imputation and justification.

All too simple, all too shallow

One of the most damaging aspects of this new teaching was that the onus in salvation was removed from God's sovereignty and placed in the subjective powers of man. It thus avoided the Biblical teaching of the Atonement. If man is only given the right motives to repent, if he can be brought to realise that Christ died to show him God's displeasure at sin and His willingness to remove man's obligations towards a broken law, then there is nothing to stop that man being saved. Indeed every man by nature has a knowledge of his duty to accept the truth of the gospel (or what the Grotians have left of it) and have himself saved. It is no wonder that the New Divinity School moved on to Finneyism and the use of psychological persuasion in the ensuing theories of mass evangelism. As Warfield says in his essay Modern Theories of the Atonement:

> There is no hint here that man needs anything more to enable him to repent than the presentation of motives calculated powerfully to induce him to repent. That is to say, there is no hint here of an adequate appreciation of the subjective effects of sin on the human heart, deadening it to the appeal of the motives to right action however powerful and requiring therefore an internal action of the Spirit of God upon it before it can repent: or of the purchase of such a gift of the Spirit by the sacrifice of Christ. As little is there any hint here of the existence of any sense of justice in God, forbidding Him to account the guilty righteous without satisfaction of guilt. All God requires for forgiveness is repentance: all the sinner needs for repentance is a moving inducement. It is all very simple, but we are afraid it does not go to the root of matters as presented either in Scripture or in the throes of our awakened heart.

Jonathan Edwards' teaching reversed

Warfield points out that though the New Divinity School 'finished by becoming the earnest advocate of a set of opinions which he (Edwards Sen.) gained his chief celebrity in demolishing', they did inherit Edwards' zeal for evangelism but developed a revivalist mentality which caused discussions and disturbances everywhere, presumably because there was no doctrine to back it up. This is a solemn warning for the present-day Reformed community in which once-orthodox preachers are now dropping the doctrines of grace yet professing that they are preaching the gospel more properly (to use their own phrase) than ever. Yet it is difficult to see what the gospel is that they are preaching apart from a high view of man's capabilities and a low view of God's sovereign grace and saving love. Such modern preaching is also being accompanied by an almost utter rejection of the teaching of the great men of the 18th century such as Gill, Hervey, Toplady, Romaine and Huntington, men who revealed the utter fallacy of theories of law, gospel, atonement and Scripture which were not anchored in the Word of God. Even the teaching of George Whitefield himself is now rejected by those who, in past years, made his doctrines popular. Whitefield's sermon *What think ye of Christ?* led to James Hervey's conversion. In this sermon Whitefield describes how Christ not only took upon Himself the punishment for our sin passively but also placed Himself under the law in His human nature, vicariously for His elect, and was obedient to it in every respect. Whitefield can thus conclude,

> Our salvation is all of God from the beginning to the end; it is not of works, lest any man should boast. Man has no hand in it; it is Christ who is made of God unto us wisdom, righteousness, sanctification, and redemption. His active obedience, as well as his passive obedience, is to be applied to poor sinners. He has fulfilled all righteousness in our stead, that we might become the righteousness of God in him.

This stand is proclaimed by many so-called 'evangelical Reformed' Christians as being Antinomian. It has less to do here with their rejection of 'revealed law' but with their rejection of the Atonement as our real Reformers; Crisp, Gill, Warfield, Hervey and Whitefield taught it.

Justification wrought out through the Atonement
Whitefield here preaches freely that justification rests alone on Christ's vicarious righteousness worked out at the Atonement. This is made possible by the God-Man who demonstrated before God and man that He was worthy to present us spotless before His Father. The great preacher adds that if any man or angel contradicts this truth, we have apostolic authority to pronounce that man or angel accursed. Sadly, all the main doctrines of Whitefield's sermon are being denied in much present-day Reformed preaching. Man's agency as co-partner in

working out salvation is now accepted as orthodox theology;[7] the ransoming nature of the Atonement is being denied along with the need for Christ's active obedience to the law and the need for our sins to be imputed to Christ and His righteousness to be imputed to the sinner. Particular redemption is now denied by the very people who re-emphasised the doctrine in the late fifties and sixties and thus pioneered the revival of the Reformed Faith.

As former leaders of the Reformed Faith have begun to leave the old paths, especially where they centre in the doctrine of Atonement, my fourth chapter will concentrate on the alternative teaching they offer, claimed to be built on the 'theological genius' of Andrew Fuller.

---

[7]According to Geoff Thomas, 'God doing all and man also doing all is the teaching of the Bible'. (ET, July, 1995, p. 11, GT's report of a talk by Iain Murray on 19th May.) After protests were made, this was subsequently given as 'God works all and man does all'. *Spurgeon v. Hyper-Calvinism*, p. 84, which hardly improves matters.

The Atonement In Modern Evangelical Thought

Chapter 4

The Atonement According to Andrew Fuller

Fuller's faulty view of law leads to a faulty view of Atonement
It was left to the Englishman Andrew Fuller, to combine the teaching of Abelard, Chandler, Neo-Platonism, Latitudinarianism and the New Divinity School and, in effect, re-introduce pure Grotianism with its affirmation of the moral government theory of the Atonement and its denial of vicarious and penal substitution. This is clearly seen in Fuller's teaching on moral and positive laws; the nature and fitness of things; divine revelation; man's natural abilities as a medium for spiritual truth and experience; and a metaphorical interpretation of Bible doctrine. Fuller outdid Grotius, in redefining the doctrines of the fall, imputation, satisfaction, substitution, ransom, redemption, atonement and Christ's being made sin for our sakes. Indeed, the only possible slogan that fits Fullerism, as his fatal error came to be called, when thinking in terms of orthodox Biblical doctrine, is, 'You name it – Fuller changed it!'

Fullerism and the modern neo-evangelical Reformed establishment
Fuller won over his followers in an ingenious manner. Apart from when speaking about the law, he closely followed traditional terminology concerning the main doctrines of the gospel, though he completely re-defined their sense content which, at times, he admitted. He was so brilliant at propagating his views that he duped many into believing that

his departure from orthodoxy was 'strict Calvinism'. Fashions in thinking come and go and Fullerism is again being marketed by holders of various moral government theories. Once again, he is being presented as the Calvinist and evangelist par excellence, especially by writers such as Michael Haykin, Chris Chun and Curt Daniel whom I feel have departed from historical Christianity more than those old bogey-men of my early student days Brunner, Barth and Bultmann. Modern Fullerites, however, do not like the epithet 'strict' and prefer to use Chandler's term 'moderate Calvinist'. If we take 'Calvinism' to mean the evangelical, Biblical, Reformed faith, then there is nothing whatsoever 'moderately' evangelical, Biblical or Reformed in Fullerism which is, as a philosophical system, immoderate to an extreme and as a gospel drastically immoral as it is a gospel of deceit. I have been castigated by modern Fullerites for condemning their philosophical stop-gap religion in the strongest terms, yet they are blind to the fact that their gospel deadens evangelism in the severest way and badly needs to be shown up for what it really is.

Early reactions to Fuller's new approach to the gospel
Fuller's new popularity through writers such as Michael Haykin, Curt Daniel, Chris Chun and Erroll Hulse is quite amazing and quite different to Fuller's contemporary acceptance. As early as 1796, Particular Baptist Abraham Booth combatted Fuller's gospel-emptying, rationalistic theories in his work *Glad Tidings to Perishing Sinners or, the Genuine Gospel a Complete Warrant for the Ungodly to Believe in Jesus*. It is quite unbelievable to me to read of Fullerites linking Booth with Fuller when they were two opposites regarding the Biblical gospel which saves. William Rushton's next generation work published in 1831 entitled *A Defence of Particular Redemption Wherein the Doctrine of Andrew Fuller Relative to the Atonement of Christ is Tried by the Word of God* has remained in print over the years as a warning against any rejection of the Biblical doctrine of the Atonement.[1] John Stevens wrote his *Help for the True Disciples of Immanuel: Being an Answer to a Book Published by the Late Rev. Andrew Fuller, entitled The Gospel Worthy of All Acceptation* in 1841, which is a detailed

---

[1] See the Primitive Publications reprint of 1973 and the Go Publications' reprint of 2007 with an Introduction by George M. Ella.

criticism on Scriptural grounds of Fuller's moral philosophy. This was followed up by his *Thoughts on God in the Salvation of His People* in 1844. John Foreman (1792-1872) published his two works on Duty-Faith in 1860. J. A. Jones of Jireh Chapel, London was so disgusted with Fuller's radical and rational Antinomianism and the way he destroyed the Christian gospel that he wrote in 1861 his *A Sketch of the Rise and Progress of Fullerism, or Duty-Faith, That Gangrene now rapidly Spreading in Many Baptist Churches*. Our modern would-be Fullerites should read these works and the contemporary secular and Christian press reports concerning Fuller's novelties of 'right reason'. Then they might tackle Fuller from a different angle instead of calling all those who oppose Fuller's gospel 'Antinomians' as the boot is certainly on the other foot. Fullerism is Antinomianism without a mask.

Many former churches and denominations are once again leaving the old Biblical paths in this new Downgrade Controversy for Fuller's mixture of Grotianism, Chandlerism, New Divinity teaching and Socinianism. It is astonishing to find professedly Reformed magazines such as Reformation Today, Banner of Truth, Founder's Journal and the Evangelical Times opening their pages to full-blown Fullerite propaganda.

Reformation Today recommends the Anti-Reformed teaching of yesterday

One of the first major attempts to re-popularise Fuller in modern times was in two publications which appeared in 1984 in Issue 82 of Reformation Today with two special recommendations of the articles by the late editor Erroll Hulse. The articles were allegedly taken from the works of American Tom Nettles but were also a departure from Nettles' doctrines and the historical overview contained in the works allegedly under review. The first article 'Why Andrew Fuller?' resembles Nettles' foreword to the Sprinkle Publications edition of Fuller's *Complete Works* re-published in 1988. It is the usual positive introduction which one expects from such a foreword. However, neither the Reformation Today essay nor the Sprinkle Publications foreword is a study in depth of Fuller's works in any way. Nettles presents Fuller as a follower of Jonathan Edwards Sen. (has he mistaken him for Jonathan

Edwards Jun.?), and as a staunch Calvinist who was thoroughly Biblical in his approach, neither modifying nor apologising for his Reformed doctrines. He is presented as a believer in sovereign grace and the driving force behind sending Carey to India. He is said to have 'altered the course not only of English Baptist history but of American Baptist history as well'.

In his book *By His Grace and For His Glory*, Nettles deals with Fuller's doctrine far more specifically and it is from this work that Hulse has selected some of Nettles' more positive views concerning Fuller, entitling them Andrew Fuller and Free Grace. Actually, their rearrangement in this way is rather unfair on Nettles as it is presented by Erroll Hulse as a special work showing the particular importance of Fuller, whereas one of the main thrusts of the complete original work was to re-establish John Gill as the great 'Bridge Over Troubled Waters' (Nettles' term) of the Baptist Movement giving him much of the credit for keeping the Particular Baptist churches and beyond on a Biblical basis. Hulse has written against John Gill, viewing him as the very opposite of Fuller, yet Nettles adorns Fuller with many feathers he claims, rightly, that Fuller had from Gill. In this we must distinguish between Fuller and modern Fullerism or Hyper-Fullerism as I prefer to call it. Furthermore, Nettles firmly establishes his own theology of the atonement as being in line with Gill's and, in his account of Fuller's view of atonement confesses that he disagrees with him. This vital factor is neatly left out by Hulse who does not acknowledge the help Fuller gained from Gill and who isolates Nettles' views of free grace from the doctrine of atonement. He portrays Nettles as arguing for Fuller's orthodoxy on the basis of total depravity and election alone. One cannot help thinking that a very balanced writer such as Nettles is being used in a most unbalanced way. This is symptomatic of Neo-Evangelicalism founded on a re-interpretation of total depravity and an emphasis on election through repentance and belief as opposed to an election secured and settled by the Atonement.

One heart and one soul with Andrew Fuller
Another modern Baptist writer, Canadian Michael Haykin, is striving to popularise Fuller, arguing that on essentials he is absolutely orthodox. He complains openly in print against those who find his defence of Fuller lacking in theological acumen. Formally he refused to

accept that Fuller was a Moral Government man, then gradually noted his tendencies to Governmentalism, confessing that this alarmed Fuller's friends. Haykin, in his work *One Heart and One Soul*, presents Fuller's theology alongside that of his friends Ryland, Sutcliffe and Carey as indebted to Governmentalism. Haykin's view is obviously that to be an evangelical Calvinist, one must be a Grotian. Strangely enough, Fuller is highly radical in limiting the work of the Spirit in redemption but Haykin describes Fuller's view of the Spirit in orthodox terms without giving sources for such orthodoxy in Fuller. So, too, Haykin writes much of Fuller's 'spirituality' a term which Fuller limits to 'morality'. I hold my brother in the faith Michael Haykin to be a very spiritually minded man who adorns Fuller wrongly with the spirituality he has himself. Indeed Haykin's new title at his Andrew Fuller Study Center is that of Professor of Spirituality. Now being a professor has something to do with academic qualifications, on this we would all agree but whoever came up with the idea that a Christian's spirituality should be reduced to an academic title? I have known street-cleaners and char-ladies of great spirituality but they were never given a professorship for their Godliness and would have laughed at the idea.

Fuller does speak of the Spirit in two brief works, 'The Inward Witness of the Spirit' and 'The Promise of the Spirit' but does not see the inner working of the Spirit as moving and compelling sinners to turn to Christ for their salvation as I believe Haykin does but as a mere external prompter and encourager, in spite of his using the term 'inward' which he, as to be expected, redefines. Indeed, the indwelling of the Spirit in the believer is absent from Fuller's theology. In man's inner reigns 'the reason and fitness of things' as in Enlightenment Liberalism such as Ephraim Lessing taught.[2]

Haykin outlines how it was through reading Joseph Bellamy, Samuel Hopkins and Jonathan Edwards Jun.[3] that Fuller and those who were 'one heart and one soul' with him, rejected 'False Calvinism' i.e. the doctrines that had been taught by Wallis, Noble, the Wallins, Gill,

---

[2] See my *Law and Gospel in the Theology of Andrew Fuller*, 2nd ed., p. 386 and index references to the Trinity in that book. God willing, I hope to publish a work on Lessing's 'Christian' Rationalism soon under the title *Gott, Offenbarung und Mensch in Lessings 'Nathan dem Weisen'*.
[3] *One Heart and One Soul*, EP, 1995, p. 139 and 300 ff..

Brine, Martin, and John Ryland Sen. to mention good men of his own denomination,[4] and embraced Grotian and New Divinity teaching. Haykin explains enthusiastically, without a shade of analytical criticism, what a 'warm welcome' Grotianism received amongst the theological heirs of Jonathan Edwards and in stating this shows the weakness in his own theological and denominational thought. Grotius was an avowed opponent of the Baptists, indeed, of any Dissenters, and as Anti-Calvinist as could be imagined, nor had Edwards anything to do with Grotianism.

The breech between Edwards Sen. and the New Divinity School denied

Haykin is apparently unaware of the gigantic breech between the theology of the New Divinity School and that of Edwards Sen.. In his book, he makes it appear that even Edwards was 'one heart and one soul' with the later theology of his own son Jonathan Edwards Jun. Haykin gives no evidence but suggests that Edwards' private notebooks – we are not told which – indicate this. Haykin is probably thinking of the rough notes Edwards made on the Medium of Moral Government which have been published from time to time in highly edited, shortened (minus the long quotes) and rearranged versions. Haykin's whole exercise in basing his new view of Edwards' theology on unpublished notes, indeed the most private of notes not meant for publication, raises the question of the propriety of such an act, as Jonathan Edwards who was keen to publish since his childhood did not think his private notes, which Haykin makes public, were representative of his thoughts. Indeed, Haykin has been telling us for many years that he will publish new material on Fuller but, as yet, has only reproduced known material edited by others.

The danger of publishing posthumous authors

Similar confusion arose concerning the supposed unpublished works of Archbishop James Ussher which, when published during his lifetime by others unknown to him, he denied were his work. He explained that they were student notes he had made for an examination chiefly on the

---

[4] Baptist stalwarts of the faith are stressed as Fuller claimed their teaching had made the Baptist movement disrespectful and appear a dunghill in society.

opinions of Thomas Cartwright which did not match his own in all places. Now modern enthusiasts, wishing to present an Ussher according to their Cartwrightean dreams, are busy producing all kinds of 'original works'.[5] We ask here if Fuller's notes on Mosheim will be declared to be Fuller's work. Apparently, Fuller's sole knowledge of the Reformation was reading through Mosheim's brief sketches. Notes made by C. S. Lewis have been published as his own, original work but he himself had obviously not thought they ought to be published, and was prevented in his efforts to burn them which he had thought best. I have seen robbed jottings of my own appear in several non-German magazines under my name without my authorisation and even found an article on Gill from my pen in the Netherlands signed by a complete stranger as being his own.

Fuller had obviously collected material from earlier days when he examined the thoughts of the Cambridge Neo-Platonists and other writers. Nevertheless, though Jonathan Edwards speaks of God's rightful moral government in his private notes, no matter whether they were his thoughts or those of others, this is quite legitimate as not all who speak of God's moral rule are Grotians. Nor can we claim from them that Edwards is a link between Grotius and New Divinity teaching. However, it is simply such an odd reference to the term that convinces Haykin that John Sutcliffe was a Grotian. Edwards, in his notes makes it crystal clear that he is distinguishing between God's moral rule through the revelation of Scripture and the idea that men can be left to their own reason. Needless to say, he completely rejects the latter proposition. Throughout these notebook jottings, Edwards maintains, with reference to a true knowledge of right and wrong, and an awareness of the purpose of life and creation, 'It is apparent, that there would be no hope that these things would ever be determined among mankind, in their present darkness and disadvantages, without a revelation'.[6] This should remove ideas that Edwards was the father of Fuller's opposite ideas.

---

[5] I discuss this topic using original documents culled from the Sheffield and Oxford archives in an appendix to my book *The Covenant of Grace and the People of God* Go Publications, 2020.
[6] Edwards' *Works*, Vol. II, Miscellaneous Observations On the Medium of Moral Government, Banner of Truth 1979 reprint, p. 485.

Judged sound by association

Equally alarming and ill-founded in Haykin's work is that he links not only Fuller and John Sutcliffe with the New Divinity School but also David Brainerd and William Carey without providing any evidence whatsoever. However, a brief perusal of Brainerd's literary remains, in spite of Haykin's hunch, will reveal how Brainerd was a fervent supporter of what Fuller disparagingly calls the 'commercial view' of the atonement. In his diary Brainerd explains how he overcame the linguistic difficulties of teaching the Indians how Christ died 'a ransom for many'. So, too, those who feel they can find any resemblance to Grotianism in William Carey's work and teaching must have a very defective theological microscope indeed! On the contrary, as much as Fuller emphasised the legal duties of the unconverted to exercise faith savingly according to the nature and fitness of things as if this were the gospel, Carey exhorted the converted to exercise the clear and precise duties they had been given at the Great Commission to go out into the world and save those who were totally incapable naturally and morally of saving themselves. Those who have carefully studied the relationship between Carey and Fuller must have noted the very many instances where Carey scolded Fuller strongly because of his lack of evangelistic acumen and misunderstandings concerning missionary strategy, and acute condemnation of the most excellent John Fountain (1767-1800) for right-wing political reasons which were totally contrary to the work of the Indian mission. Happily, we still profit from Fountain's Mission Hymns though Fuller rejected their purport.

Friends of two conflicting minds

Carey and Fuller were certainly of two very conflicting minds concerning the spreading of the gospel and its Biblical basis. Indeed, Fuller mocked Carey's theology of evangelism in cooperation with Christians of other evangelical denominations as a 'pleasant dream' and refused to support it. This led to several breaks between the Baptist Missionary Society (BMS) and Indian missions as also between Carey and his brother and sister missionaries of other denominations. Indeed, it can be truly said that Fuller's policies, continued by Ryland Jun. after Fuller's death, led to the end of the Serampore Trio's work and witness. It certainly led to great disappointment within the Calcutta and Serampore missionary fold. There were, moreover, other Baptists at work in India whose engagement was far closer to the Biblical ideal called into life by Christ's command recorded in Matthew 28. One cannot judge Baptist involvement in India by Fuller's lack of traditional Baptist principles.

The Banner of Truth and 'provincial' theology

Writing in his biography of Jonathan Edwards published in 1987, Iain Murray of the Banner of Truth Trust stresses how the New Divinity School saw things radically different from Jonathan Edwards Sen. with both Hopkins and Edwards Jun. paving the way for later Finneyism. Murray, without going into any detail whatsoever, dismisses the New Divinity teaching as metaphysical and, using the words of B. B. Warfield, declares them to be 'provincial'. This reminds me of Fuller's criticism of Priestly though he himself was termed 'worse than Priestly'. Yet Murray must have known from his reading of the period that it was the New Divinity men who had radically influenced Andrew Fuller whose 'provincial theology' Murray, backed by Maurice Roberts, has advocated strongly since writing his book on Edwards, introducing him as the answer to the supposed Hyper-Calvinism of John Gill.

Gill's theology, admittedly went above and beyond Calvin's in many areas but these were where he, like Heinrich Bullinger (1504-1575) and Martin Bucer (1491-1551) subdued Calvin's extremes. These Christian stalwarts did not make themselves 'Hyper-Calvinistic' by any means in curbing Calvin's rather fatalistic doctrines but rather clarified and improved them. This, of course, led Bullinger to scold Calvin for giving the impression that God was the author of sin and moved Bucer to show Calvin, with his high ideas of being 'President' of the Genevan Church founded by others, that every Christian was an office-bearer in God's service. Most 'Calvinists' nowadays tend happily to view Calvinism through Bullinger's and Bucer's eyes and list 'firsts' of Calvin which he merely took over from these two men, Zwingli, Melanchthon and many others for his compilation. Here we can compare this historical mistake with that regarding Carey who built on the work of over seventy-five British and Continental missionaries before him and continued his work under their support.

August Lang in his *The Source of Calvin's Institutes* (1936) has shown Calvin's huge dependence on Bucer as also Francois Wendel in his work *Calvin* of 1963. Marc van Campen's *Martin Bucer een vergeten reformator (1491-1551)* of 1991 gives us more information on this dependence as does also Ford Lewis Battles in his *Analysis of the Institutes of the Christian Religion* and other works from the 1970s. This led Gustav Anrich to claim even earlier in his 1914 work *Martin Bucer* that his subject was 'The Father of Calvinism'. We must also think of Frenchman Francois Lambert who was preaching what most of us call 'Calvinism' around 1520 and Jacques Lefèvre (c.1455-c.1536) was preaching justification by faith alone from the book of Romans in 1512, long before even Luther. Indeed, whilst Luther was in hiding and had not yet published on his main teaching, Lambert was preaching the Reformation openly in Erfurt in Latin as he knew no German at the time. Later he led the faculty at Germany's first Protestant university in Marburg and invited Luther to join him. Luther declined as he had hoped for Lambert's post but a good number of his colleagues joined Marburg University where this writer had the privilege of studying for his doctorate in theology. Actually, the French, Poles, Germans, Swiss and Dutch were all preaching 'Calvinism' before Calvin.

The Broken Voice of Years
The theology expressed anonymously in the notorious Voice of Years article in the July 1988 Banner of Truth Magazine for which Iain Murray claimed responsibility, portrays the very New Divinity theology that Murray formerly claimed was 'provincial' and is far from being 'Calvinistic' in any sense of the word. Murray had obviously changed his theological mind. The scandal caused by the U-turn of Banner of Truth theology even hit the Dutch dailies, one newspaper carrying a whole series of Letters to the Editor on new Banner of Truth thinking, chiefly caused by a letter from W. Smit criticising the Banner of Truth's new stand. One Dutch writer named Iain Murray in particular and the Banner of Truth in general as being obsessed with the idea of Hyper-Calvinism which was making them paranoid in their opposition. It was bemoaned that the spirit of Sidney Norton no longer played any part in Banner of Truth thinking. This matter became of so much importance for the brethren in the Netherlands that Dr K. van der Zwaag took up over a dozen pages in his massive 1098 paged book *Afwachten*

of verwachten? Die toe-eigening des heils in historisch en theologisch perspectief, to give both sides of the argument, particularly highlighting growing criticism of the Banner of Truth's new divinity. Around this time, I received a scolding letter from Maurice Roberts denouncing William Huntington though he had only read one brief book by him challenging Arminianism which Roberts ought also, in my opinion, to be challenging. In one letter from Roberts rejecting my analysis of Fuller's theology he pronounced Fuller the greatest theologian of his age. This goes back to a quote from Spurgeon as misinterpreted by Haykin. Banner of Truth evidence for such a sweeping statement has never been offered. So, too, at the time Murray sent me a copy of an article entitled Portrait of an Antinomian which he attributed to Fuller, claiming it was a condemnation of William Huntington's theology. Huntington's name did not appear in this article, nor did it portray Huntington's theology in any way. It did, however, throw a great deal of light on Fuller's own highly questionable theological position. When I quoted from the article that Murray had sent me in a reply to the Banner of Truth's condemnation of Huntington, I was told in print by Robert Oliver writing in the Banner of Truth magazine that there was no proof that Fuller was thinking of Huntington when he wrote the article. However, this was just what Murray had affirmed and was why I criticised it. I still have Murray's letter as evidence of this fact and the cutting he enclosed.

Huntington and the eternal standard of God's Law
Just as it is most strange that Fullerites call Gill an Antinomian though he held to the eternal nature of the Law, eternally anchored in the Covenant of Grace, a doctrine Fullerites combat, Fullerite criticism of Huntington as an Antinomian is equally weird. Huntington taught that revealed law was God's own standard for Himself and for His People and would be the Standard in all eternity and this was revealed in the atoning work of Christ. Again, this sound theology is combatted by Fullerites purely out of Antinomian reasons. Though I would not call Fullerites 'Hyper-Calvinists' as I have never encountered such an Aunt Sally as they set up, they are indeed, at least when compared to Gill and

Huntington, 'Antinomians'. An Antinomian cannot have a sound view of the Atonement.

Fuller's general theology has been closely dealt with in other works[7] but let us look specifically here to his writings pertaining to his Moral Government shortcomings as they challenge the Biblical doctrine of the Atonement.

Fuller and the fitness of things

Fuller's system is often so close to that of Grotius and Chandler as to make no difference. He is especially Grotian in his view of the Jews as following revealed law but Christians opting for the nature and fitness of things. Fuller quite overlooks the status of true, believing Jews in the Old Testament represented by Moses, Abraham and all the prophets. His legalistic view of the Mosaic Law totally ignores Moses' insistence on its gospel-tenor which points to an atoning salvation in Christ by whose stripes we are healed. This is the gospel witnessed to in both Testaments. Fuller's view which entails harsh criticism of the Jews whether believers or unbelievers thus helped to launch the New Covenant Theology movement and former Fullerites and Banner of Truth writers such as Tom Wells and David Gay have now become its modern spokesmen.

Writing to the Church at Serampore as an 'absentee bishop', telling them how to manage their affairs, Fuller gives them a nice piece of Grotianism to help them with problems of church discipline. He informs the brethren in his obvious ignorance of pan-Biblical Covenant theology that:

> The form and order of the Christian church, much more than that of the Jewish church, are founded on the reason and fitness of things. Under the former dispensation the duties of religion were mostly positive; and were of course prescribed with the nicest precision, and the most exact minuteness. Under the gospel they are chiefly moral, and, consequently, require only the suggestion of general principles. In conforming to the one, it was

---

[7] See my books *William Huntington: Pastor of Providence, John Gill and the Cause of God and Truth* and *Law and Gospel in the Theology of Andrew Fuller*, also my Focus article *A Gospel Unworthy of Any Acceptation* and my book *The Covenant of Grace and the People of God* besides this present work.

necessary that men should keep their eye incessantly on the rule; but in complying with the other, there is more occasion for fixing it upon the end.[8]

Here someone should have reminded Fuller of the Messianic teaching of the Old Testament and the fact that all doctrine relating to the goal or 'end time' found in the New Testament is taken from the Old as our Reformers were very quick and able to point out. There is no evidence whatsoever to show that Fuller ever studied these matters but if he did he had not grasped their message.

Fuller's faulty view of the ancient church
In this rather Jesuit-minded letter Fuller goes on to argue that the form and order of the Christian church needed no pattern as Christians were endued with 'a holy wisdom, to discern and pursue on all occasions what was good and right'. Here we have the teleological ideal of the ancient Greeks that life in harmony with Natural Law produces the maximum good. So, too, we wonder what 'Church' Fuller is talking about. As he argues that Christian churches other than his own are 'seduced by Jezebel' and that Old Testament believers belonged to a different Church, is Fuller limiting the Church to his own followers, few as they were at the time? Was the Atonement in his view for the Baptist Missionary Society, of highly mixed doctrines, alone? The message of Hebrews is that we Gentiles have joined the Old Testament Church which goes back beyond Abraham. We are thus in the same Church as our Father Abraham. The NCT teach that somehow Jews will eventually be grafted into the Gentile Church but the Bible teaches that we have already been grafted into sound Old Testament stock. Every believer is found in the bosom of Abraham as the old Negro slaves knew but not Fuller. Belief in the Old Testament was not a belief in nationalism and legalism but belief in God's Covenant of Grace just as it is today. The message of Gabriel to the budding New Testament Church was the same as he gave the Old Testament Church in that the

---

[8] Fuller's emphasis. See Principles of Church Discipline, *Works*, Vol. III, p. 452.

one Church was growing out of God's eternal Covenant with man which covers all time.

Fuller's side-step

Fuller, realising he was in danger of stepping outside of the Biblical view of law and divine precepts here, raises the question, 'Will not the considering of these things as moral, rather than positive (i.e. revealed)[9], open a way for the introduction of human inventions into the church of God?' His answer is, 'Why should it?' He then goes on to make one of the many compromises he often makes, either because of the uncertainty of his position or because he did not wish to appear radical. He argues that though the greater part of what belongs to the organisation and discipline of the church is founded in the fitness of things, we must have some form of divine revelation to guide us, providing we do not adhere too minutely to its precepts and examples. This is still better, Fuller argues, 'than to exercise the liberty to prefer what may appear fit and right to us'. Even this rough rule does not cover everything for Fuller, however, as he argues there are indeed positive rules in the New Testament similar to the patterns laid down by Moses such as baptism and the Lord's Supper, which must be kept 'as they were delivered'. How Fuller believed that these were 'delivered' is entirely another matter as he added the two Biblical celebrations to his list of legal morals, quite robbing them of their gospel purport. Chapter 5 will discuss the follies of a merely moral understanding of Law and Gospel which provides no atonement.

---

[9] My explanation.

Chapter 5

No 'Moral Law' Atones for Sin

Challenging the idea of a moral law

The idea of 'moral law' so much promoted in modern evangelical, Reformed circles is open to serious question as it proposes a gospel quite different from Biblical standards and is defined differently to pre-Grotian usage as we have seen in Gill's correction of Grotianism. 'Moral Law' based on 'Natural Law' is actually a non-theological term handed down from ancient Greek thinking and has become part of the cultural thought of the Western World. The Greeks taught that any obligation to any law was a matter of reason and rational insight and the very idea of law was strictly teleological, merely reflecting the necessities of man in his pursuit of happiness. Indeed, Fuller's law philosophy reflects Aristotelian legal thinking as expressed in Book Five of his Nicomachean Ethics in its dualism of 'natural' and 'conventional' law with the difference that Fuller sees such bare rational thinking as something 'religious'. The judicial sense of law, however, which Aristotle saw, reflects a corrective element outside of man, forcing him to accept or reject the will of another, be it a political entity or God. It is an instrument to assist man in conforming to the requirements of others or Another. God's friend Moses[1] saw both natural and conventional typological law not as a means of force but as a means of grace, the one being merged with and not separated from the other.

Christianity is not man's 'natural' ideal but God's supernatural will

The Christian view of law is not 'moral' in the traditional sense of the word as it is not man's natural ideal but God's ideal of how man should be. Christian morals are revealed and not deduced by reason.

The Biblical, and therefore Christian, idea of Law is thus not only judicial but supremely theological, soteriological and eschatological. It is an essential part of God's plan of salvation in preparing a people for Himself and cannot be forced out of it. 'Moral law' directs man to a basic longing to pull himself up by his own boot-strings as per Greek rationalism. Divine Law, as revealed in Scripture, provides a means of fulfilling the Law on the sinner's behalf by the God-Man who alone can do so and provide man with the helping Hand he needs. This is the purpose of the Atonement. Man cannot work out an At-one-ment with God through his fallen understanding of 'reason and the fitness of things'. He is entirely unreasonable and unfit for such a task.

The new ten-point 'Calvinism'

During the later eighties and throughout the nineties until the present day, we have been bombarded with a new legalism propagated through evangelical and Reformed media. These publishing houses and para-church organisations insist, in the name of 'Reformed religion', that keeping the Ten Commandments, otherwise named the Decalogue, as a cut-down, stand-alone, and ripped from its Biblical context and Old Testament teaching on them, is all that is necessary for a life of faith. No heed is paid to the fact that Moses wrote Genesis, Exodus, Leviticus, Numbers and Deuteronomy as the founding books of the Bible and as a gospel commentary on the Ten Commandments. Moses showed that one cannot cut off Law from Gospel as the tenor of both reveal one gospel which is the Father's Covenant of Grace with His Son. The Torah or Pentateuch of which the Ten Commandments are but a tiny

---

[1] Exodus 33:11.

part, points back to man's fall through Adam and forwards to justification by faith in the Messiah Christ and not by works righteousness. The present obsession with but a fraction of the entire Mosaic Law, cut entirely out of its evangelical context, brings with it a moralism based on an anti-Mosaic Neonomianism. This is presented as 'moral law' or 'true religion' but it is not the religion of the Bible. The false argument here is that Christ did not place Himself under the whole Law as He was always above it, but gave Himself as a token sacrifice, fulfilling a token Law as an example of how He wished his Bride to live. Orthodox theologians such as John Milton with whom such as Rationalist Andrew Fuller strongly disagreed for obvious reasons, believed that man must die or Someone in his stead, saying:

> Some other able, and as willing, pay
> The rigid satisfaction, death for death.[2]

Against this atoning and saving doctrine, Fuller proclaimed he knew better and stated:

> The law made no such condition or provision, nor was it indifferent to the Lawgiver who should suffer, the sinner or another on his behalf. The language of the law to the transgressor was not, Thou shalt die or someone on thy behalf, but simply, Thou shalt die: and had it literally taken its course, every child of man must have perished. The sufferings of Christ in our stead, therefore are not a punishment inflicted in the ordinary course of justice, but an extraordinary interposition of infinite wisdom and love; not contrary to, but above the law, deviating from the letter, but more than preserving the spirit of it. Such, Brethren, as well as I am able to explain them are my views of the substitution of Christ.[3]

---

[2] *Paradise Lost*, Book III, 210-212.
[3] Conversations on Substitution, *Works*, Vol. II, p. 689.

The Ten Commandments alone do not sum up the Gospel

This is what comes from isolating the Ten Commandments from the gospel of Christ in which God embedded them through Moses. It ignores all God's provisions in using the Law to point to Christ by preaching salvation in the Coming One, foretold in the Old Testament teaching concerning sacrifices, scapegoats and the doctrine of justification by faith in the Messiah. Such modern 'moral apostles' leave out the Old Testament teaching regarding Christ completely by rejecting the whole Law and Gospel which points to Him. The entire Old Testament is one with the New in proclaiming the vicarious and substitutionary death of Christ who put Himself fully under His own Law, the Just for the unjust, for our total salvation. Death did not take its course for Christ's flock because Christ's death intervened, fulfilling time's purpose and the Will of God. The entire doctrine of the Atonement has to do with the Just One dying for the unjust.

Moral man is a law unto himself

There is no atonement in moralism as Christ teaches that left to his moral-law-ism man becomes a law unto himself. This includes the unlawful use of the so-called 'moral law' or the entire Mosaic Law. This substitution of morals for Biblical Christianity certainly earns the titles 'Hyper-moralism' and 'Antinomianism'. Even secular writers such as Alexander Grau in his 'Hypermoral', a book well worth reading, acknowledge this. It is the rational Hyper-moralists in our churches who now define the orthodox faith as 'Hyper-Calvinism' and 'Antinomianism', though partakers of such faith believe in the doctrine of Grace and the responsibility of man to the whole Law and Gospel as contained in the whole Bible from Genesis to Revelation. We alone have not reduced the Bible message to the Ten Commandments or less.

Ten Commandments counted on nine fingers and less

It is also interesting to see how even the former Ten Commandment moralists are reducing the commandments in number, eliminating those which go against their own moral precepts. Fuller himself cancelled the commandment on adultery in his glaringly immoral advice to the Indian mission, advocating divorce for those Baptists married to a non-Baptist, leaving them free to court another woman. So, too, many Fullerites have dropped the commandment regarding the Sabbath.

I remember my surprise after writing my published tribute to William Huntington and describing his all-comprehensive view of the Law. Several Neonomian moralistic publishing houses on both sides of the Atlantic responded by calling Huntington an Antinomian because he had a pan-Biblical understanding of the Law which they had reduced to their eight, nine or ten point faith built merely on their cut-down view of the Law. I was called the same for standing in the shadow of Crisp, Gill, Brine, Huntington, Button, Ryland Sen., Martin, Stevens, Toplady, Foreman, Rushton, Wright, Hawker and Doudney who were representatives of different denominations but united in the same Christ. On his website Maurice Roberts, a former Banner of Truth editor, still lashes out at those who defend a comprehensive Biblical view of both Law and Gospel because they refuse to join his moral club and be 'one of the boys'. Morals divide, Christ unites. Sectarianism is, however, seldom 'Christian' and rarely 'moral' in the Christian sense.

The double morals of the moralists
Some years ago, I wrote to a major critic of Huntington who was then another editor of a leading Reformed British magazine. This 'Reformed' man had just published an article in his magazine advocating Sunday trading. I pointed out to him that Huntington had refused a lucrative job because it involved working on the Sabbath yet the editor called him 'an Antinomian without a mask'. Back came the written answer that in his Sunday trading the editor honoured the Lord of the Sabbath, implying that Huntington did not in his abstinence from such work. This is the 'double moral' of the moralist. This hypocritical eight, nine or ten point token 'moral' religion, called erroneously 'Evangelical Calvinism' is neither 'Evangelical' nor 'Calvinism' and is still spreading as a cancer throughout evangelical, Reformed churches. Huntington did not meet the myopic conditions of the editor's moral club and was thus denigrated for not being like-short-sighted.

'Moral Law' provides no salvation
There is no saving factor in man's fallen appreciation of the Scriptures. Typical of this deification of the supposed 'moral law' is David Prince's Southern Baptist blogsite named 'Andrew Fuller Fridays' proclaiming

'The Moral Law the Rule of Conduct for Believers'. A moral view of but a small part of Scripture provides no spirituality and no salvation and no understanding of the Scriptures as a whole. The Scriptures preach forgiveness and reconciliation with God and provide a *vade mecum* throughout a life in Christ outside of moral codes defined by man. Even if man could form his life within the morality of the Ten Commandments, this would have no relevance to salvation. This was the sin of the Pharisees and scribes. Moralism does not point to any form of atonement whatsoever. Morality as practised by mankind is a religion of intolerance which separates one clique from the other. Christianity is a religion of forgiveness and acceptance for lost sinners whether 'moral', 'amoral' or 'immoral'. Thanks be to God, Christ died for the ungodly! Christ makes it quite clear in His teaching that when we feel that all moral laws are being obeyed, we are still only doing law-duties and still have attained no atonement for our sins. In Luke 17:9, 10, the Great Reconciler says:

> Doth he thank that servant because he did the things that were commanded him? I trow not. So likewise ye, when ye shall have done all those things which are commanded you, say, We are unprofitable servants: we have done that which was our duty to do.

Human behaviour at its very best is only human behaviour at best and goes not one step beyond it. Morality, or rather the religion of moralism, merely shows us that we need something far greater from outside which frees us from such Fall-thinking. Those who wish to climb up the moral ladder so that by an acknowledgement of duties they can reach or continue in saving faith are again called to soberness by the Scriptures which warn us: 'Let him that thinketh he standeth take heed lest he fall'.[4]

A dead-end gospel

The truth is that morality-based, make-believe religions such as the modernistic teaching on the duty-faith awareness of 'the fitness and reasonableness of things' in fallen man are dead-end gospels of works

---

[4] 1 Corinthians 10:12.

righteousness, which clearly and simply show the unrighteousness of their origins and goals. No human ideology saves from sin. The moral-law mentality is totally void of a sense of meaning concerning its own function and the reconciliation that only God can provide.

'Morals' are not always 'moral'

It is however, argued that morals are good things and even such a moraliser as John Gill sought to live a moral life. This is an unfair argument. We are not talking about the same things. 'Morals' can never lead to faith and are not always 'moral' in the sense that they are edifying and uplifting in our walk of faith. Indeed, the term 'moral' has been emptied of true Biblical meaning by followers of the 'well-meant offer', 'duty-faith', 'moral law' enthusiasts. It is this Gill complained about and he is still criticised for his 'Back to the Bible' appeal concerning Christian morality by such free-will Rationalists as Curt Daniel and Sam Waldron. They have exchanged Christianity for Enlightenment reasoning concerning man's abilities to will himself into God's grace. Gill saw all that was morally edifying as coming from the gracious heart of God. Not from the supposed Fullerite 'reasonableness of things' propagated by the old Liberals and fallen man's alleged awareness of his duty to believe as a moral instrument towards salvation. The fact is that this late-modernistic view of 'morals' has been depleted of any truly moral content. The Christian gospel throughout the Bible teaches that we are saved by grace and not works. The 'morality' of grace is different to works morality. This limiting of the faith to keeping a supposed 'Moral Law' is only a means to an unknown selfish end. The priest who hides in his cloister and whips himself to be good, is good for nothing!

Rocking the missionary boat in India

It was this narrow 'moral' legalistic stance taken by Fuller to which he added a too narrow, legalistic interpretation of Baptism and the Lord's Supper which 'rocked the boat' of Indian Missions. This caused much anxiety within the Baptist India Mission and split the international and inter-denominational missionary movement in India down the middle. Baptist missionaries, who fell to the Socinianism of the churches which

Fuller merged with his Particular and General Baptists before changing their names, antagonised their evangelical missionary brethren in India but also fostered faulty doctrines into the native languages through most deficient 'translations'. Fuller's condemnation of Carey's co-missionaries as 'seduced by Jezebel'; his idea of converting Indians as a means of making them obedient to the British Raj; his policy of divorce from non-Baptists and freedom to marry Baptists to keep Baptist churches 'pure' and his demand that the missionaries should accept his politics ruined the Indian mission. It was all highly immoral besides being a travesty of the gospel. It was a work of profound lawlessness and immorality. Indeed, Carey had to protest that Fuller's political criticisms of Fountain were 'killing' him and Carey called Ryland's interference 'evil'. Carey also differed strongly from Fuller in their concepts of the theology of ecclesiology, the theology of evangelism and regarding colonial politics. Whatever friendship they had, Fuller brought this friendship to a breaking point time and time again. Indeed, Carey often held the ropes for Fuller though Fuller let go of the ropes holding Carey.

Church order based on 'the fitness of things' not Scripture

Warning his readers it would be expecting too much to look for Scriptural authority respecting the form, order and organisation of the Christian church, Fuller argues he will prove that such a form, order and organisation of the New Testament church can be derived from 'the fitness of things', and he goes on to describe his idea of New Testament practice according to the 'genius of Christianity'. Non-Fullerites would feel quite at a loss here as Fuller continually advises them not to take Christ's precepts literally, leaving only 'general principles' as a guide which he interprets in a very singular way. He misunderstands God's revelations to the Old Testament peoples as being merely 'legal' and sees the New Testament as being founded on moral principles and not Law. He was, of course, quite wrong on both counts.

Fuller on moral and positive precepts

Fuller argues the Grotian way more fully in his *On Moral and Positive Obedience* which was surprisingly an annual pastoral letter to the local Baptist Association pastors though there is only pseudo-intellectualism and rationalism in it and nothing 'pastoral'. In this work, Fuller lays great store on the right use of reason or 'right reason' as he calls it. The word reason signifies to Fuller 'the fitness of things'. This is the way, he argues, the apostles used it when they said, 'It is not reason that we should leave the word of God, and serve tables';[5] that is, 'it is not fit or proper'. Right reason, Fuller tells us, 'is perfect and immutable, remaining always the same' and further, 'No Divine truth can disagree' with it. Such reason may, however, 'be above and contrary to' man's reasoning which is shattered by sin, blindness and prejudice. Fuller, however, in stressing that right reason may not of necessity contradict man's reasoning, obviously feels that man is somehow capable of using right reason, though he does not outline how reason, used rightly, can atone for sin. So, for Fuller, it is the practical use of right reason which distinguishes New Testament teaching from the Old which he believes was law-bound as we have seen from the above quote from Fuller's *Principles of Church Discipline*.[6] Jews were unreasonable he claims but the people of New Testament times are reasonable beings. Furthermore, according to Fuller, the Old hindered man from using his reason as he relied on 'positive law' whereas the New encourages reason. This is keeping with Fuller's own reasoning which rules that man is not dead in trespasses and sins as God could not reason with a dead man. He only speaks to one capable of hearing and responding. Presumably Fuller, who is often Anti-Semitic, thought the Jews were incapable of such an exercise but Gentiles are. This is why Fuller argues in his *The Gospel Worthy of All Acceptation*:

> Or if the inability of sinners to believe in Christ were of the same nature as that of a dead body in a grave to rise up and walk, it were absurd to suppose that they would on this account fall under the Divine censure. No man is reproved for not doing that which is naturally impossible; but sinners are reproved for not believing, and given to understand that it is solely owing to their

[5] *Works*, Vol. III, Moral and Positive Obedience, p. 357.
[6] *Works*, Vol. III, p. 452. In Fuller's *Complete Works* hitherto published we find this reference in 'Principles of Church Discipline' under the title 'Thoughts on the Principles' which Fuller sent to the Baptist missionaries in Serampore. This is found on p. 831 in the one volume Banner of Truth reprint.

criminal ignorance, pride, dishonesty of heart, and aversion from God.[7]

Is Fuller referring to dead Jews or dead Gentiles here or both? Here, too, Fuller is de-theologising sin which he sees as 'criminal ignorance' due to lack of right reason. The Biblical truth is that man's duplicity and responsibility in sinning against God cannot be put down to 'ignorance' and a failure to be reasonable. All the symptoms of man's enmity against God, Fuller reasons, do not point to physical and spiritual death, nor even moral inability, but merely to an 'unwillingness to believe'. This is his mock fall. The real fall, according to Fuller, comes when Christ is rejected on hearing the gospel because man then refuses to use his inherent capabilities to believe in Christ savingly. Again, this is pure Grotianism and not the Reformed, evangelical, Protestant faith.

Fuller's Grotian principle of two standards of 'right'

In Fuller's pastoral letter *On Moral and Positive Obedience*, he teaches that there are eternals such as the order of nature and temporals such as God's Law and revelations to man which are entirely arbitrary. The latter are right only because God commanded them and have no relation to the intrinsic nature of God's own character, nor to the 'fitness of things'. Echoing Chandler, Fuller reinterprets Philippians 4:8:

> Whatsoever things are true, whatsoever things are honest, whatsoever things are just, whatsoever things are pure, whatsoever things are lovely, whatsoever things are of *good report*;[8] if there be any virtue, and if there be any praise, think on these things.

Like Chandler, he emphasises that Paul is teaching that the moral law is implanted in the minds of men. Like Chandler, he does not seem to realise that the standard for true, honest, just, pure and lovely things – things which lead to a good report – are Scriptural standards, i.e. revealed standards, given because they reflect God's own unchangeable character. Revealed precepts, however, are to Fuller in 'positive' form

---

[7] *Works*, Vol. II, p. 355.
[8] Fuller's emphasis.

and have no absolute authority as they 'arise merely from the sovereign will of the Law-giver'. The use of the word 'merely' here speaks volumes regarding Fuller's ambiguous belief in God. As an example of the latter, 'positive' law, Fuller gives:

Wherefore I beseech you, be ye followers of me[9]

Be ye followers of me, even as I also am of Christ.[10]

Now I praise you brethren, that you remember me in all things, as I delivered them to you.[11]

Brethren be followers together of me, and mark them that walk so as ye have us for an example.[12]

He then argues that Philippians 4:8:

Whatsoever things are true, whatsoever things are honest, whatsoever things are just, whatsoever things are pure, whatsoever things are lovely, whatsoever things are of good report; If there be any virtue, and if there be any praise, think on these things,

is commanding what is right but 1 Corinthians 4:16, 17:

Wherefore I beseech you, be ye followers of me. For this cause have I sent unto you Timotheus, who is my beloved son, and faithful in the Lord, who shall bring you into remembrance of my ways which be in Christ, as I reach everywhere in every church,

is right because it is commanded and adds:

---

[9] 1 Corinthians 4:16.
[10] 1 Corinthians 11:1.
[11] 1 Corinthians 11:2.
[12] Philippians 3:17.

> The great principles of the former are of perpetual obligation, and know no other variety than that which arises from the varying of relations and conditions; but those of the latter may be binding at one period of time, and utterly abolished in another.

Again, Fuller is using his own trust in 'right reason' to judge these things. He does not seem to realise that we have learnt to follow Christ through the written testimony of such as Paul and that the teaching Paul claims in 1 Corinthians 4 he has from Christ has become the Word of God itself and is a value for eternity. In rejecting everything that God has revealed including Law and Gospel as arbitrary and temporary works of God in favour of Natural Law and Natural Religion, Fuller rejects the immutable and eternal Being of God and replaces Him with a product of his own will which is atheistic Rationalism.

Fuller's cautions concerning the commandments of Christ
In his eagerness to find what he calls 'general principles' in the Bible, Fuller is highly critical of the exact words and precepts of Christ Himself, arguing:

> the commandments of Christ, however, are not all of the same kind, so neither is our obedience required to be yielded in all respects on the same principles.

Fuller means by this that we must use our right reason to discern when Christ is speaking according to fixed eternal moral laws or is merely giving 'positive' instruction. We must thus use our fallen 'right reason' to judge Christ's commandments and discern whether they are 'moral' or 'positive'. We see here that Fuller is again using the word 'positive' to mean 'negative'. Fuller would have us believe that this is orthodox theology claiming, 'The distinction of obedience into moral and positive is far from novel'. This may well be the case. The faulty thinking might be as old as Methuselah but it is still human reason and not gospel revelation. Without this distinction, however, Fuller tells us we will never be able to understand Scripture. He goes on to express what is moral and what is positive in Scripture by saying:

We can clearly perceive that it were inconsistent with the perfections of God not to have required us to love him and one another, or to have allowed of the contrary. Children also must needs be required to 'obey their parents; for this is right'. But it is not thus in positive institutions. Whatever wisdom there may be in them, and whatever discernment in us, we could not have known them had they not been expressly revealed; nor are they ever enforced as being right in themselves, but merely as being of Divine appointment. Of them we may say, Had it pleased God, he might in various instances have enjoined the opposites; but of the other, we are not allowed to suppose it possible, or consistent with righteousness, to require anything different from that which is required.

Man's obligation to the moral law, Fuller goes on to argue, is coeval with his creation 'but it was not till God had planted a garden in Eden, and there put the man he had formed, and expressly prohibited the fruit of one of the trees on pain of death, that he came under a positive law. The former would approve itself to his conscience as according with the nature of things; the latter as being commanded by the Creator'. Fuller seems never to have heard of a 'seared conscience' and man's fallen inability to obey God's Word. So, too, Fuller is obviously saying that God kept to 'moral laws' before Creation but dropped them for arbitrary 'positive' laws after creation. This astonishing disbelief in God's immutable nature is the basis on which Fuller builds his 'Gospel worthy of all acceptation'. Who is Fuller, and with him many would-be Rationalists, trying to kid?

Fuller's use of right reason is wrong
It is interesting to note that Fuller in the above quote uses Ephesians 6:1 concerning children's obedience in a manner showing that he is already implementing his rule of 'right reason' to stress the importance of his moral law over positive law. Fuller misquotes the verse in Ephesians merely to promote his rationalism. The Scripture reads, 'Children obey your parents in the Lord: for this is right'. This would be, according to Fuller, a positive command not a nebulous 'moral' command. To get

over this difficulty, Fuller has omitted the words 'in the Lord' as they obviously refer to post-Edenic revelation expressing what Fuller calls positive law. Children are to obey their parents according to Fuller, not because the Lord in His revelation so wills it as His Divine standard but because what is right commands this. This 'right' is older and therefore more absolute than the revealed will of God, according to Fuller. This idea of 'right' is coeval with man and thus prior to the revealed Word of God in Scripture. Yet Fuller has to corrupt the Biblical message to get over his point.

Fuller is totally confused by his own utilitarian religion
Actually, as becomes clear on reading through Fuller's *On Moral and Positive Obedience*, the author is advocating a completely utilitarian, rational way of life[13] and a de-theologising and a de-Scripturalising of Christianity. Fuller, indeed, claims here that he finds the utility of his views apparent. Fuller rather contradicts himself in his brief commentary on one of Robert Hall's *Fast Sermons* where he questions that 'morality' is founded in 'utility'. However, morality as here defined is confessing what is 'fit' or 'unfit' and the reasons he gives for this are, in spite of his denial, strictly utilitarian. Thus utility is founded in morality for Fuller.[14] Similarly, Fuller argues ostensibly against Socinianism, Baxterism and Arminianism yet he actually argues so often in their favour.

Fuller gives a host of examples as to what Christian action or ordinance is 'moral' and what is 'positive' but he confuses his own distinctions when applying them to the revealed Word of God and their outcome in Christian behaviour. The pattern of behaviour which he presents in separating the moral from the positive may show much rational sense to those who think that way, but it is obviously not Scriptural or even 'Christian'. Nevertheless, after setting up clear distinctions between what is 'moral' and what is 'positive', Fuller is so full of exceptions where he finds that the moral is positive or the positive is moral that irrational chaos is the result. Fuller gets himself tied up in his own view of 'the fitness of things'. This is because Fuller was always changing his system of Rationalism and morality. He had

---

[13] See p. 357.
[14] See the Banner of Truth one volume edition of Fuller's *Works*, p. 994.

no anchor in God's immutable will for his own but sought his anchor in things 'fitting and reasonable' which, nevertheless often appeared to him as 'unfitting' and 'unreasonable'. When one has no norm anyone's guess may rule. This forwards-backwards march is especially seen in today's New Covenant Theology philosophy which boasts of reserving the right to alter their system at will.

Facing both ways on moral law

After telling his readers, for instance, that man's knowledge of the moral law is coeval with man and that man has the natural wherewithal to understand this, Fuller dampens our moral enthusiasm by confessing, 'If, on the other hand, we do everything according to the letter of the moral precepts, we shall often overlook the true intent of them, and do that which is manifestly wrong'.[15] Indeed, Fuller seems to be constantly looking for what is 'manifestly right' and what is 'manifestly wrong' by reinterpreting the precepts of Christ and the patterns of behaviour laid down in the gospel according to what he calls 'parity of reasoning' and presenting them as new laws for right reasoning, though he is obviously always plagued by second thoughts on the matter and alters his course without removing his former zig-zag route from his writings. It is perhaps not being too unkind to Fuller to suggest that because he defines what is 'moral' and thus eternal and what is 'positive' and thus temporal quite arbitrarily, he has no fixed guide to recommend for our Christian walk. It is thus no wonder that Fullerites call orthodox Christians Antinomians as the latter see the Mosaic Law as an essential, eternal part of God's everlasting covenant (1 Corinthians 4:16) with His Son for the salvation of mankind but Fullerites have their ever changing 'right reason' to go by and are totally confused by their 'moral' and 'positive' legalistic mix-up.

Fuller's faulty view of the Covenant of Grace

Fuller claims that the old covenant of works has been abolished for sinner and saint alike yet his doctrine of a penal gospel and rules for right thinking are really a new covenant of works based on the gospel.

---

[15] Op. cit. p. 354.

The Truth is that what Fullerites call 'the old covenant of works', is not 'old' but eternal as it reveals the Character of God and was placed within the eternal Covenant of Grace because of man's transgressions and with it the promise of forgiveness to those who understand its tenor. That is God's will in creating the Covenant as a means of drawing in the people of God. Fuller creates his own 'covenant of works' by redefining what Law within Gospel is. Separating the Old Testament covenantal promises from the New divides the Gospel. This is Fuller's enigma and again we see how NCT has developed out of such Fullerite ideas. Though Fuller has such a low view of the Law, and might therefore with absolute fairness be called an Antinomian, he is, nevertheless, an extreme legalist. However, his legalistic views based allegedly on the 'fitness' and 'reasonableness' of things are purely arbitrary and of his own invention.

There is no purpose in Fuller's gospel

Fuller's often mentioned 'end' to which his idea of gospel revelation is a mere figurative 'means' is never actually revealed or fully reasoned out in his system. Thus there is no solid hope of salvation in his teaching as it by-passes the Atonement. The Biblical way to heaven in Fuller's map of salvation is marked out in winding paths of symbols, of signs, of imagery and metaphor illustrated with pseudo-philosophic axioms which can only totally confuse and disorientate the Christian pilgrim. Wherever one follows Fuller's reasoning one never seems to come to the end of the chain. He constantly requires his readers to make do during the search for his 'end' with a pious kind of utilitarian 'situation ethics' which can only lead to utter scepticism as to what is truth. All his talk of moral and positive obedience is, as Gill told Chandler in similar words, mere pseudo-intellectual verbal waffle to cover up his distrust of revealed religion.

No law substitute for a full Atonement of grace

Neither the Moral Influence Theory, nor the Governmental Theory, nor their combination in Fuller's teaching provide a solution to the problem of law and sin. The Moralist says that Christ's example should prompt us to love Him and the Governmentalist tells us that the fact of Christ's deterrent death ought to frighten us into obedience. Fuller appeals more to 'law' but to an unlawful law; a law which is nowhere to be found in

Scripture. He takes man's gaze from the Atonement which is necessary for the divine law to be fulfilled and places it on a moral or natural law which, for him, is not an eternal representation of God's righteousness but claims that it is a metaphor to tell the criminal (rather than the sinner) to love Christ as if he had never apostatised and in fulfilling this duty he will be saved[16].

Fullerism does not deal with the guilt of man and Atonement for it
In Fullerism love combined with fear produce duty which leads to salvation but this is not one whit better than the mock-gospel Grotius, Chandler and Hopkins give us. It does not deal with the guilt of man. It does not deal with sin as sin and does not even begin to answer the question of how a man may get right with an angry God. Indeed, Fuller depicts God as being narrowly but lovingly benevolent to the point of exhibiting blindness to justice and mercy. Fuller subjectifies the Atonement as he teaches that actual at-one-ment is instigated by personal repentance and faith. He thus robs the Atonement of its objective, historical display of mercy in which Christ covered His Bride's sins there and then on the cross. The Atonement is thus also robbed of the very benevolence of which Fuller boasts. Fuller and his modern followers equally rob the Atonement of its justice as they deny that it was at Calvary that the ransom was paid once and for all time.

Chapter 6 of this book will deal with the superiority of revealed law and gospel over Grotian thinking and the actual and factual outworking of the Atonement as opposed to Fullerite tokenism and symbolism.

---

[16] See especially The Gospel Worthy of All Acceptation, *Works*, Vol. II, pp. 375, 376.

Chapter 6

Understanding the Law Lawfully

Fuller's theology belittles the Divine imperative

Modern Neonomians and Antinomians who speak of a figurative imputation, redemption and reconciliation have traditionally criticised upholders of the doctrine of Grace for teaching the eternal validity of God's Law. There is no divine imperative in the law in the Moral Government theory as there is in the gospel of the Bible found in both Testaments. In Governmentalism man's basic desire is depicted as being personal happiness or the general good. Fuller swerves in his exposition of the Divine imperative according to whether he was reading the earlier or the later New England divines at the time. In *The Gospel Worthy of All Acceptation,* Fuller shows clearly his dependence on Bellamy and his *The Holy Nature of the Christian Religion* and reveals clear signs of Hopkins' thoughts mixed with other earlier and later New Divinity theories.

Fuller admitted himself that he had changed his views radically on the subject though his followers continue to quote Fuller's earlier and later altered views as if they were Fuller's constant or final views, thus adding to their theological chaos. Time and time again, we find Fuller arguing that the Biblical law is teleological and must be seen as a general rule of advice and catalogue of principles whereby man must guard himself against becoming bogged down in the finer points. There are no jots and tittles to Fuller's law but a broad reliance on what Fuller calls 'the spirit' which is invariably 'the nature and fitness of things'.

True Law needed not fake laws

Moses insisted on following the tenor of the Law which pointed to faith but Fuller's moral law is a mere psychological rule of conduct, outlining duties according to natural abilities. It is thus not a true Law at all and thus cannot be an aid to faith and a guide into the Covenant of Grace. Fuller's positive law is also without imperatives as it is merely a temporal accommodation to God's supposed arbitrary will and needs the moral law to interpret it aright. Both of Fuller's laws, the 'moral' which is immoral and the 'positive' which is negative, however, reveal a very legal system running contrary to God's Law. Fuller's view of the gospel places the emphasis on the law-bound duty of a sinner to exercise faith savingly and not on the grace of God in supplying man with what the law could never awake in man and never provide him with.[1] In Fuller's system law is but a 'moral' gospel but his gospel is not Law in the Mosaic, therefore God's, sense but merely a legalistic Neonomian means to encourage sinners to keep the Fullerite law-gospel. Thus, in boasting of their gospel which they say is worthy of all acceptation, Fullerites are abusing the call to evangelise by presenting man with a covenant of works and not the Covenant of Grace. They have turned the faith-bringing gospel provisions of Christ into a duty-bound, legal system that Moses never intended as he emphasised the tenor and spirit of the Law and not its letter.

Governmentalism has a totally false view of law

There is obviously, as far as fallen man is concerned, nothing natural at all in so-called 'Natural Law'. Even if there were such a law, man would have as little understanding of it as he would have ability to save himself through adhering to it. The message of Romans 2 is that man in his fallen nature has become a law unto himself and is thus without excuse for his state. Without atoning mercies, he is lost. Natural Law as we see it in its fallen status will be wound up when Christ comes to take His people home to their New Jerusalem.

---

[1] Acts 13:39.

Fuller confuses his version of natural law with his version of moral law as he teaches that it is moral law which is provided by natural religion and the law which each person has by nature. His gospel of 'the nature and fitness of things' could only be thought successful if it could be proven that man's natural abilities have not suffered from his fall into sin and if, as Fuller taught, man's reason and conscience were still the immaculate image of God in man. The revealed Word of God shows that such a perfection is not the lot of fallen man and fallen man has not even the natural sense to see this, so natural law whether intact or fallen is of no saving use to him.

The superiority of Revealed Law over so-called 'Natural Law'
Both 'Natural Law' and 'Moral law', of themselves, know no penalties other than man's not reaching the ultimate end of personal bliss which the Bible – and experience – show to be fallen man's inevitable goal. They are also laws which provide no means for them to be kept, as Governmentalists and Fullerites claim that not even Christ has kept them fully for man as he did not place Himself under the Law but above it. Besides, even if He had placed Himself under the Law in Fullerite thinking, the Moral Influence people do not believe that obedience and what it gains can be transferred or imputed. Those who accept Biblical Law are ill-advised to use a conflict of terms such as 'moral' and 'positive' which invariably brings a conflict of ideas with it. The Biblical pattern of Law goes far beyond ideas of natural, moral, positive or conventional laws. The Bible speaks of the Mosaic Law and of God's decrees regarding its fulfilment in the Law of Christ (Galatians 6:2) and the Law of Faith (Romans 3:27). These laws show that no saving faith can be produced by duties to any works-only law because if salvation could be sought by such duties it would then be of works and not faith. Faith however, is a gift of God which comes through Christ's atoning intervention in our lives and has no relation to law-duties but is entirely of grace.

No Atonement if Christ died 'above the Law'
Those who teach, following Grotius and Fuller, that Christ's sufferings and death were above the Law rule out Christ's vicarious sufferings for

those with whom he identified Himself who were under the Law. It is the Law that cursed man under it and so Christ had to carry the punishment for this broken Law equally under it. Had He not placed Himself under the Law and took on its curse through His sinless body, there would have been no Atonement. This is the great deficit in the gospel of defenders of Fullerism such as Haykin, Chun and Daniel. They speak very much of a warranted salvation through duties but they circumnavigate the gospel truth of the Atonement in a circumlocution of non-gospel words which is nothing but a denial of Christ's work on the cross. The cheek of it all is that this gospel of deceit is trumpeted abroad as 'the gospel worthy of all acceptation'.

The law of duty-faith at variance with Scripture

The Governmental law of duty-faith, therefore, is at variance with Scripture. It is thus spiritually profitable to keep to Scriptural terms of law as they convey Christian concepts and show the full scope of what is expected of man and how these expectations can be met in the saving work of Father, Son and Holy Spirit. These laws do not neglect the bliss of man but provide a means of knowing God and enjoying him for ever. Such a knowledge and such a union, however, can only come about when the Lawgiver is perfectly satisfied. This satisfaction is obtained in the Atonement which was the act of Christ whereby He took upon Himself our sins and suffered punishment for them on our behalf, thus releasing His elect from all the penalties, but not the obligations and responsibilities of God's law. These obligations and responsibilities are taken up in our union with Christ and we now do not serve the law as a taskmaster but serve the lawgiver Himself personally in Christ, looking to our Saviour for strength to live out His righteousness, supported by the indwelling of the Holy Spirit and the continuing assistance of God's holy Word.

New Testament teaching seen as 'an evasion' of the truth

It is symptomatic of modern Fullerites that they support their founder fully in this aberration of holy truth. They actually feel, following Fuller, that to argue that there are New Testament precepts concerning grace in the New Testament which add to our interpretation of the decalogue and are objects of faith is 'mere evasion'[2] and beside the point! Robert Oliver in his numerous attempts to defend Fuller, rejects William Huntington's condemnation of Christian Pharisees who believe in the justifying powers of the law and the full gospel being revealed in the decalogue as if it were a mere legal code. For them the sole moral standard of the Christian life clearly 'evades' the full gospel truth. It is an inability to grasp Huntington's point that a so-called moral law can never be the sole rule of conduct for the Christian. Moses, of course, never taught such nonsense. Huntington viewed the Decalogue and its fulfilment from the point of view of the revelation in Christ concerning His everlasting gospel. If the so-called 'Moral Law' had been a sufficient norm for Christians and if it were truly the sum of Old Testament gospel revelation, Huntington argued, this would have rendered the New Testament superfluous. To concentrate on what the law says to the exclusion of the gospel in which it is embedded throughout the Bible is clearly the blindest of evasion tactics. God's eternal standard goes hand in hand with God's eternal gospel, indeed, they are one. Even in this matter, however, Fuller was highly inconsistent. His essays on moral and positive law show that he rid even the ten commandments of 'positive' precepts at times. Fuller always suffered under his own vocabulary as he constantly redefined words.

The idea that all which is necessary to saving faith is to be found in the Ten Commandments which Fullerites call their 'moral law' is neither the theology of the Old nor the New Testament.

The gospel according to make-believe
The Governmental view of the whole plan of salvation, i.e. the whole gospel as it is in Christ Jesus, is a matter of make-believe metaphor. The doctrines of baptism and the Lord's Supper which Fuller interprets in a completely legal way and not in a gospel way are the only doctrines that Fuller claims signify what they really are. Yet even here Fuller has totally misunderstood the two sacraments and explains away their spiritual and ecclesiological relevance. All other doctrines, as seen by Fuller are not couched in real, concrete terms but are highly

---

[2] Banner of Truth Magazine, Issues 373, p. 12; 376, p. 12.

metaphorical or merely *de jure*. This reflects the Grotian and Fullerite idea of revealed religion being but a covering for the 'nature and fitness of things' which comprise its rationale. Such a religion can thus never approach to a teaching of actual union with Christ, based on Christ's objective atonement and Christ's imputed righteousness as taught literally by the New Testament and followed by the Reformers, Puritans and earlier leaders of the Evangelical Awakening. The last thing that Fuller does is look for the literal meaning of a Biblical doctrine.

Putting on Christ

The emphasis on the practical outcome of the new man's union with Christ described vividly in the Bible as 'putting on Christ' has caused much protest amongst Fullerite Neo-evangelicals in recent years who claim that sovereign grace is thus emphasised too much leaving the believer with a mere passive sanctification. They want to know more about working out their own salvation. Under the misleading title 'An Appraisal of William Huntington', written in Issue 298 of the Banner of Truth Magazine, 1988, the anonymous author criticised Huntington for believing in the actual imputation of man's sin to Christ and Christ's righteousness to the new man. For this display of trust in what the Scriptures actually say, Huntington was called an Antinomian by the nameless accuser. As the systematic doctrinal views aired had nothing to do with *The Voice of Years*, a book which was allegedly being reviewed in the article, and hardly applied in the form given to Huntington, it was obvious that the writer was merely using the book and the subject for some other sinister purpose. Furthermore, the writer, whoever it really was, must be criticised for using the work of a most questionable writer and scoffer indeed and pawning this off as the truth, the whole truth and nothing but the truth. Naturally for the anonymous author, who was leaning on Fuller's review of *The Voice of Years*, he continued in the same slanderous vein. Neither *The Voice of Years* author nor Fuller analysed Huntington's theology in any way, but though *The Voice of Years* author sought to be balanced in part, Fuller knew no such balance and criticised Huntington mercilessly without a single quote to back up his quite unbalanced case. Though shielding the Banner of Truth author with the cloak of anonymity, the Editorial Manager, Rev. Iain Murray, accepted full responsibility for inserting this dagger, with the excuse that it would open up what he called 'an important controversy'.[3] He was not disappointed as the article was designed to split the Reformed churches down the middle. When I wrote to the Editorial board in protest, I was told by the editor that he was not so much campaigning against Huntington but holding him up as a figure to ward off young Christians from Antinomianism. This was quite a surprise as Huntington taught that the Law of God was eternal and that on the Day of Judgment, it would be used by God in separating the sheep from the goats. He was neither an Antinomian nor a Neonomian but a man who, like David, loved the Law and saw it as a means of grace. I was told that Huntington was a 'theoretical' Antinomian whereas his accusers, when compared to the real Huntington, were real practising Antinomians. Yet the many letters of readers which protested against this dumbing down of Reformed religion were given hardly a mention and one contribution was so edited as to make it say the opposite of what was intended. When I protested against the misuse of my own correspondence with the Editorial Board, the then new editor, Maurice Roberts told me in a written reply that my protest was 'unworthy' of me. Several other protestors published their letters separately to make sure that the truth was known. I answered with several published essays on Huntington's theology and my defence of Huntington in the wee book *Weighed in the Balance*, pointing out the inaccuracy of the Banner of Truth's misuse of Huntington. The curious fact here is that the four or five correspondents who had written with their complaints regarding the Banner of Truth's handling of Huntington had read most, if not all, his works whereas the Banner of Truth editor confessed he had but read one work of Huntington's which was against Arminianism and this was enough to condemn all his other works. Sadly, ignorance is the main weapon in pseudo-evangelical warfare.

The fact that Huntington was being criticised for believing sound doctrines that were held by a number of authors whose works were formerly printed by the Banner of Truth, (one only has to think of Thomas Goodwin, John Owen and Louis Berkhof), shows that this Christian publishing house was actually announcing a new trend in their

---

[3] Issue 378, Banner of Truth Magazine, p. 22.

theological thinking. Other writers such as Witsius, Trail and Warfield have been warmly recommended in the Banner of Truth pages in the past but presumably would find no favourable mention in those pages now as they hold to doctrines of grace completely opposed to the new Banner of Truth position and identical to Huntington's.[4]

Avowed opponents of the doctrine of actual imputation

The Banner of Truth author of the anonymous accusations against Huntington's most successful teaching and preaching implied that Huntington did not believe in a judicial imputation because he believed in an actual one. Governmentalists, of course, believe that the one element cancels the other out. Judgment, however, in God's care of His elect always goes hand in hand with mercy (grace). The Banner of Truth idea was inherited from the Socinians who are avowed opponents of the doctrine of actual imputation. Huntington, on strong Biblical evidence, had emphasised that Christ's imputed righteousness was both judicial and real. This was the very kernel of the triumphant message James Hervey had for John Wesley and his Arminian denial of imputation.[5] Huntington was merely taking up Hervey's Scriptural mantle, maintaining that sinners could be clothed with Christ's righteousness. The joint friend of Hervey and Huntington, William Romaine, described the orthodox teaching on imputation in his sermon The Lord Our Righteousness based on Isaiah 45:8 and preached before the University of Oxford, March 20, 1757:

> There is no salvation without righteousness, and it is of the Lord's free grace that he (the sinner) is received as righteous, through the righteousness of Christ imputed to him by faith. Christ's righteousness can be made ours only by imputation. As our sins were actually imputed to him, so his righteousness is actually imputed to us. The Lord laid upon him the iniquity of us all, and therefore he was wounded for our transgressions, and was

---

[4] Since I originally wrote these words the Banner of Truth have come up with an 'Easy Reader' of Trail's fine work on justification which they, like a similar 'update' on a work by Bunyan, have heavily altered to suit Fullerite thinking and make Trail 'Banner of Truth compatible'.
[5] See my article, *Whose Righteousness Saves Us?*, Bible League Quarterly, July-September, 1991, pp. 436-442. See also my *James Hervey: Preacher of Righteousness*, Go Publications, 1997 for Hervey's personal contact and correspondence with Wesley.

bruised for our iniquities. As he thus took our sins upon himself, so we by faith take his righteousness upon us, and by it are saved.[6]

The Banner of Truth author obviously believed that imputation was merely a judicial 'as if' ruling or a kind of make-believe on God's part. Here, the Banner of Truth was following the Socinian, Grotian, Fullerite trend whereby the doctrine of actual imputation, whether Adam's sin to mankind or the elect's sin to Christ or Christ's righteousness to the elect, has been rationalised out of their thinking. Needless to say, the Banner of Truth eventually denounced William Romaine himself as an Antinomian alongside Huntington. When they claimed in their magazine and sister magazines that I, too, was an Antinomian and a Hyper-Calvinist, I felt placed in honourable company.

A refreshing word from an unexpected quarter
I have had trouble with the Banner of Truth on a number of issues which has led them to assume and declare in their magazine that I do not believe in preaching Christ to sinners. What a horribly false thought! However, the magazine was going through a Wesleyan phase at the time so one can understand that they had become weak on imputation. Happily, in the cause of God and truth, it does appear that they have moved back to a Biblical basis on their doctrine of imputation. On doing some intense research into the subject of imputation, caused by brethren in two chat groups who accused me of teaching that Christ was sinful, I read a most beautiful, moving sermon by Geoff Thomas of the Banner of Truth who put the doctrine of Imputation of Sin to Christ into golden words of Biblical wisdom which cannot really be bettered. He said:

God made him who had no sin to be sin for us, so that in him we might become the righteousness of God (2 Corinthians 5:20,

---

[6] *The Whole Works of the Late Reverend William Romaine A. M.*, London, 1837, p. 789. Exciting news is that this sermon and other sermons of Romaine are being reprinted in cheap but sturdy editions by the Christian Bookshop, Ossett. The bookshop is also reprinting, Crisp, Hawker, Gill, Brine and a number of other forgotten heroes of the faith. This work is being paralleled in the States by the Baptist Standard Bearer.

21). So Paul is saying something absolutely breath taking about Golgotha. Something great was actually achieved in the agonizing death of Jesus which could not have been achieved if Jesus had not died that death. It was this, that on Calvary 'God made him who had no sin to be sin for us'. God was there imputing our sin to Christ. He was really laying sin on him. We can say it in a dozen ways but the message is always the same: He was accounting Christ to be a sinner. He was charging Jesus with our guilt. He was ascribing to the spotless Son the shame and blame of our bad behaviour. He was reckoning to the account of our Lord our sins and making him answer for us. In our place God the Son was being condemned. Jesus was being made accountable for what we have done. God was making his Son answer for our wrongdoing, and Jesus was willingly and freely choosing to be made sin for us. The Father and the Son were in harmonious agreement that because of their great mutual and eternal love for us this could be the only way that we fallen sons of Adam most certainly will be redeemed. Something in the very nature of who God is requires that death inevitably has to be the wages of sin. Without the shedding of blood there can be no remission. That is how the only God that exists is.

Thank you Geoff Thomas for this sweet testimony to the great suffering Christ went through in order to save our worthless souls and may we be ever thankful and full of wonder and praise at this great exchange – our sin for Christ's righteousness. You have pointed the way to the very heart of our loving God and helped us to find a welcome place in it.

In Chapter 7, I shall discuss how Fullerites condemn the atoning properties of the work of Christ in justification and sanctification and outline the gospel nearness of the Old Paths to New Divinity and the modern Fullerite gospel substitute.

Chapter 7

The Old Paths versus New Divinity

Scripture contra fallen 'Right Reason' exemplified by William Huntington and Andrew Fuller

The Halcyon Days of the Banner of Truth
The work of the Banner of Truth Trust proved a great encouragement in my spiritual development as a young Christian and I became an enthusiastic reader of their magazine from the late fifties on. Throughout the following years, especially during the seventies and eighties, I was able to break away from my work in Sweden and Germany to attend a number of inspiring Leicester Conferences which blessed the soul of so many pastors and teachers and gave them a love for Reformed doctrines and personal holiness. In those early halcyon days of theological unity and brotherly love, we young men believed we were on the verge of a great revival and a return to the Old Paths of evangelism and soul-care which had become overgrown with the weeds of Liberal theology. We were all prepared, under the leadership of such fine men as Sidney Houghton, Sidney Norton and Iain Murray, to clean up those paths and lead the way to worldwide revival.

Introduced to Huntington at a Banner of Truth Conference

At that time, the name of William Huntington was often on the lips of the conference delegates. This man of poor origins and little education was mightily used of God in the saving of souls and his numerous works were read avidly by all social classes both at home and abroad. From a preacher in the fields and dock-yards, Huntington became pastor of an ever growing church which became the greatest in London. The members gave so much money away for the work of the gospel that even Huntington critics, such as Rowland Hill of Surrey Chapel, sent their members to beg at the door of Huntington's chapel when the people left after the service. Needless to say, Huntington's second-hand works were precious items for those who wished to have a Christian mentor they could understand and follow. Those who brought them to the Leicester Conference could be sure of a quick sale. It was thus there that I purchased my first collections of Huntington's letters. These were then supplemented quickly by Bensley's and Collingridge's editions of Huntington's further works. Books such as *Moses Unveiled in the Face of Christ, The Justification of a Sinner* and *On the Dimensions of Eternal Love*, to name but a few gems, thrilled my soul. Huntington's *Letters on Ministerial Qualifications* was just the kind of material the conference pastors needed.

The Old Paths challenged

This widespread love of Huntington was to change radically amongst Banner of Truth leaders, followed sadly by a vociferous minority of their most devoted fans who now began to hurl the charge of Antinomianism and Hyper-Calvinism at anyone who chose to remain on the Old Paths. As mentioned previously, the July 1988 issue of the Banner of Truth Magazine featured an anonymous and scathing, indeed scandalous, attack on Huntington's testimony. This groundless and base assault was presented under the misleading title of An Appraisal of William Huntington by an anonymous author, an unusual step for the magazine. The word 'appraisal', etymologically speaking, has to do with 'praise' but the article, said falsely to be taken from a small, anonymous book named *The Voice of Years*, contained no praise but was full of mixed-up Fullerite, New Divinity theology which was certainly not found in *The Voice of Years*, bad as the book is. However, much of the tone and content of the Banner of Truth article is to be found rather in a review of *The Voice of Years*, penned by Andrew Fuller who introduced New Divinity and Liberalism into English evangelical theology during Huntington's day.[1]

In the 'appraisal', the nameless accuser claimed:

> William Huntington (1745-1813) was an Antinomian who maintained the following doctrines:
> (1) The elect are justified from all eternity, an act of which their justification in this world by faith is only a manifestation; (2) that God sees no sin in believers, and is never angry with them; (3) that the imputation of our sins to Christ, and of His righteousness to us, was actual, not judicial; (4) that faith, repentance, and holy obedience are covenant conditions on the part of Christ, not on our part; (5) that sanctification is no evidence of justification but rather renders it more obscure. These doctrines form the general creed of all theoretical Antinomians, more or less.

Groundless accusations

Such grave accusations needed to be backed by convincing examples from the condemned person's works. However, the anonymous accuser gave no primary evidence for his severe allegations thus making himself guilty of vicious gossip. Though the author mentioned some of Huntington's 'good points' such as his being plain and natural, Scriptural, experimental, contemplative and laborious, he took this all back when listing the so-called 'bad points'. He did not go so far as Fuller who claimed that all Huntington's good points had nothing to do with a Christian's witness, nevertheless, he calls Huntington conceited, dogmatical, vindictive, infallible, inaccessible, political and anti-literal ending his harangue with the pious-sounding words, 'We should not follow him but the personal example of Christ'.

On reading this tasteless tirade, I sent a refutation of its moral, historical, and theological errors to the Banner of Truth for publication.

---

[1] *Works*, Vol. III, p. 762 ff..

I had hitherto been in good standing with the magazine who had published a number of essays from my pen on Huntington's contemporaries. This time, Iain Murray refused to publish my letter, claiming responsibility for the article and adding that he had nothing personally against Huntington but he wished to scare young Christians away from Antinomianism. This reminded me of the research I was doing on Arthur Miller's *The Crucible*. Miller had claimed that the American Puritans were 'absolute evil' so that he could persuade play-goers to turn from them and adopt his radicalism. Here Miller the dramatist of fiction joins hands with Murray the maker of religious fiction. Happily the Bible League Quarterly confessed to a strong love for the works and teaching of Huntington and published my defence of Huntington.[2]

It was now obvious to me that Huntington was out of fashion at the Banner of Truth and Fullerism now reigned. Since then Fuller has indeed become the House Tutor of the Banner of Truth and whenever men of God such as Huntington, Gill, Toplady, Romaine or Crisp are castigated by these purveyors of doctrinal fashion, Fuller is used as an antidote. Sadly, these Fullerites appear to know their mentor as little as they know Huntington. Here I would like to take up Huntington's thoroughly Reformed views of the doctrines aired by the 1988 Banner of Truth Magazine article and place them alongside Fuller's contrary doctrines of 'right reason' which are in all cases Antinomian in relation to the law and anti-evangelistic in relation to the gospel.

Justification
According to the Banner of Truth, Huntington taught that 'The elect are justified from all eternity, an act of which their justification in this world by faith is only a manifestation', so 'proving' that he was an Antinomian. Today's Banner of Truth denies that man's justification is settled eternally in heaven. For them justification is merely a forensic term and does not refer to a factitive, operative and causative transforming of sinners. Justification is not a Divine decree and has nothing to do with reconciliation and regeneration. Justification is merely a legal 'as if' pronouncement or formal recognition after the believer comes to faith. Thus Banner of Truth ignores the fundamental

---

[2] Op. cit., Jan-Mar, 1990, pp. 305-312.

and Scriptural meaning of justification which goes far beyond being a mere declarative acknowledgement of the sinner's repentance. For them, justification is for the already just.[3] It is a mere tautology. This contradicts the earlier teaching of the Banner of Truth.[4]

Huntington summarises his numerous writings on the subject in his *The Justification of a Sinner and Satan's Law-Suit With Him*.[5] Like our Reformers, he viewed justification as the doctrine which includes all doctrines, embracing all the blessings of salvation which Christ has gained for His elect. Justification is a transforming work of grace annexed with blessings (pp. 104, 105) and consists of election (pp. 75, 157), union with Christ from eternity (pp. 73, 75, 157), the removal of condemnation (pp. 77, 105), effectual calling (p. 154), the purging of blood (pp. 102, 112), cleansing from unrighteousness (p. 85), imputed righteousness (pp. 99, 101, 102), redemption (pp. 86, 157), regeneration (pp. 24, 65), the forgiveness of sins (p. 59), repentance (pp. 24 ff., 61), a new creature (pp. 73, 94), 'holy workfolks' (p. 119), true holiness and sanctification (pp. 86, 157), ordination, adoption and sonship (p. 97), being made righteous (pp. 86, 101), the granting of faith (p. 101), Christ's obedience (p. 101), the granting of an inheritance (p. 110), and is for sinners as sinners (pp. 4, 101). Here we see Huntington follows God's Word as in, for instance, Acts 13:38-41; Romans 3:20-26; 5:1; 5:16; 5:19; 8:1, 2; 8:33; 13:48; Galatians 2:16; 3:24-26; 4:5, 6; 1 Timothy 3:16 and Titus 3:7.

The Covenant of Grace begins in eternity and is eternal

Huntington begins in eternity with God's covenant with Christ to form a people of God and place them securely in union with the Son. Justification is not dependent on time but on God's decrees centred in the work of Christ as Covenant Keeper. Thus the elect sinner's justification is anchored in eternity for eternity and revealed in time to the justified sinner (p. 730). Justification is not legal fiction but the sinner is made a new creation and fitted out for heaven.

---

[3] See *Collected Writings of John Murray*, Vol. II, Justification.
[4] See Berkhof's *Systematic Theology*, Banner of Truth, 1959. My mother presented me with this volume as soon as it came out.
[5] Collingridge, 1856 edit., Vol. II. Comments are from this version as it has a modern reprint.

Fuller disagrees completely. He isolates justification from the redemptive work of Christ. His ideas are principally based on Natural Law which he believed was obscured by revealed law, so he is the Antinomian, not Huntington. For Fuller, the sole rule of faith for Jews and Christians alike is the Moral Law which reflects Natural Law, true moral government and right reason.[6] Fuller reduces justification to a formal acknowledgement following the repentance of the sinner. Justification is a judicial recognition of the sinner's mind in his fallen awareness of his duty to believe in Christ savingly. This is prior to his growth in sanctification through the exercising of his natural abilities in keeping the Moral Law. Even the work of the Spirit, which Fuller sees as a mere external influence through the example of others, does not equip the Christian with any abilities he did not have before his conversion (Vol. 2, pp. 546, 547). Justification for Fuller comes through recognizing 'the nature, reason and fitness of things' but it comes solely to the already-godly. Such a person becomes godly by being aware of God by nature and the moral law which gives him a 'holy disposition' and teaches him to accept any further revelation which God gives him (Vol. 2, p. 349 ff., Vol. 3, p. 781) re-interpreted through the eyes of right reason. He is then moved by the gospel through a process in the mind to repent and then declared righteous by God. The atonement is thus objectively for all but subjectively and conditionally for those only who have a mind for it (Vol. 2, p. 709). When this mind turns to Christ in repentance, the atonement becomes objective for him.

God justifies the ungodly

Huntington opens his essay on justification by declaring that justification comes when the sinner is still at enmity with God. It is a work entirely of grace. Fuller disagrees. When expounding Romans 4:5 in his *Remarks on God's Justifying the Ungodly* (Vol. 3, pp. 714-719), Fuller rationalizes away the literal meaning of the text. He says that as this is such a unique, difficult passage, we must interpret it in line with other Scripture. When interpretations clash with the rest of Scripture, we must reject them. When Paul says he is the chief of sinners it obviously does not mean that he was 'one of the worst of characters' so when the word 'ungodly' is used, it does not mean that at the time of

---

[6] The Sprinkle Publications three volume edition is used throughout as it is still in print.

justification that the sinner was at enmity with God. Fuller thus asks, 'Do the Scriptures, which form the statute-book of heaven, and fully express the mind of God, pronounce any man pardoned or justified in his sight, while his heart is in a state of enmity with God?' To this, he answers 'No'. However, Romans 4:5 is far from peculiar and unclear. Romans 5:10 tells us that our reconciliation with God came whilst we were His enemies and Romans 4:25 tells us that our Lord was delivered up because of our offences and was raised again for our justification. Romans 4:8 teaches that God does not impute sin to his elect. As Fuller scorns imputation, he cannot grasp the meaning of sin and righteousness and does not understand such arguments. This caused Abraham Booth to pronounce Fuller 'lost'.

In justification, God clearly deals with us whilst we are offensive to Him. No says Fuller. There is no justification without prior repentance and belief, thus Romans 4:5 cannot mean the actual state of the mind of the sinner before justification in relationship to God. Fuller thus reclassifies the meaning of 'ungodly' to mean that it does not describe the state of unsaved sinners but the character of believers who are, nevertheless still sinners. They are the ungodly godly. Huntington answers that our justification has nothing to do with our own righteousness which is non-existent but with God's electing love, rescuing us from our own fallen state. Faith is given us to accept and understand what God in Christ has done for us. Faith is thus the God-given awareness, receptor and appropriator of our justification but not the work which earns it.

Huntington on the chastening of God's children
The Banner of Truth author maintains that for Huntington 'God sees no sin in believers, and is never angry with them'. Of course, this shows a total ignorance of Huntington's works and my correspondence with the Banner of Truth editors on four of their anti-Huntington articles confirmed this. In doing research for their lengthy anti-Huntington articles (if they did any research at all), these editors and contributors had only to read Huntington's *Contemplations on the God of Israel* concerning the sinfulness of even the elect. Here, the author discusses the elects' communion with God with his dearest friend J. Jenkins, and

outlines how the Lord rebukes and rebuffs the erring believer and how He chastises His dear ones. 'Whom the Lord loves, He chastens', was a thought Huntington had with him daily. As Huntington says in his *The Justification of a Sinner* concerning the believer, 'Every time he sins against his Father and Redeemer, having the law of God and the rule of judgment written on his heart, he arraigns himself'. If he neglects to do this, God will surely do so because 'If we would judge ourselves we should not be judged; but when we are chastened, we are judged of the Lord, that we should not be condemned with the world (1 Corinthians 11:31, 32)'.[7] Indeed, the Banner of Truth editors must know that this was a regular topic of scorn with Fuller who complained that the Huntingtonians were always complaining about their sinfulness before God. For Fuller, even this was a mark of Antinomianism!

Sin in Fullerism is not taken as seriously as it is in traditionally Reformed literature and the Banner of Truth's criticism of Huntington's view of sin and the status of a believer, throws much light on their own deviation from Scriptural paths in these doctrines. Their views of sin and belief are obviously radically different from Huntington's as one would expect from those who put forward Fuller's New Divinity teaching as an antidote against Biblical theology and piety. Huntington, for instance, believed that man is totally dead in trespasses and sins. He is dead to the overtures of the gospel, buried by his own transgressions. He knows nothing about a natural ability to commune with God. A corpse has only the ability to stink. So Huntington can safely say in accordance with Scripture that:

A free-willer can no more raise himself up, and go to the Saviour by his own power than a dead corpse can raise itself out of the grave, and go to the judgment seat.[8]

Denial of total depravity influences Fuller's doctrine of Atonement
Fuller denies that fallen man is totally depraved, claiming that this is figurative language which must be relativised and he denies that fallen man is dead to the gospel. There are no impossibilities for natural man

[7] Collingridge, Vol. 2, p. 105.
[8] Collingridge, Vol. 2, p. 69.

to communicate as such with God as he has the same powers to believe as not to believe.[9] If man were dead in trespasses and sins, Fuller argues, he would have no sense of his duty to exercise faith savingly and would have no ears for God's call. Huntington retorts:

> It requires more power to quicken and raise up a dead soul to spiritual life, than it does to raise up a dead body. The mouldered dust will make no more resistance than the passive earth did while God formed Adam; but the rebellious soul will resist to the last; like a desperate criminal under sentence, it will kill or be killed.[10]

Not so, says Fuller:

> If the inability of sinners to believe in Christ were of the same nature as that of a dead body in a grave to rise up and walk, it were absurd to suppose that they would on this account fall under the divine censure.[11]

Fuller can say this as he does not accept the Biblical doctrine of the Fall and does not accept that the divine censure has already fallen on all men and pronounced them dead in trespasses and sins. For Fuller, the Fall is the result of not following the inner duty to believe in Christ savingly and the rejection of Christ. This is the doctrine of New Divinity which teaches that man is on probation until he accepts or rejects Christ.[12] That probation ended according to Scripture with the fall of Adam. Man is not on probation. He broke his probation in Eden. Now men are imprisoned in their sins and need a ransom to be bailed out which only Christ can pay. But the Biblical doctrine of ransom does not fit into Fuller's system, either. No ransom means no atonement.

[9] *Works*, Vol. 2, p. 357; Vol. 3, p. 678.
[10] Collingridge, p. 69.
[11] *Works*, Vol. 2, p. 355.
[12] Bellamy, *True Religion Delineated*, pp. 7-9.

Mankind has no natural ability to turn to God

The idea that all men have the natural ability to respond to God permeates all Fuller's teaching on the atonement. In his essay *Substitution* which is a denial of the Biblical doctrine of the vicarious work of Christ, Fuller maintains that the atonement must be sufficient for all because if it were not, inviting men to Christ would be to ask sinners to do what is *naturally impossible* (Fuller's emphasis). For Fuller, God would never offer Christ freely to all sinners unless it were possible for them to respond. A universal atonement combined with natural abilities allows the sinner to make his compliance (Fuller's word) necessary when the 'free offer' comes. Fuller says he admits of the 'difficulties' in his theory but 'it belongs to the general subject of reconciling the purposes of God and the agency of man'. If one has theological difficulties, it appears, one must always preserve the 'agency of man' in salvation as any emphasis on God's grace and the demerits of man is 'Antinomian'.

For Huntington, any theological system which speaks in paradoxical riddles and of a God dependent on man's agency is 'Antinomianism unmasked' as it belittles sin and leaves the believer to believe in himself. Personally, I hold the repeated Banner of Truth statement that salvation ensues when God is prepared to work His all and fallen man is prepared to do his all,[13] to be sheer blasphemy. Of the self-righteous, Antinomian Christian who belittled his own depravity Huntington said in *Contemplations*:

> Even under this calm of peace and tranquillity, there is no godly sorrow flowing out to God; no condemning, hating, and abhorring self; nor any real tears of pious grief, mourning over a suffering Saviour; no repentance towards the Lord, nor heartfelt gratitude to him, nor real thanks and praises for his long-suffering, undeserved, and unexpected clemency.[14]

Fuller scorns this form of piety. He explains away personal holiness, condemns those who believe in total depravity as showing the first sign of Antinomianism, complaining that such wear 'a cunning smile in their

[13] See Iain Murray's *Spurgeon versus Hyper-Calvinism*, p. 84.
[14] Collingridge, Vol. 2, p. 307.

countenances, profess to be as bad as Satan himself; manifestly with the design of being thought deep Christians, thoroughly acquainted with the plague of their own heart'.[15] Fuller did not appear to know his own heart half so well.

The Banner of Truth's faulty view of imputation

The Banner of Truth claims that in Huntington's theology, 'the imputation of our sins to Christ, and of His righteousness to us, was actual, not judicial', without explaining what they mean. Such an explanation is called for given the Banner of Truth's own dodgy, figurative interpretations. When attacking Huntington, they soft-pedal on this issue, excuse Fuller's explaining away of the Biblical doctrine and attack defenders of Huntington's doctrine with wild misrepresentations. Thus Robert Oliver covers 13 pages in far-fetched criticism of this kind in a 'review' of my Huntington biography[16] and presents Fuller in contrast as 'the greatest theologian in the world'.[17] Oliver refers to Booth's disagreement with Fuller on imputation but does not mention that Booth pronounced Fuller because of this 'lost'. Oliver does add his own conviction which is:

> The present reviewer is happier with Booth's presentation of his case than Fuller's but it is important to see that Fuller was guarding against the ideas of imputed holiness.

Oliver presents no evidence for this excusing hunch and accuses me in his article of confusing imputation with the indwelling of the Holy Spirit. This merely highlights Oliver's own difficulty in coming to terms with the Biblical doctrine of imputation other than regarding it in some vague and undefined metaphorical way.[18] I maintain with Huntington that the faith which justifies is the fruit of the Holy Spirit

---

[15] *Works*, Vol. II, p. 745.

[16] A new edition of *William Huntington: Pastor of Providence* has recently been published by Go Publications.

[17] Oliver says this on the authority of another writer who attributes it to Spurgeon.

[18] See Fuller's *Works*, Vol. III, Defence of the Doctrine of Imputed Righteousness. Whenever Fuller entitles a work as a defence or vindication one can expect the opposite due to his altering the meaning of terms.

(Galatians 5:16) and the justification which Christ gives us is His very own which is 'in the Spirit' (1 Timothy 3:16). Moreover, I believe that the blessing of Abraham comes upon believers through Jesus Christ that we might receive the promises of the Spirit through faith (Galatians 3:14). I agree with Huntington and the Scriptures concerning the Lord's people of whom it is said, 'But ye are washed, but ye are sanctified, but ye are justified in the name of the Lord Jesus, and by the Spirit of our God' (1 Corinthians 6:12).

The Holy Spirit plays no important role in Fuller's theology. Indeed in his treatise named *The Inward Witness of the Spirit*,[19] Fuller mentions the Spirit only once in the whole book and that is merely as an external influence. So, too, contrary to the Scriptures, the Banner of Truth appears from the above to deny the accompanying work of the Spirit in justification and imputation. The Banner of Truth claim to represent Calvinism but Calvin made it plain followed by Huntington that the faith which justifies through the imputed righteousness of Christ is the principle work of the Holy Spirit.[20]

Oliver says he is not happy with Fuller's figurative interpretation, yet rejects any actual and concrete benefits the elect receive in having their sins imputed to Christ and Christ's righteousness to them in justification. Oliver needs to explain what a 'figurative imputation' is and why Huntington's belief in a 'real imputation' is wrong. He must also explain why he believes that a man who takes Scripture literally is an 'Antinomian' and give his reasons for isolating righteousness from imputation, sanctification and holiness. Our pioneer Reformers knew of no such separation.

For Huntington, imputed righteousness was the wedding garment given to the elect in preparation for the Marriage Supper of the Lamb. Christ clothes His own with righteousness (Isaiah 61:10) in the same way as the loving father clothed the Prodigal son on his return. Such a garment and such a righteousness is not the product or the deserts of the receiver, but it is truly his as a gift.[21] In his beautiful, inspiring work *Dimensions of Eternal Love*, Huntington speaks of 'the righteousness of God which is by faith of Jesus Christ unto all and upon all them that

---

[19] *Works*, Vol. 1, p. 624 ff..
[20] *Institutes*, 3, 2:34, Chapter 17.
[21] Collingridge, Vol. 2, p. 86.

believe' (Romans 3:22), emphasizing that this righteousness is not our own but is freely given to those who do not deserve it. In the Atonement, for Huntington:

> Christ wrought out this righteousness for us; God the Father accepts it, and places it to our account, and imputes it freely. The gospel reveals it, the Holy Spirit applies it to the hand of an appropriating faith, and makes it manifest to the sinner's conscience; conscience enjoys it, and finds peace to be the effect of it. Thus we, 'are justified freely from all things from which we could not be justified by the law of Moses' (Acts 13:39).[22]

When Huntington speaks like this the Banner of Truth accuses him of 'spiritualising'. However, when they themselves 'spiritualise' or rather 'rationalise away' justification and imputation, they call their critics who interpret Scripture by Scripture 'Antinomians'. When Fuller describes the coming to himself of the Prodigal, there is no imputed righteousness for him in the story. Fuller merely claims that the son came to his senses, realised what material benefits he had forfeited at his father's and 'what was right and fit' and returned home.[23] Huntington tells us that the Prodigal saw that he had sinned against Heaven and in his father's sight and was unworthy to be called his son. For Fuller, the Prodigal's salvation was solely in his realizing where he was better off. Certainly Huntington's interpretation is the more Scriptural.[24]

Huntington argues like this because he believes that Christ put Himself under the Law and obeyed every jot and tittle on our behalf. Fuller cannot think like this as he believes that Christ had no need to place Himself under the law. Fuller admitted that he had changed his mind several times on imputation, as he did on justification. However, as Fuller's moral government theory grew more complex and his simple trust in the words of Scripture diminished, he fell more and more into

---

[22] Collingridge, Vol. 2, pp. 395, 396.
[23] *Works*, Vol. 2, p. 485.
[24] Luke 15:18, 19.

the rationalism of the Latitudinarians and New Divinity. Thus Fuller cannot be recommended as a shepherd of souls.

The Banner of Truth points out tirelessly how Fuller revived the churches and missionary thinking and gives him the praise due to William Carey and over a hundred years of British and Continental work done before him. They refuse to face the facts that Fuller was no great evangelist, had a church far smaller than his so-called Antinomian fellow pastors and lived to see his Association churches shrink under his theology and go Liberal whilst churches such as those of the Huntingtonians' grew to bursting point. This was also true of the work of the following generation of 'Antinomian' ministers such as Robert Hawker, whereas Fuller's Northampton Association officially denounced the Scriptures as the infallible Word of God. Fuller's policies brought Arianism and division to the Indian Church and looked on the Indians as inferior beings who could not rule themselves therefore must be ruled by Britain. These ideas caused the Black Hole of Calcutta and the Indian Mutiny.

It must be said in fairness that in one doctrine, Fuller is even more Biblical than the Banner of Truth. In his metaphorical, 'as if' interpretations of imputation and justification, he, nevertheless, refers constantly to the old man in Adam and the new man in Christ. According to the Banner of Truth, however, the old man has been done away with and Christians are new men only.[25] It is thus no wonder that the Banner of Truth is now courting Arminian Wesley, famed for his doctrine of Christian perfection!

Christ fulfils all the conditions needed for an Atonement

Huntington, according to the Banner of Truth, held that 'faith, repentance, and holy obedience are covenant conditions on the part of Christ, not on our part', which, they claim, is Antinomianism. This criticism reveals the Banner of Truth's own Antinomianism in altering the nature of the Mosaic Law, the Covenant of Grace and the Rule of Faith. They demand the impossible, i.e. that the sinner must overcome certain obstacles before attaining God's justification.

Huntington, believed that the covenant of grace is established in eternity where believers are placed in union with Christ. This is

---

[25] See Issue 92, *Paul's Use of the term 'The Old Man'* by Donald MacLeod.

Election. Fuller claims that this union is not from eternity but is created when the sinner meets the conditions of faith. Huntington argues that all covenant conditions are met by Christ, the originator, keeper and fulfiller of the covenant, according to God's eternal decrees regarding His elect. Christ is the Author and Finisher of every believer's faith. By means of Christ's work in eternity for His Bride, culminating in His vicarious work in the fulness of time, Christ graciously grants her repentance, faith and a fulfilled law, without which no man can be saved. As no man is able to exercise the repentance, faith and obedience required by both law and gospel, Christ steps in as the vicarious representative and substitute for those in union with Him.[26] In following Fuller in denying this, the Banner of Truth is challenging both orthodox Christianity and the completeness of Christ's atoning, penal, vicarious work both in time and eternity.

The true dimensions of eternal love
Huntington argues in his *Dimensions of Eternal Love* that as the elect are condemned by the law, faith, repentance and obedience to that law is impossible for even them in their natural state. But Christ fulfilled the law on their behalf, 'He shall make reconciliation for iniquity, and bring in everlasting righteousness' (Daniel 9:24). Such a reconciliation and bringing in of everlasting righteousness is solely Christ's doing because, 'By the obedience of one shall many be made righteous' (Romans 5:19). Fuller denies that Christ made Himself obedient to the law vicariously for His Bride, the elect Church. He claims that Christ neither placed Himself against nor under the law 'but rather above the law, deviating from the letter, but more than preserving the spirit of it'.[27] Christ is thus not the believer's Substitute but his super-human guide. Huntington, of course, believed that Christ as God is above the law and more than its teaching, but argues that He came as a Man under law to fulfil the conditions men could not. It would have been enough for man to have kept the law to attain an Edenic state but this no man after the Fall could do. So Christ had to do it for him, granting him above and over an earthly garden, a greater inheritance in Heaven. Christ

---

[26] Op. cit. pp. 394, 395.
[27] *Works*, Vol. 2, p. 689.

redeemed His Bride through His obedience as a man, our human Substitute, who truly kept both the letter and spirit of the law for our sakes. It was the law that slew man, not something above it or more than it, so it was through obedience to the law, under the law only that man could be given life. Thus Huntington emphasises that Christ was 'made under the law, to redeem them that were under the law'.[28]

Law repentance neither atones nor justifies

Fuller sees man's repentance as the way to justification. The Banner of Truth views repentance as being a condition placed on man. In his *Contemplations on the God of Israel*, Huntington teaches that repentance is the work of the Spirit and is thus a gift of grace. That Huntington's stance is Scriptural is testified by the Word. Acts 5:31 tells us 'Him hath God exalted with his right hand to be a Prince and Saviour, for to give repentance to Israel, and forgiveness of sins'. This is obviously a reference to Christ acting on an unbeliever in giving him repentance and faith before any previous belief is shown. Fuller might claim that this is a one-off text which demands special interpretation, but in vain. Acts 11:18, Romans 2:4, and 2 Timothy 2:25 all stress that it is God who leads to repentance; God who grants repentance and God who 'peradventure' i.e. according to His will, gives repentance.

Thus, Huntington did not regard faith, obedience and repentance as conditions to be met by natural, fallen man. He explains in his *Dimensions* that the righteousness of God comes by the faith of Christ, not man's faith (Romans 3:21, 22), and that the gift of righteousness reigns in us through Jesus Christ (Romans 5:17).[29] This faith and righteousness of Christ is claimed by the Banner of Truth to be a condition based on man's agency as if a fallen sinner or even an elect saint could give himself Christ's faith and righteousness, grant himself repentance and give himself the power to be obedient to the law. This they call 'duty-faith' but one can only exercise a duty to faith once it has been given. Faith is never given as a reward for duties obeyed. Unfulfilled law-duties merely doom sinners. Christ's faith given to man reprieves him and gives him a saving faith which no law-keeping could procure for him. This is made clear in Acts 13:39 and Romans 4:16.

---

[28] Collingridge, Vol. 2, p. 203.
[29] Collingridge, Vol. 2, p. 397.

Fuller, following Bellamy of the New Divinity School, taught that keeping the law perfectly would eventually lead to faith in Christ. Huntington taught that even if we kept the law perfectly, this might restore an Adam to Eden but certainly not a sinner to Christ because the believer's status in Christ is greater than that of Adam in Eden. Fuller set himself the impossible and unnecessary task of making Adams of us all. This is the gospel he calls *Worthy of All Acceptation.*[30] The Bible tells us, that the salvation which might have been found in the first Adam was merely of an earthly, natural kind whereas that found in the last Adam (Christ) fits us out with a spiritual, heavenly body (1 Corinthians 15:45-49).

Robert Oliver on 'morals'

Oliver attacks Huntington for not holding that the so-called 'moral law' is the complete rule for right faith.[31] In his essay *Faith in Christ Being a Requirement of the Moral Law*, Fuller argues that one can approach God in Christ through following one's law duties and that 'If love to God include faith in Christ wherever he is revealed by the gospel, then the moral law, which expressly requires the former, must also require the latter'. In his *The Law Established in a Life of Faith*, Huntington reveals the weakness of such a position, arguing that the work of the Law is to discover sin and condemn man. It furnishes the unjustified sinner with an accuser before God and thus the Law separates the sinner completely from his Maker. The Law, however, cannot subdue sin; it cannot give the sinner dominion over it; it cannot give man a second chance nor lift the sentence of death from him. The Law knows no pardon and can neither give life to the sinner nor quicken him spiritually. The Law cannot justify a man nor even bring a man to the Saviour of itself without God's effectual call. Huntington concludes that it is scandalous to argue that the Law contains all the injunctions and powers of the gospel. It has its own work to do as also the *Rule of Faith and the Rule of Christ.*[32] Those who confuse them, as he believed

---

[30] *Works*, Vol. 2, p. 323 ff..
[31] Banner of Truth Magazine, Issue 376, p. 12 ff..
[32] This Huntington held in common with the Marrow Men as also his doctrine of offering Christ within the Covenant of Grace. Fuller condemned the Marrow Men, too, presumably because he

Fuller did, confuse Law with gospel and thus have no true Law and no true gospel.

Sanctification accompanies Justification in the Atonement

Huntington, according to the Banner of Truth, taught 'that sanctification is no evidence of justification but rather renders it more obscure' but finds no evidence in Huntington's works to defend their misjudgment. In understanding the Banner of Truth's misconception of Huntington's theology, we must note four things. Firstly, according to Robert Oliver, the Banner of Truth's standard of sanctification is supplied solely by the Moral Law which they see, following Fuller, as comprehending all duty, binding on all men, believers and unbelievers alike.[33] When Huntington, argues that if everything necessary to faith was in the Old Testament, we would have no need for a New, Oliver and Murray, following Fuller calls this an evasion of the issue.[34] Clearly they are the ones who are evading the gospel issue in their preference for a legal religion. Secondly, the Banner of Truth, unlike our Reformers and Huntington, separate justification radically from sanctification and teach that sanctification follows justification but is not part of the justifying process. However, as they claim that justification is merely 'as if' and does not transform the unbeliever in any way, they apparently expect sanctification and holiness to derive from the 'holy disposition' (Fuller's term) which arises from practising duty-faith. Thirdly, the Banner of Truth confuses the doctrine of sanctification with the doctrine of good works. For them, the performance of good works is the sanctifying process. Huntington believed that in justification, the sinner was sanctified and set apart in order to live a godly life which entailed being led by the Spirit and indwelt by Christ, so that holiness might ensue. Sanctification thus did not render justification obscure but clearly accompanied justification and was one of its blessings. Indeed, when our Reformers wrote of sanctification in the Latin language common to them, they used the word synonymously with *beatificationem* linking it with Romans 4:6-8

---

felt that 'gospel offers' were not within God's Covenant but outside. This is the only reason I can find to explain why Huntington is condemned as a 'no offers of salvation' man by Banner of Truth writers, though this was an essential part of his preaching.

[33] Op. cit. p. 12.

[34] Banner of Truth Magazine, Issues 376, p. 12; 273, p. 12.

referring to the justification of Abraham.[35] This is exactly the position of Huntington who writes of 'the sentence of justification and the blessings annexed to it', showing that for him, as for our Reformers, justification was both a legal release from condemnation and a causal and sanctifying work in the believer.[36] This is good Pauline theology. However, the Banner of Truth's New Divinity stand on justification and sanctification obscures the plain teaching of Paul. They have thus no credentials to judge Huntington as they themselves have no grasp of the subject. Sanctification does for the Banner of Truth what justification does for Huntington, the difference being that Huntington looks to God directly for his sanctification whereas the Banner of Truth looks to God indirectly through the good works and law-keeping of the believer. This hazardous Banner of Truth view puts them under the charge of Neonomianism (a form of Antinomianism) as they appear to believe that justification does not secure the sinner's salvation and sanctification and they must be supplemented by post-conversion sincere obedience to the law but without its curse. This is in keeping with their view that no salvation is possible without the sinner's compliance and agency. Fourthly, it is well known that those who originally called Huntington an Antinomian were 'evangelical' 'free-thinkers' who followed Martin Madan in condemning those who would not support a plurality of wives as acting contrary to Old Testament principles. Such hypocrisy exists in Huntington's modern critics who are quick to cry 'Antinomian' of others but bend Old Testament principles this way and that to suit their own taste. In 1993 Iain Murray promoted Sunday trading of Banner of Truth books in the Banner of Truth Magazine, so I wrote to him, informing him that though he called Huntington an Antinomian and a breaker of the Ten Commandments, Huntington had given up a good labouring job because it entailed working on the Sabbath. Mr Murray replied that he was aware that some Christians were against Sunday trading but he did not share this view. 'The great thing is', he wrote, 'that we agree with Newton's words *How dull the Sabbath Day without the Sabbath Lord*'. Huntington believed he could not honour the Lord and work or trade on the Sabbath. Murray

---

[35] See Bullinger's *Decades*, Vol. I, Sermon VI, Justification by Faith.
[36] Collingridge, Vol. 2, p. 104.

thought that he could. Thus who is the greatest Antinomian? Huntington wanted the Lord's Day for fellowship with the Lord, Murray wanted to set up traders' tables. Murray ought to have at least borne Luke 6:42 in mind before criticizing others.

First seek the Kingdom of Heaven

Happily, Huntington wrote much on sanctification, holiness and the moral law. He taught that first one must seek the King and His Kingdom of Heaven and then all else will be added, teaching 'But now the righteousness of God without the law is manifested, being witnessed by the law and the prophets; even the righteousness of God, which is by faith of Jesus Christ unto all and upon all them that believe' (Romans 3:21, 22).[37] 'The law of the Spirit of life in Christ Jesus hath made me free from the law of sin and death' (Romans 8:2).[38] The believer's standard of sanctification is thus Christ and all that Christ teaches. 'He is made of God sanctification and redemption' (1 Corinthians 1:30). The entire Trinity, however, were concerned in this work 'Elect according to the foreknowledge of God the Father, through sanctification of the Spirit, unto obedience and sprinkling of the blood of Jesus Christ' (1 Peter 1:2).[39] Here we see that it is Christ's atoning work which secured our Election then and there on the cross. Because this central Biblical emphasis places sanctification in the realms of election, justification and redemption, those who believe that faith is to be found in the law pronounce Huntington an Antinomian without reading his applications of the Scriptural truths in his daily walk with God. But Huntington maintains that to neglect seeking Christ first and obtaining faith in Him and confusing the law with faith is to use the law unlawfully. That the law has a most important place in Christian teaching is, nevertheless, emphasized by Huntington who says:

> But some may reply, 'Do you make void the law through faith?' No; Paul says that preaching faith establishes the law, and that nothing else will or can do it. It establishes the righteousness of the law, which is fulfilled in every believer, though not by him.

---

[37] Collingridge, Vol. 2, p. 395.
[38] *Ibid.* p. 179.
[39] *Ibid*, p. 157.

It establishes the law in the hand of the Father to his own elect, as a rod of correction and a schoolmaster; and, in the hand of justice, to all the wicked; and as a killing commandment to all the reprobate and bond children.[40]

Huntington had allegedly no Christian 'virtue'

Faced with the clear evidence that Huntington preaches the whole law and the whole gospel, his Banner of Truth critics evade the issues by claiming that Huntington's piety was empty of Christian virtue and accuse him of teaching a passive doctrine of sanctification, void of Christian conduct[41] enforced by an anti-literal understanding of the Bible.[42] It is here that the Banner of Truth are at their meanest. In an effort to force their readers to believe that Huntington was not a practising Christian, they claim he ignored the poor, spiritualizing away texts referring to them. Yet Huntington preached constantly on the social responsibility of his people and the various sermons he preached on Matthew 25:36 and the application of this text in private letters were most literal and to the point. He argued that it was no using preaching to men with an empty stomach and campaigned for cheaper prices on food for the poor. This included all men everywhere and not merely those of the flock.[43] He denounced those who separated conduct from doctrine as the worst of Antinomians and Pharisees, preaching time and time again that they should not be weary in well-doing. Oliver takes Huntington to task here for what he calls 'Huntington's abusive language' in calling Antinomians and Pharisees such, but he and the other Banner of Truth writers use a whole series of 'theological swearwords' against Huntington themselves for taking a more literal path than themselves. Oliver, for instance, calls Huntington 'abusive' for referring objectively to the 'killing' nature of the law, though Paul testifies to this literal truth in Romans 7:9-11. On the other hand, as we have seen, Banner of Truth criticism is mostly against Huntington's

---

[40] Banner of Truth Magazine, Issue 376, p. 14.
[41] *Ibid*, p. 14.
[42] Banner of Truth Magazine, Issue 298, p. 11.
[43] See *Contemplations on the God of Israel*, Collingridge, Vol. 2, pp. 312-320.

literal rendering of texts relating to imputation, justification, sanctification, the indwelling of Christ and the Spirit which Banner of Truth writers interpret clean away from their basic and clearest meanings. When Huntington is 'literal' his enemies claim this is illiteracy or 'spiritualising the meaning away'. As they have not grasped the meaning, who are they to judge?

Maurice Roberts and the Rule and the Riddle

When Maurice Roberts took over the Banner of Truth editorship from Iain Murray, I wrote to him questioning his condemnation of Huntington and praise of Fuller, asking him for his textual proof. In his reply he re-affirmed that he held Fuller to be one of the great theologians of his age and confessed that after thinking ill of Huntington he decided to check his opinions and read *The Rule and the Riddle* which confirmed them. He gave no textual evidence regarding either Fuller whom he had obviously not studied in depth, nor Huntington. However, in *The Rule and the Riddle*, Huntington refers to one who called him an Antinomian for denying that following the Mosaic Law was the only rule of life for a Christian. Huntington points out that this is misusing the law and asks:

> If I am an Antinomian, only because I cannot find any text in God's book that calls the law of Moses the believer's only rule of life, what must this man be?' The answer is clear: 'An Antinomian without a mask'.

Chapter 8 will now consider how Atonement transformed the Fall.

Chapter 8

The Atonement in Relation to the Fall

The Scriptures conclude all under sin

It is fundamental to the preaching of the gospel of salvation that our hearers understand from the outset that all have sinned and fallen short of the glory of God. One may preach the Atonement to no avail whatsoever if our hearers take it for granted that the man next to them in the pew is being addressed and not themselves. Thus the Great Commission we read about in Matthew 28:18-20 primarily addresses the basic need of fallen man, that without Christ and His reconciling death, he is lost. This work of reconciliation is expressed in 2 Corinthians 5:17-21 as:

> Therefore if any man be in Christ, he is a new creature: old things are passed away; behold, all things are become new. And all things are of God, who hath reconciled us to himself by Jesus Christ, and hath given to us the ministry of reconciliation; To wit, that God was in Christ, reconciling the world unto himself, not imputing their trespasses unto them; and hath committed unto us the word of reconciliation. Now then we are ambassadors for Christ, as though God did beseech you by us: we pray you in Christ's stead, be ye reconciled to God. For he hath made him to be sin for us, who knew no sin; that we might be made the righteousness of God in him.

117

Sin refers to God's law alone

The word 'sin' is a rarity nowadays and like the gospel words 'holiness' and 'righteousness', might soon disappear from our vocabulary. Modern critics of our Authorized Version such as Alan Clifford tell us we ought to translate the Bible into the language of the streets. Sadly, the streets of our western 'civilization' do not have words like holiness, righteousness, reconciliation, propitiation and, of course Atonement. Clifford has come up with a number of suggestions which besides being way off the theological mark have not been used in the streets for as many generations as the old terms used in the King James Version. It is no use looking for another modern word for 'sin' in the streets as 'sin' is still the most modern word we have and which describes the state of every street, road, rail, tram and aeroplane traveller.

Modern evangelists now refer to sin merely in its 'moral' implications and not in its lethal implications. Who dares to preach nowadays that 'The soul that sinneth, he shall die'. People who preach this truth in the very streets from which some would pick up a new Bible translation risk being charged for 'hate crimes'. One preacher well known to me has been told that he ought to submit his sermons to the thought control of local politicians before preaching them. Our Orwellian Big Brothers are watching us.

The reasons for rescuing sin and salvation from the theories of the moral prophets are clear: 'Sin' in its Biblical meaning is the opposite of holiness and righteousness. These two latter terms relate solely to the Person of God who takes away sin and grants holiness and righteousness. There are no such attributes in the person of fallen man. Thus, there can be no awareness of sin where there is no awareness of our sovereign, absolute and holy God. 'Moral behaviour', however is usually understood as indicating subjection to a human code. Where there is no sense of sin, there can be no sense of righteousness though the sinner may strive to be 'moral'. Our holy God has given us a clear definition of sin in His Word. God's eternal nature is revealed to us in His Law which is God's standard not only for all time but for all eternity. Sin is the rejection of this standard. Neither God's standards, nor the Word that contains them, will ever pass away. We can only understand what sin is in this context. Thus Paul said, 'I had not known sin, but by the law: for I had not known lust, except the law had said,

Thou shalt not covet'.[1] Without God's Law, we can neither understand ourselves nor God, however moral our propensities might be.

The temporal and eternal functions of the Law

Grotius, Fuller and the NCT, claim that God has no eternal laws in spite of Christ's teaching, 'Till heaven and earth pass, one jot and one tittle shall in no wise pass from the law, till all be fulfilled'.[2] The significance of the words 'when all is fulfilled', is taken to mean by many that after this world is no more and the Day of Judgment has passed there will be no more Law as a revelation of God's standards which Fuller claims are arbitrary. Here we must realise the generality of the Law which reflects on both saints and sinners. For the former it is God's eternal standard, for the latter it is a means of condemning their sin. When sin is no more, God will not be less righteous and holy and His character expressed in the Law remains as it always was, is, and will be. Romans Chapters 3 and 7 show the function of the Law. It holds up before us a mirror of our own sinful state so that 'every mouth may be stopped, and all the world may become guilty before God'.[3] The Law is not there as the righteous-making arm of God to justify us by our efforts to keep it. It is there to reveal to us our damnable nature and to show us that the wages of sin is death. Salvation allows us to live in holiness and righteousness in conformity to God's eternal standards expressed in the Law. Thus, although the Law reveals God's righteousness to us, at the same time it reveals our sin and shame. Fallen man cannot justify himself by the deeds of the Law as the Law finds no righteousness in man. The Law reveals that 'all have sinned and come (fallen) short of the glory of God'.[4] This side of the Law teaches that it is appointed unto man once to die, and then comes judgment. Once the Law has judged all, its condemning purpose has been fulfilled but not its saving purpose as once saved always saved. However, as the Law reveals to us the standards which God has set up Himself because they reveal His very nature and Christ has fulfilled that Law on our behalf, this standard

---

[1] Romans 7:7.
[2] Matthew 5:18.
[3] Romans 3:19.
[4] Romans 3:23.

remains as eternal as God. From the side of man, he learns to understand the Law aright. From the side of God, He always keeps to it as it is His self-revelation.

Confused teaching as to the nature of sin

In my over sixty years of Christian witness, I find that people are most uncertain in their understanding of sin's nature. Here, I believe, the various theological schools and denominational dogmas have grievously clouded our picture of sin's nature and thus made it more difficult for us to understand salvation. Sin has been analysed and dissected so much that we have lost the overall picture of what sin really is. Indeed, one cannot deal with sin in its entirety without consulting God's plan of dealing with it in its entirety.

Most theologians distinguish between actual and original sin, as if the former left us guilty but the latter innocent. Some speak of intentional and unintentional sin as if the latter were less sinful than the former. Others speak of 'mortal sins', and sins of 'presumption', 'commission' and 'omission'. Then we are told that there are Seven Deadly Sins as if all other sins were not deadly. Some theologians tell us that sin is merely a moral propensity or tendency and not a post-fall natural handicap common to all. This leads them to teach that sin is in the will alone which our natural abilities can control. In short, most definitions of sin tend to explain away or ignore elements of sin which the Bible condemns.

Others believe that certain rites and rituals can excuse or even remove certain sins. They attribute powers of forgiveness and rewards to baptism, the Lord's Supper, martyr death, penitence, good deeds and so-called prayers which cleanse. In the slum area in which I was brought up were some of the lowest rogues but their 'religion' sent them to confessions once a week and they came home feeling they were as innocent as the non-fallen angels. Such ideas pervade throughout all our institutional and denominational churches.

As a right understanding of sin is fundamental to a correct knowledge of how Christ's salvation is accomplished, it is no wonder that Christians are at sixes and sevens over the latter when there is so much disagreement about the former. So, too, one cannot analyse sin into different sins as there are no varieties of sin. Sin is plainly and simply enmity towards God shown through disobedience. This leads to confusion in the minds of sinners and it is thus no surprise to find that a number of the many words for sin in the Old Testament refer to 'confusion'. We may paraphrase Daniel 9:7, 8: O Lord, righteousness belongeth unto thee, but unto us confusion.

Sin seen in the right context

Analytic and systematic attitudes to sin do not deal with sin in the context of Christ's understanding of it. They deal merely with aspects of the confusion which often lead to further confusion. After all, Christ took upon Himself the wages of sin as sin, not as a collection of individual separate parts of sin, on our behalf. Sin must thus always be seen from two perspectives, the Law that condemns it as a whole and Christ who fulfils it as a whole. Thus any treatment of sin which ignores either the condemnation of the Law or the extent to which Christ went to fulfil it vicariously is not Scriptural and therefore cannot be effectual. This view is often criticised as being dualistic, i.e. that it views salvation as dealing with two absolutes and opposites, the Law versus the Gospel, Moses versus Christ, Old Testament thinking versus the New. This is an unbiblical way of getting out of the dilemma in which sin leaves us. Christ is portrayed in the Scriptures as being Creator of all and Lord over all. He is the Divine Lawgiver, fulfilling all the teaching of the Old Testament in Himself. Indeed, Christ does not regard the Law as His opposite but as His own instrument in condemning sin in order to save sinners. The Law is an essential part of Christ's atoning work.

The Atonement is thus all about how Christ put a stop to this infernal spread of human pollution which we call sin. It would be helpful here, I believe, to look more thoroughly at the work of Satan in the affairs of men as the defeat of Satan is an essential part of Christ's cross work.

How sin marred all

The initial problem concerning sin is how it started and how it spread. And how it marred all: not just man but the whole of creation. Immediately, the traditional term 'original sin', comes to mind though its various definitions have caused the churches perhaps as much strife as the doctrines of baptism and the Lord's supper. From a Scriptural point of view, sin is neither original to man nor is man the originator of sin, though he in Adam was the first to fall under its grip. Nor was man the original sinner. However, as salvation from sin is designed for man alone, Biblical references focus more on man's sin than what sin was prior to him. If 'original sin' is used to mean that death embraced all mankind ever after Adam's death, the term would have strong significance but this is not as it is usually defined in analytical or systematic theology which I have learnt to abhor. Given the variety of views expressing how sin came into the world and spread, Daniel 9:7, 8, proves a touchstone in discerning their validity. 'Original sin' does not refer to a sin we did not commit but that all sinners are sinful in that they live at enmity with God.

Sin in Heaven
Revelation 12:7-9 tells us of the war in Heaven where Archangel Michael and his angels was challenged by the dragon and his angels. The dragon was defeated and we read that he 'was cast out, that old serpent, called the Devil, and Satan, which deceiveth the whole world: he was cast out into the earth, and his angels were cast out with him'.

Thus, when we open our Bible at Genesis, after reading of the creation of Adam and Eve, we find them living in innocence and happiness as God's stewards of Eden. Suddenly this idyll is broken by the appearance of Eve's tempter, the devil, the lord of Sin. He tells her that if she disobeys God's rule not to eat of the fruit of the central tree in the garden she will not die, as God has warned, but she will become god-like and be given all knowledge. As we know, Eve saw how laden the tree was with good fruit, and the temptation proved too much for her and her husband. This alone shows Adam and Eve initially knew what was good. It was evil they knew nothing of. Now they wanted to know everything and be wise according to Satan's standards which were all rebellion against God. They joined Satan in his rebellion. Satan was thrown out of Heaven but God made a way back for mankind.

Wise in goodness and simple in evil
It is interesting to note that the gospel of salvation always refers back to this initial act when Adam and Eve became wise in a condemnatory way. They were not content to know 'good' alone, they wanted to know 'evil'. In Paul's last chapter to the Romans and his last words before going over to the general greetings in verse 19, the Apostle says 'I

would have you wise unto that which is good, and simple concerning evil. And the God of peace shall bruise Satan under your feet shortly. The grace of our Lord Jesus Christ be with you. Amen'.

Here Paul is emphasising that where sin reigns, grace reigns all the more and those who have been captured by the devil's evil power, can be rescued by Christ's good and almighty power which can 'make us wise unto salvation through faith which is in Christ Jesus'. This is the wisdom of God and not that of the Serpent. Adam's own faith failed him, the faith of the Second Adam, Christ, imputed to us, never fails.

Sin came by the transgression of one man only

We may query this on the grounds that Eve sinned first and then Adam so this verse should read either 'by one woman' or, 'by the primal woman and man'; but Adam was first given the responsibility not to eat of the forbidden fruit before Eve was created.[5] Eve's knowledge of the tree would have thus come from Adam who had been directly appointed to follow God's ruling. Also, Adam was the head of Eve and Eve was not made of the dust of the earth as the entire animal creation and Adam, but formed from Adam himself. The term 'woman' means 'from man', thus signifying that the two were one flesh.[6]

Sin's punishment passed on to all subsequent mankind

Just as Eve was naturally part of Adam, so were all who came from him. When Adam sinned, entire mankind sinned, because Adam and Eve were the sole progenitors of future mankind. Indeed, God designed entire mankind from their initial father Adam as an ethnic unity with no distinctions regarding their nature either in relation to God or to their fellow-men. This we see clearly outlined in Acts 17:24-27:

> God that made the world and all things therein … made of one blood all nations of men for to dwell on all the face of the earth, and hath determined the times before appointed, and the bounds of their habitation; that they should seek the Lord, if haply they might feel after him, and find him.

---

[5] Genesis 2:16-18.
[6] Genesis 2:23.

Obviously, this verse was written with the Fall in view and the chance of salvation. There is thus no man who is not the offspring of Adam and shares his very sinful being. There is no racism which comes from Heaven and no racism in Heaven. There is also no 'gender war' in Heaven as we shall all be like the angels.

Sin and death reign since Adam

This is a most debatable point in modern theology as the doctrine of imputation has come seriously under fire whether regarding Adam's sin imputed to his offspring, our sin imputed to Christ, or Christ's righteousness imputed to sinners. Some deny imputation outright arguing that mankind cannot be held responsible for their progenitor's sins, nor can Christ be made responsible for our sins, nor can Christ's faith and righteousness be God's gifts to His adopted children. Others say there was no true imputation because of an actual state i.e. Adam's guilt being passed on to his offspring, our guilt to Christ, Christ's righteousness to us, but that God chose to treat us as if this were the case, thus the term is merely metaphorical. This discussion becomes meaningless when applied to pre-Mosaic times. Death reigned from Adam to Moses because sin did. There are no post-Adamic 'holy innocents'. Sin, however, was 'imputed' where the Law was broken: i.e. the term imputation refers to an actual, non-metaphorical judgment of God on the lawless. 'Imputed sin' means real sin that condemns all. 'Imputed righteousness' is real righteousness given to those whom Christ makes righteous in sharing His righteousness with them as he died for His entire Flock.

Death through sin is every man's lot, though he might not have sinned just like Adam

In the eighteenth century, Jonathan Edwards, a great theologian but a fond dabbler in philosophical riddles, taught that man must be seen both as a natural and as a moral being. He did this to make it allegedly easier to analyse the effect of sin on man. However, sin is an entity in itself which cannot be split into further attributes which are then to be analysed separately. So is man in relation to his Maker. As a student of Psychology under the best Christian Professor imaginable, we students at Uppsala were taught what man really is as an essential part of studying his problems.

Some of Edwards' followers, particularly of the New Divinity School, took the analytical idea further and separated totally in man what Scripture sees as a unity. Mankind cannot be divided into moral and natural parts with regard to sin as he is sinful in the same sin throughout his whole being. To postulate that man is morally sinful but naturally innocent is to ignore the Scriptural definition of man as being 'sold under sin'. Thus a number of Edwards' students, including his son of the same name, developed a dualistic theology of man in his nature and man as a moral being, seeing all that has to do with sin and faith merely in the moral sphere, leaving his natural capacities Adam-like. Furthermore, the moral side of man was attributed to his will so by the time this New Divinity reached England under Andrew Fuller, it had dwindled to 'I can if I will' which was a further simplification of the categorical imperative of the Enlightenment 'You ought therefore you can'. All things were thought possible of man, ignoring the testimony of Jesus in Mark 9:23 who truly said 'All things are possible' but added, 'to him that believeth'. One can only take this to mean that all things are not possible for those hindered by disbelief.

The wages of sin relate to the whole man viewed as a unity and his physical damnation and death are very much part of his natural depravity. Natural, or moral, call man's attributes what you will, they are all fallen and all damned because the wages of sin is death.

Many teach that infants, strangers to the gospel, those of limited ability and the deranged are innocent in God's sight, having only 'original sin', inherited from Adam. Each person, they say, must proceed from innocence to guilt by imitating Adam before being proclaimed guilty by God. However, this verse teaches that death comes to all because all have sinned, even if they have not sinned exactly as Adam. 'Death reigned from Adam to Moses, even over them that had not sinned after the similitude of Adam's transgression who is the figure of him that was to come.'[7]

I take this to mean, with the commentary given in the entire chapter going on into the next, that the gospel was with man from the moment he sinned and was widely declared as such by Moses' Law of Grace

---

[7] Romans 5:14.

125

which pointed to the way of salvation made necessary because of the abundance of man's transgressions and the greater need for grace.

The first human sinner is a figure of Christ
An astonishing insight into the mind of God is revealed here. Though Adam was the earthly father of sin, his marriage to Eve is presented as a lasting ideal, reaffirmed by Christ[8] and used as a picture of Christ and His Bride, the Church. Furthermore, Adam, despite his sin, points us to Christ, the great Restorer of the Fall who is therefore called the Second Adam in the Scriptures. Thus Paul can conclude in Romans 5:17, 'For if by one man's offence death reigned by one; much more they which receive abundance of grace and of the gift of righteousness shall reign in life by one Jesus Christ'.

How sin finds us out
Following the Old Testament warning to those who reject the Lord, 'Be sure your sins will find you out',[9] and the above cited Scripture passages, we see how the Scriptures conclude all under sin and show us how sin entered into and spread through the world. We may know all about this yet still do not recognise sin when it confronts us. A knowledge of the letter of the Scriptures does not of necessity bring with it an understanding of what the Spirit wishes to tell us by it. Furthermore, nothing is condemned more in Scripture than paying lip-service only to the law. This kind of behaviour, we read, makes staunch hypocrites but weak Christians whom sin has not yet found out.

Man is paradoxically a law lover
Most of us, however, love laws. We like to show others how good we are at keeping them and how bad others are who neglect them. As soon as we form a church, we draw up a constitution and a list of 'Thou Shalts' and 'Thou Shalt Nots' which so often become our Traditions of the Elders and our justification for our odd behaviour and hard hearts. There is nothing like a good pat on our own shoulders to boost our own egos. The Bible calls such self-deceivers 'hypocrites' which means 'actors' or 'impostors'. It also means, in English idiom, one who acts

---

[8] Genesis 2:24; Matthew 19:5.
[9] Numbers 32:23.

the goat and makes a fool of himself. There was a good custom in the old days of decorating church pews and the parson's stall with goat heads, to remind both worshippers and preachers that they were not there to practise hypocrisy but to be God's sheep, not the devil's goats.

It is the clear teaching of Scripture that such self-complacent outward law-abiders are the worst sinners. Indeed, we read that the letter kills but the Spirit quickens us. In other words, those who feel that they can live law-like under their own steam are misusing the Law and to misuse the Law is sin and the wages of sin is death. The Law is there to drive us into the arms of the Spirit, whom Christ tells us, will make everything plain. Without the Spirit, the Law is a dead letter for spiritually dead people. The purpose of the Law is to make sinners in the sense that it reveals them as such.

Here modern evangelism stands on thin ice. We are invariably told that God punishes the sinner and that is what Hell is all about. But Hell is not God's prison for the eternal punishment of sinners. Sin is wholly the product of man. When the Scriptures tell us that the wages of sin is death they are talking about man's suicide not God's punishment. Perhaps we have caused too many difficulties in understanding sin as we have swept all man's misdemeanours, rebellion, transgressions, errors, offences, felonies and the like under one carpet we call 'sin'. There are at least six terms in the New Testament for 'sin'. All point to man's failings, not to God's doings. They all point to the fact that man has elected himself to the Godhead and is at enmity with God. Sin is man's infirmity just as righteousness and salvation is God's healing.

Correcting the abuse of the Law
A large part of Christ's ministry was to correct the abuse of His Law and to define clearly the consequences of breaking it. The heart of this teaching is found in Christ's numerous speeches beginning with 'Ye have heard that it was said by them of old time ... But I say unto you'. Here, Jesus points out that the self-righteous have selected a misunderstood Law, detached it from its clear, wider, spiritual meaning, and, feeling they have kept to the very letter, judge themselves righteous enough if not righteous over-much! We can take Matthew 5:28 as a fitting example:

Ye have heard that it was said by them of old time, Thou shalt not commit adultery: But I say unto you that whosoever looketh on a woman to lust after her hath committed adultery with her already in his heart.

As Moses and the Prophets pointed out, we should follow the tenor of the Law, that is its Spirit and not the letter having blocked out all that it is saying to us. Some strive to confuse the issue here and belittle sin by saying that Christ is squabbling with Moses and showing the temporary nature of revealed law and thus any demand for eternal moral standards on God's part is a human invention. Perish the thought! Christ is pointing out that His divine law is being misused to give sinners hope of life when, in reality, their spiritual death is being proclaimed. He is pointing out that Moses, Christ's own Old Testament expositor, and God's friend, implemented the law so it covered both deed and thought. Christ expounds the full and complete Law in His authority as the Lawgiver, and not handing out the Law piece-meal with the traditional, man-honouring and God-forgetting methods of the scribes as we read in the concluding verse[10] of this 'Sermon on the Mount', 'For he taught them as one having authority and not as the scribes'.

Outside and inside application

The self-righteous man looks only at his own outside appearance, but God searches his heart. The same Law that condemns adultery, also condemns the letter-keeper here because it also condemns the one who commits adultery in his heart and covets another man's wife. We know from the sad example of David that the very best of men are not immune to this kind of sin and David's adulterous thoughts and actions were used by God to drive him to his knees and pray such deep prayers of repentance as we find in Psalm 51. When David was on his knees in repentant prayer, he was in the place the Law was designed to put him. Nevertheless, David knew he was not forced to his knees by his own efforts. They had produced his sin in thought and deed. They had caused him to stand in his own self-pride. It was God who caused him to fall on his knees. David then realised that this was the Spirit's work and thus prayed in his repentance for God to give him a new, contrite heart

---

[10] Matthew 7:29.

and not take the Holy Spirit from him. David learnt the hard way, as we all must, but this way is the only way for sinners.

Where sin abounds, grace much more abounds
According to the Scriptures the work of Law is a work of grace so that the sinner may stand before his Lord and Saviour with no false ideas of himself. This good, gospel use of the Law is called using the Law lawfully in Scripture, i.e. giving the Law its correct function and application.[11] Grace enlightens us by making us blind to all forms of righteousness other than Christ's own righteousness. Though sin slays us, grace redeems us when Christ says to us personally 'Cast thy burden upon the Lord, and He shall sustain thee. He shall never suffer the righteous to be moved'.[12]

Christ, not the Law, is God's full Covenant revelation
The Law is not God's total revelation to man. If it were, there would be no story of salvation which we know to be the main teaching of the Christian gospel based on God's Word. The Ten Commandments, indeed, are only a small part of God's revelation to Moses concerning the purpose of the Law revealed through God's grace. His expositions of God's righteousness which the Law depicts cover several books of the Bible and there are many commentaries on it from other writers in Scripture. It reveals most positively the righteousness of God but also His forgiving grace to those of His People who admit they are lost until God saves them.

The shadow side of the Law is that it does not help us to gain that righteousness which we have rejected in our sin. This is not the Law's fault, nor does it show any weakness in the Holy Law. It is entirely due to our sinful state. In other words, if we are to be saved, it must be from some source outside of the Law yet a source to which the Law points. That is the function of the Law. This is why the Scriptures speak of the Law as a schoolmaster who brings us, like the old Greek pedagogues brought their Roman masters' children to school, to Christ, who is God

---

[11] 1 Timothy 1:8.
[12] Psalm 55:22.

incarnate.[13] Paul tells us in Romans 3 that we should give up all hope of finding salvation in and through the Law and concentrate on the righteousness of God. This righteousness is plain to see, says Paul, through the work of the Law and the prophets who point to Christ. This Christ, Paul teaches, is the One:

> Whom God hath set forth to be a propitiation through faith in his blood, to declare his righteousness for the remission of sins that are past, through the forbearance of God.[14]

Paul explains that there are two sides to the teaching of the Law. The one is the condemning side and the other is the forgiving, propitiating, restoring and justifying side of God's nature. This is why great evangelists such as John Gill always pointed to the dual action of the Covenant, to condemn sin, and yet justify the sinner. The Law was always of Grace as it opened the door to forgiveness and cleansing. This shows that the Law was not merely judicial but combined justice and mercy. Paul repeats, broadens and deepens this doctrine in Galatians 3 where he tells us that Christ has redeemed us from the curse of the law, being made a curse for us. Christ has paid the penalty of sin for us that we may be pronounced innocent before God. We are justified through the faith exercised by Christ in going to the cross as our vicarious and victorious representative.[15] Thus, even our faith is a vicarious, substitutionary work of Christ who risked all, trusting in the promises of the Father, that we, in Him, might gain all.

As we have seen above, where sin is, Satan is at hand so we must deal in Chapter 9 with the way Christ defeated Satan in His Atonement.

---

[13] Galatians 3:24, 25.
[14] Romans 3:25.
[15] Galatians 2:16.

Chapter 9

The Atonement and our Deliverance from Satan

Who is Satan and what Character has he?

Satan is introduced in Scripture under a variety of names such as the devil, Satan, the accuser, the tempter, the ruler of this age, the evil one, the dragon, the serpent, a roaring lion, the destroyer, the enemy, Beelzebub, Lucifer, a father of unbelievers or unbelief and a liar from the beginning, according to the variety of actions he takes against God and man. He is also, which is not often noted, called a 'son of God'.

The devil does not hold us ransom

Many who believe in our being ransomed wrongly believe that Christ ransoms us from the devil's control. The devil, however, has no ownership over us, so the idea of ransoming us from the devil, often aired in sub-Christian literature, does not stand to debate. However, the devil has had strong claims on us since Adam and Eve sinned through his temptations. Adam fell under such temptations but we see that our Redeemer Christ, who came to deliver us from Satan's claims, was also tempted by him but He withstood those temptations as the Second Adam and thus was counted worthy of representing man before God.

The Serpent

Satan is first introduced in Genesis 3:1 as a serpent (nachash) because of his subtlety and beguiling nature but whether this was a true or assumed form is irrelevant to the evil which came through his encounter with Eve. Since then humans have always abhorred creepy, crawly, slimy creatures which have no legs to stand up on. The New Testament writers also use the name 'serpent' to depict Satan as in 2 Corinthians 11:3, 'But I fear, lest by any means, as the serpent beguiled Eve through his subtlety, so your minds should be corrupted from the simplicity that is in Christ'. Here Paul is warning the churches that the serpent is still at work now in the form of those who would present them with a false picture of Jesus. This could only lead to a false spirit and a false gospel. It is obvious that Paul sees the serpent in his days as especially beguiling the churches. I do sincerely believe and fear that Satan is even more subtly at work in our churches than ever and many churches are now but a chaos of the cults. This is certainly a sign that the serpent fears for the end and is, as it were, working overtime to do as much damage as possible before his final defeat when death which follows sin shall be no more. It is thus no surprise to find John in the book of Revelation teaching the serpent's end when he says:

> And there was war in heaven: Michael and his angels fought against the dragon; and the dragon fought and his angels. And prevailed not; neither was their place found anymore in heaven. And the great dragon was cast out, that old serpent, called the Devil and Satan, which deceiveth the whole world: he was cast out into the earth, and his angels were cast out with him. And I heard a loud voice saying in heaven, Now is come salvation, and strength, and the kingdom of our God, and the power of his Christ: for the accuser of our brethren is cast down, which accused them before our God day and night.[1]

The devil is our accuser before God

The name 'devil' is old Anglo Saxon and is akin to the Latin term 'diabolus' and the Greek 'diabolos' which means one who throws us about like a ball, pierces us through and through, or one who informs against us as in Luke 16:1, whether he be man or devil. As the devil cannot be trusted, his accusations are called 'slander' or 'treachery' in

---

[1] Revelation 12:7-12

Scripture as in 1 Timothy 3:11 and 2 Timothy 3:3 which tell us that when humans are slanderers they are doing the work of the devil. Even amongst the Apostles, we find that there are those led by the devil, a fact that will be commented on later in this chapter.

Since the Fall, the devil has been our accuser but he is powerless to wrench us from Christ's arms. John goes on to show how the serpent fought Christ and his people but lost the battle and his fate is sealed. In my childish imagination prompted by a physics lesson at school, I thought of the serpent being thrown into an astronomical wormhole (which means 'serpent hole') for a thousand years before coming out at the other end and landing in some sort of exploding black hole. Regardless of how we 'adults' might imagine this, it means the end of the serpent alias the devil and all his works.

To be truthful, Christ challenged the devil to do his worst but woe be to the man who has similar ideas. The point was that we sinners have fallen to the devil's temptations but Christ, the true Man could not have been truly incarnated as Man among men, if He had not shown that He could withstand the devil. So, we find that as soon as Christ started His ministry, He was tempted by the devil in an area where the devil could show and utilise all his powers. We read in Matthew 4:1ff.: 'Then was Jesus led up of the Spirit into the wilderness to be tempted of the devil. And when he had fasted forty days and forty nights, he was afterward an hungred'.

Here we note that Christ knew what trials were ahead of Him as Man suffering for men and spent the time at His disposal in conversation with His Father in preparation for His ordeal. In such times, we too ought to always pray and not faint in the face of trouble.[2]

We read on: 'And when the tempter came to him, he said, If thou be the Son of God, command that these stones be made bread. But he answered and said, It is written, Man shall not live by bread alone, but by every word that proceedeth out of the mouth of God'.

Of course, the devil knew that Christ was hungry and also knew that Christ could order food and water to be produced from the most unusual natural elements as He did when He was with Moses in the Wilderness.

---

[2] Luke 18:1.

What the devil did not understand was that He was going about godly business living on the Word of God which was the food He needed at the time.

> Then the devil taketh him up into the holy city, and setteth him on a pinnacle of the temple, And saith unto him, If thou be the Son of God, cast thyself down: for it is written, He shall give his angels charge concerning thee: and in their hands they shall bear thee up, lest at any time thou dash thy foot against a stone.

Here the devil had cottoned on to the way Christ was thinking and showed that he, too, knew his Old Testament in which he had featured so often. However, who knew the Word of God better than God's own Son, the Creator of all things with the Holy Spirit and co-equal with the Father? So Christ could put the devil in his place and told him straight: 'Thou shalt not tempt the Lord thy God'.

Then we read: 'Again, the devil taketh him up into an exceeding high mountain, and sheweth him all the kingdoms of the world, and the glory of them; And saith unto him, All these things will I give thee, if thou wilt fall down and worship me'.

I have read many commentators on this passage whom I believe to be quite erroneous. One says:

> Satan's promise in Matthew 4:8, 9 and Luke 4:6, 7 to give Jesus all the kingdoms of the earth implies that all those kingdoms belong to him. The fact that Jesus does not dispute Satan's promise indicates that the authors of those gospels believed this to be true.

We never read that Christ has given up His role as Creator and Preserver of this world until the Elect are gathered in. Nor do we read that God has signed over the world to Satan who is the Accuser of this world but has no ownership over it even if he is called 'the god' of this world, alias 'the Father of Lies'. Even if he roars like an angry lion in this world, he is still on God's leash. The devil did not worship God, nor did he serve Him, the true Owner. Thus he was in no position to bargain with Christ whom he could not bluff.

Once I was a member of a Baptist pastors' online chat group and the subject of Christ's temptations cropped up. I was astonished that the majority of members from several countries were adamant in their belief that Christ's temptations were not real as applied to Christ's human nature. He was not tempted as man, they said, because if Christ were really tempted, it would mean that He could sin. Of course, I responded with the gospel fact that Christ was 'tempted in all points like as we are, yet without sin'.[3] I also explained that: 'For in that he himself hath suffered being tempted, he is able to succour them that are tempted'.[4]

My brethren rejected my evidence feeling that mine was a false interpretation. Christ withstood the devil, they said because He was God in man not because he was a Man amongst men and suffered as a Brother amongst brothers. Up to this time, after being in Christ from youth to old age, I had never realised that so many modern evangelical pastors could be Docetists. They were thus as far from the truth as our Muslim friends who believe that Christ did not suffer on the cross but someone or something in His stead. If Christ as Man could not be tempted, how could he represent those who are tempted and fall? He went through all that the devil can summon up in his powers to deceive us but with the Man Christ Jesus, it did not work. Still today we find Christians who deny that Christ took upon Himself a mortal body so that we with Him could be resurrected with an immortal body. After all, this is clearly what Scripture says, not only referring to our mortality but also to that of Christ. What are the Biblical facts?

John 1:14 tells us: 'And the Word was made flesh, and dwelt among us, (and we beheld his glory, the glory as of the only begotten of the Father,) full of grace and truth'. And, Romans 8:3 comments on this by saying: 'For what the Law could not do, in that it was weak through the flesh, God sending his own Son in the likeness of sinful flesh, and for sin, condemned sin in the flesh'.

The word for 'likeness' here ομοιωματι (omoioomati) does not mean 'in a similar form' but in the same form. Jesus took on our flesh to condemn our sin in our flesh. To argue that our flesh is not mortal needs

---

[3] Hebrews 4:15.
[4] Hebrews 2:18.

quite a bit of extra-Biblical imagination as Paul tells us in Romans 8:11 that God who raised up Christ from the dead, that is from mortality to immortality because Christ truly died bodily, will also raise us up from mortality to immortality as also witnessed by 1 Corinthians 15:53, 54.[5] Christ became mortal when He took on our mortality. I take it that this is what is meant by Philippians 2:7, 8:

> But made himself of no reputation, and took upon himself the form of a servant, and was made in the likeness of men. And being found in fashion as a man, he humbled himself, and became obedient unto death, even the death on the cross.

Here again, the word for 'form', 'likeness' and 'fashion' are concrete words depicting flesh and blood and not some phantasmal or celestial substance. Where New Testament teaching reaches our gaze, there is always Old Testament teaching behind it and here we see the Suffering Servant so vividly and emotionally portrayed by Isaiah who knew his Christ.

So, to finish off the battle of temptation between Christ and the devil which was far from being the last battle, we read:

> Then saith Jesus unto him, Get thee hence, Satan: for it is written, Thou shalt worship the Lord thy God, and him only shalt thou serve. Then the devil leaveth him, and, behold, angels came and ministered unto him.[6]

This story ought to be read by every NCT follower who believes that when Christ came, He abolished the Old Testament teaching and inaugurated a New Law. Christ tells the tempting devil that He is the author and finisher of creation as outlined in God's Old Testament gospel which, of course, Christ knew far better than the devil. However Christ is not here leaning on his Godhead but is acting as the perfect Man who lives accordingly to the letter and tenor of the Divine Word. This was then the Old Testament Torah which the devil refused to acknowledge like the NCT followers of today.

---

[5] See also 2 Corinthians 4:11 and 2 Corinthians 5:4.
[6] See also Mark 1:12, 13, and Luke 4:1-13.

After showing that when the devil is resisted, he will flee, Jesus now openly confessed His Sonship and position as the Messiah and Redeemer expounding Isaiah 61:1 ff. and preached deliverance from Satan's treachery.[7] This took place in Nazareth where Christ was raised and He now showed His fellow-citizens to what purpose He was born.

Beelzebub or Lord of the Flies
We read in Matthew, Mark and Luke that the devil has another name, especially amongst the scoffing Pharisees which is that of Beelzebub. So when the Pharisees and the Jerusalem Scribes who were unbelievers regarding the Scriptures, saw Christ healing and casting out devils,[8] they claimed that Jesus was acting on Beelzebub's orders whom they termed 'the prince of the devils'. They obviously professed to know more about Beelzebub than they knew of Christ foretold by Isaiah. Isaiah had condemned the clerical intelligentsia of Jerusalem and believed the old city was even then in the hands of the evil one, hence he spoke of the destruction of Jerusalem, paving the way for the New Jerusalem of true, worldwide believers.

We must ask here from where these misled students of their own Torah had obtained their information about Beelzebub as it was strictly a term used by enemies of the true Jewish faith. The term is appears to be a form of Baal-Zebub, the 'Lord of the Flies', an ancient Ekronite[9] god which seems to have been a humoristic version of Canaanite Baal-Zebul, the 'Lord of the High Places'. Whatever the etymology, Beelzebub was brought low by Christ who called him Satan.

Ekron was a leading Philistine city in the days of Moses and is mentioned in Joshua 15:45 as one of the foreign areas given to the Children of Judah after the Exodus and was situated on the border near Judah and Dan on the edge of what is now called the Gaza Strip. In a recent television interview concerning Israel's plan to annex large parts of Palestine which were traditionally non-Jewish, it was claimed that the area around Ekron was promised to the children of Israel in Moses'

---

[7] See Luke 4:16-21.
[8] Luke 15:14-20.
[9] Inhabitants of the most northerly of the five towns belonging to the lords of the Philistines, about 11 miles north of Gath.

day in the Bible and thus belongs to modern Israel. This historical right is claimed by many Israeli politicians for all of Palestine. This is false as the Gaza Strip where the Philistines lived was exempted by God from annexation by the children of Israel. Genesis 15:18-21; 21:22-27; 26:28-39 and Exodus 13:17 all refer to the Philistines' exclusion from the Refugees' occupations obviously because of the peace treaties the Patriarchs had drawn up with the Philistines and because of the different religions. The Children of Israel mingled with the Philistines, who grew in power over Israel until the days of Samson and their religious rites were kept alive by renegade Jews. By this time, it was difficult to tell who was a Jew and who was a Philistine as they were quite mixed.

Even in the Exodus battles, when the Refugees took Ekron by force, the city-state was reclaimed by the Philistines repeatedly. Even after the Settlement it became an object of conflict between Judah and Dan as to which tribe should take over what. Ekron was one of the many 'Gentile' areas taken over in the Promised Land. The long list of peoples of other languages and religions which were merged with the Children of Israel into what became for a brief time 'Israel' quite contradicts the idea that Israel was merely populated by Joseph's family which moved to Egypt. Before leaving Egypt, the people of that time whom we wrongly call Jews (a name derived later from 'Judah' who split off from Israel) was a mixed race of nationalities as the Genesis story tells us.

It appears that Ekron could not accept Jewish rule until well into King Hezekiah's reign after which it ceased to be further mentioned in the Old Testament. The city-state apparently refused to give up its Canaanite religion but its city or tribal god was remembered as a personification of evil. Not only the Ekronites but also the Jebusites and other peoples who were not defeated by the Children of Israel were absorbed into Israel bringing their Canaanite religion with them. Jerusalem takes its name from the Jebusites who were non-Jews. This perhaps explains why the prophets always viewed Jerusalem as the centre of opposition to the Messianic faith. It is clear that the Scribes and Pharisees of Jerusalem had Canaanite roots in their religion and later took on Persian philosophical and religious elements which still dominate much of the Jewish faith, especially the 'traditions of the elders'. They were thus more at home with Beelzebub than the God of the Torah. Perhaps the UN had an eye for this when in 1947/8 they claimed that Jerusalem must remain an international city.

The fictive idea that the Jews were genetically of one blood and spiritually of one faith still haunts our Christian view of the gospel and our witness to the Jews. Indeed, the German churches have banned missionary work to the Jews with the explanation that they are already the people of God. There are strong elements in society which would also ban witnessing to any other religion on the same basis. Already in our schools we are learning that religious knowledge may only be spread in the form prescribed by narrow-minded, uneducated party politicians who are basically irreligious. Here in Germany we teachers are still free to pray with our pupils and students, read the Bible to and with them and witness to Christ in lessons. In the States and Britain this is impossible as I heard in a U.S.A. Gideon Conference in which I took part. Several minor parties are, however, now campaigning in Germany and are telling us we are blind and must follow the blind.

The NCT has lost a true understanding of the people of God

The idea of the NCT that the Mosaic Law which they usually reduced to nine commandments, leaving out God's rulings regarding the Sabbath was a solely Jewish national covenant does not take into consideration the mixture of Jews and Gentiles and different religions which existed with growing extension until the time of Christ. Yet the same gospel which believing Jews like Isaiah and Jeremiah preached came to be preached worldwide and not merely locally amongst the Gentiles thus finally breaking down all distinctions between Jews and Gentiles. It is also significant to note that when the NCT criticise the Old Testament peoples as being legalists only, they are thinking of the unbelieving, pagan element, in the Old Testament and not on the faith of the Patriarchs, Moses, the Prophets and the Apostles in Christ. If one looks on law without gospel as the NCT do in the Old Testament, and then reject law and gospel together, one has no basis for a New Covenant Theology which, according to Scripture started before Sinai.

The destroyer

In the Old Testament the word Abaddon which means 'place of destruction' is used for hell or sheol and is translated in the New Testament as Apollyon. In Revelation 9:11 Apollyon is called 'the angel of the bottomless pit' and identified with those who would not repent who 'worship devils, and idols of gold, and silver, and brass, and stone, and of wood: which neither can see, nor hear, nor walk'.

I cannot help but see a touch of humour in such a definition pointing out the futility of a life outside of Christ, as also the futility of a life down a bottomless pit, accepting that the devil is referred to here.[10]

Satan and his pseudonyms

A usual name for the devil used in Scripture is 'Satan', meaning the accuser, adversary or enemy, who feels he can legally claim us for himself as one law-breaker who has led others to join him in his evil deeds. However, Satan can claim nothing from God as he does not own us, nor is he anywhere equal to God in arguing with Him but his defeat was declared as soon as he caused man to fall. This is why Christ is called our Advocate as He pleads for His Bride before the Throne of Grace against the accuser.

Satan was at work from the dawn of time

One of the oldest books in the Bible, apparently dating back to pre-Mosaic times, if not before the Abrahamic age, depicts the story of God's servant Job who learnt to know Satan as his accuser, enemy and would-be destroyer. It presents difficulties to some as they say Satan is banned to earth but in the Book of Job seemingly moves around freely in Heaven. The text does not support such an understanding. First, Heaven is not a locality surrounded by borders but is everywhere where God reigns in His everlastingness and borderless Kingdom. This was the teaching of Moses when in Deuteronomy 30:4 he says, 'If any of thine be driven out unto the uttermost parts of heaven, from thence will the Lord thy God gather thee, and from thence will he fetch thee'. Moses continues to outline the scope of Heaven which also embraces the earth and says in verse 19 'call heaven and earth to record this day against you, that I have set before you life and death, blessing and cursing: therefore choose life, that both thou and thy seed shall live'. This extension of Heaven, or Heavens[11] is also echoed by the Prophets as in Nehemiah 1:9 where we read:

---

[10] Revelation 9:11-21.

[11] The Hebrew word is used in its plural form as in 'The Heavens declare His glory'.

But if ye turn unto me, and keep my commandments, and do them; though there were of you cast out into the uttermost parts of heaven, yet will I gather them from thence, and will bring them unto the place that I have chosen to set my name there.

Heaven is where God is active and that is everywhere. Of those who campaign against God, He says:

Though they dig into hell, thence shall my hand take them; though they climb up to heaven, thence will I bring them down. And though they hide themselves in the top of Carmel, I will search and take them out thence; and though they be hid from my sight in the bottom of the sea, thence will I command the serpent, and he shall bite them.[12]

Second, in Job 1:6-11, we find God calling in a council of 'the sons of God' to the presence of God but we are not told that the scene is set in Heaven as opposed to on earth. Furthermore, Satan tells God that he has being going to and fro on the earth and it is on the earth that he seeks permission to tempt the patience of Job. We thus read:

Now there was a day when the sons of God came to present themselves before the LORD, and Satan came also among them. And the LORD said unto Satan, Whence comest thou? Then Satan answered the LORD, and said, From going to and fro in the earth, and from walking up and down in it. And the LORD said unto Satan, Hast thou considered my servant Job, that there is none like him in the earth, a perfect and an upright man, one that feareth God, and escheweth evil? Then Satan answered the LORD, and said, Doth Job fear God for nought? Hast not thou made an hedge about him, and about his house, and about all that he hath on every side? thou hast blessed the work of his hands, and his substance is increased in the land. But put forth thine hand now, and touch all that he hath, and he will curse thee to thy face.

---

[12] Amos 8:2, 3.

We note that Satan, though a son of God, had no powers of his own above those which were permitted of God, so Satan has to go begging to obtain his goal. He is not satisfied with merely robbing Job of most of his family but has to beg at God's hand again in order to destroy Job personally.

So on the next occasion of being called before God to explain his ways Satan said:

> Skin for skin, yea, all that a man hath will he give for his life. But put forth thine hand now, and touch his bone and his flesh, and he will curse thee to thy face. And the Lord said unto Satan, Behold, he is in thine hand; but save his life.[13]

It is frightening to me to see how God tried Job to the uttermost but how great is the child of God under the fiercest temptation when God is at his side and enables one to say with Job:

> For I know that my Redeemer liveth, and that he shall stand at the latter day upon the earth: and though after my skin worms destroy this body, yet in my flesh shall I see God. Whom I shall see for myself, and mine eyes shall behold.[14]

Furthermore, we read that 'So the Lord blessed the latter end of Job more than his beginning'.[15]

Job and Peter compared

In Jesus' teaching we find a parallel between God permitting Satan's attacks on Job and Jesus' dealings with both Satan and Peter. We thus read in Luke 22:31:

> And the Lord said, Simon, Simon, behold Satan hath desired to have you, that he might sift you as wheat. But I have prayed for thee, that thy faith fail not: and when thou art converted, strengthen the brethren.

---

[13] Job 2:4, 5.
[14] Job 19:25-27.
[15] Job 42:12.

Nevertheless, Christ had to rebuke Peter several times severely and had even told him that he was an agent of Satan, saying:

> Get thee behind me Satan: thou art an offence unto me: for thou savourest not the things that be of God, but those that be of man.[16]

As in the case of Job, we do not read that the evil work of Satan was forbidden by the Lord but obviously allowed and are told that Jesus was praying for the unbelieving disciple who was to repeatedly deny Him. Yet Christ, who always had Satan under control told Peter the truth. He would be converted, pardoned and made effective in the Gospel and become a strength to the brethren. We know, too, that we have the same Advocate with the Father as had Peter who continually prays for us. The story of Simon Peter strengthens us in this trust.

Judas Iscariot fared differently
The case of Judas Iscariot in relation to Jesus and the devil was different. Peter would be converted but Judas not. He was 'the Son of Perdition' of whom Christ said 'Have not I chosen you twelve and one of you is a devil?'[17] So Luke 22:3-6 tells us that 'Satan entered' Judas so that he betrayed Christ and on realising what he had done Judas hanged himself. Here, it is obvious that Christ allowed Satan to enter Judas so that His work could be fulfilled. So may those who think we stand very near Christ, take heed lest we fall. However, it is one thing to betray Christ and another thing to doubt His work in our lives and here the case of Doubting Thomas helps to remove such similar doubts.

The Bible distinguishes between believing and unbelieving Jews
People may doubt my emphasis made in this work and others that the Jews as a people were never more than a mixture of ethnic Jews and ethnic Gentiles and were under two conflicting gospels in the Old Testament through which time only a remnant were saved. Yet Christ openly declares this fact as recorded by John 8:44 where He says to a

---

[16] Matthew 16:23.
[17] John 6:70.

number who falsely referred to Abraham as their 'father' (that is as the father of the faithful), that they follow the father of the unfaithful, Satan. So he says:

> Ye are of your father the devil, and the lusts of your father ye will do. He was a murderer from the beginning, and abode not in the truth, because there is no truth in him. When he speaketh a lie, he speaketh of his own: for he is a liar and the father of it. And because I tell you the truth, ye believe me not.

If you think this is rather hard on the unbelieving Jews, then you must read Isaiah both on the believing remnant and the unbelieving rest of the Old Testament peoples as portrayed in my book *The Covenant of Grace and the People of God*.

Satan contra God's Word

The parable of the sower depicted in Matthew 13:3 ff.; Mark 4:3 ff. and Luke 8:5 ff., finds Satan referred to by name as the one who corrupts the good seed which is the Word of God. This shows how we Christians should honour God's Word in all we do and say and never criticise its theology by 'experiments in interpretation' or by striving to understand the Scriptures according to philosophical or pseudo-scientific fashions. A case in point is viewing the Bible in evolutionary terms. As these terms vary from generation to generation and each generation puts forward new theories of science, we see the folly of taking that which is eternal in God's Word and looking at it as if it were time-bound. Today's science, on the whole, merely views God's Heavens as a corruptible and ever changing phenomena. We Christians believe in an uncorrupted Saviour who is the same yesterday, today and forever and has overcome the corrupted world. May all our scientists learn that the earth is the Lord's and the fulness thereof and that we Christians believe in new Heavens and a new earth wherein dwelleth righteousness.[18]

Why can Adam be forgiven but not the devil?

Many who think merely of a God of Love who cannot condemn anyone are puzzled by the fact that there is hope given to Adam and his posterity

---

[18] 2 Peter 3:13.

but not to Satan with all his works. My explanation is that Satan was not made in the likeness of God and fell and was not alone in falling as a number of other celestial beings fell with him. Adam was made in the likeness of God and could return to that status through repentance and faith. The devil's very nature prohibited this as he did not have the wherewithal in God's wisdom and the Godhead's plan for Christ's Bride who were elected never to fall. The devil who was called a 'son of God'[19] was nevertheless a liar from the beginning and was a prodigal that could never return to his Father. Adam was not a liar from the beginning and the way of repentance and belief and reconciliation with God was laid before him. What happened to the fallen angels need not happen to fallen mankind. Jesus in his incarnation was made 'so much better than the angels'. I take it that this is thus the status of man who has been given by inheritance a 'more excellent name' than the angels who worship the Incarnate Christ as true man.[20] As all the members of Christ's Bride are classified as being 'in Christ' and Christ in us is 'our hope of glory', the angels even worship Christ's Elect but Satan would not worship either God or His chosen people and thus lowered himself below man to a status beyond salvation. The angels were there to communicate between heaven and earth as ambassadors of God but Satan lost this position and received the rank of a lowly animal. Thus Adam became the prototype of the incarnate Second Adam who put right all his wrongs. Adam was also the proto-type of the unbeliever just as Christ was the proto-type of the believer.

Lucifer

Many Christians believe the Devil was once a beautiful angel named Lucifer who defied God and fell from grace. This assumption that he is a fallen angel is often based the book of Isaiah in the Bible which says, 'How art thou fallen from heaven, O Lucifer, son of the morning! How art thou cut down to the ground, which didst weaken the nations'.[21]

Here Isaiah who always preached with a worldwide view, including both Jews and Gentiles knew that the nations were being delivered from

---

[19] Job 1:6.
[20] Hebrews 1:1-6.
[21] Isaiah 14:12.

the grasp of Satan through the Suffering Servant of God. This he emphasises throughout his lengthy work, especially chapter 52 where we read of the vicariously suffering Christ:

> So shall he sprinkle many nations; the kings shall shut their mouths at him: for that which had not been told them shall they see; and that which they had not heard shall they consider.[22]

The word 'consider' here reminds one of Hebrews 12:3 and the teaching of the whole chapter which presents Christ as One who endured man's shame to free him from sin's curse.

In chapter 55 Isaiah tells us of the everlasting Covenant (v. 3) with Isaiah's thirsting hearers and those of yet unknown nations (v. 5) who will flock to the Holy One of Israel because He has glorified God. This fills me with the conviction that though the Fullerites of this world present us with a false gospel and the NCT withhold from sinners the solution to their sins, God will yet save His People by ways undreamed of by those that scoff at Him. Fancy the NCT protesting against us for not believing that the Old Testament was for unbelieving Jews only who were solely under a political national covenant. It is easy to be deaf to God's Word when one hides ones ears and eyes from God and turns to another loud and noisy but meaningless gospel.

Apart from tormenting Job, we find Satan interfering in David's calling, in advising him to number his people so he can estimate his forces instead of relying on the Lord.[23] There was already a sign of a split in the young Kingdom as Judah was more or less autonomous from Israel. Now the tribes of Levi and Benjamin rebelled alongside David's closest advisor Joab. The result was that God 'smote Israel' and David was given grace to repent. I feel it so strange nowadays that both Christian and Israeli zealots demand that the full Davidic earthly kingdom should be restored to modern Israel as if there were a traditional godly right to this land. In truth, it did not endure forty years and had to be continually chastised by God for unbelief, starting at Jerusalem which was apparently the worst hit. It very rarely indeed placed a living trust in God and was continually being reduced and split

---

[22] Isaiah 52:13-15.
[23] 1 Chronicles 21:1.

up through its rebellion against God. No wonder the Prophets longed for a New Jerusalem under no other guidance than the Grace of God on the world remnant, as, of course, the Gentile nations were no better than old Israel and Judah. The Bible tells us that 'the Devil sinneth from the beginning' and blind unbelievers still pride themselves in following him. John's words are of note here as he upholds the Law against sinners though NCT tells us that the Law was abrogated before John wrote his epistles. John, however, tells us:

> Whosoever committeth sin transgresseth also the law: for sin is the transgression of the law. And ye know that he was manifested to take away our sins; and in him is no sin. Whosoever abideth in him sinneth not: whosoever sinneth hath not seen him, neither known him. Little children, let no man deceive you: he that doeth righteousness is righteous, even as he is righteous. He that committeth sin is of the devil; for the devil sinneth from the beginning. For this purpose the Son of God was manifested, that he might destroy the works of the devil.[24]

Here, of course, is the problem some have in wondering if they are not God's children as they still sin in their Adamic body. However, so did Abraham, so did Moses and so did David and so do all of us. Yet, when our accuser comes, we have an advocate with the Father who pleads for us. This shows how God's Law is merged with grace, mercy and justice which join hands.

Conclusion

Crucial to the doctrine of Atonement is the mentioning here of the destruction of Satan and all his works as also taught by that Old Testament commentator, the author of the book of Hebrews, who says:

> For as much then as the children are partakers of flesh and blood, he also himself like-wise took part of the same; that

---

[24] 1 John 3:4-8.

through death he might destroy him that had the power of death, that is the devil.[25]

Thus a very essential part of the work of reconciliation was to put the Devil at bay and to rescue His Bride from the grip of the devil. In the most practical terms possible the Atonement annulled the Devil's claims on sinful mankind. This is obviously what is meant by the binding of Satan and the satisfaction that was made to appease both the Saviour and the saved. This satisfaction cannot be understood without looking into the results of a two-way imputation – of man's sin to Christ and Christ's righteousness to man which is considered in the next chapter.

---

[25] Hebrews 2:14.

Chapter 10

Righteousness and Sin Imputed
in the Atonement

The imputation of sin to Christ is not merely symbolic

The main Scripture passage which moved me to write this chapter was
2 Corinthians 5:21: 'For he hath made him to be sin for us who knew
no sin: that we might be made the righteousness of God in him'.

First of all, I wish to examine the modern pseudo-Reformed idea that
imputation, whether of our sin to Christ or His righteousness to us, is
merely a use of figurative imagery and metaphor.

A most crucial doctrine

The doctrine that our sin was imputed to Christ for which He suffered
death and that Christ's righteousness is imputed to us so that we may
live, is one of the most crucial doctrines of the Church. But how are we
to take it? Is it a fact that cannot be interpreted away or is it merely a
metaphor or piece of imagery which can be taken this way or that? Are
we all free to read into it what we will? If imputation is merely
figurative why do these modern 'evangelical' scoffers not come up with
the real thing?

Through the influence of Andrew Fuller[1] and other symbolists, the
idea has captivated many in the so-called 'Reformed' camp that
doctrines like 'imputation' and 'justification' are always 'putative',

---

[1] See index to Fuller's *Works* and especially the chapter entitled Imputation, in Fuller's
Justification, *Works*, Vol. III, pp. 720, 721.

which means 'supposed' or 'forensic', which means 'legal'. In other words, we are not to take the supposed, legal metaphor or pieces of imagery of our Christian doctrine as indicating a final actuality and reality, or indeed, anything concrete. Supporters of the 'as if' or 'putative' school apparently see them as merely hints on the way to further enlightenment. John Murray is very adamant about this in his essay on justification and if one reads Phillip R. Johnson's Blogsite on 2 Corinthians 5:21, you will see how this idea of imagery rather than fact is defended. But where does it lead to?

Arguing dogmatically that his is the only interpretation possible, Johnson describes vicarious punishment and substitution in the words:

> He (Christ) became, in a figurative sense and in a judicial sense, the embodiment and the symbol of our wickedness.

This is how Johnson understands 2 Corinthians 5:21, but if Christ were made sin merely in a figurative, judicial and symbolic sense, how can this satisfy God's justice? If I paid a fine for my crime in stage-money, arguing that it was a figurative payment, my sentence could not possibly be lifted through such a senseless gesture. What reality is behind the metaphors? Johnson and his circle merely argue from one piece of imagery to another, never discovering the antitype behind the types or the reality behind the shadows. Their figurative gymnastics lead them to a mock-gospel without a literal, concrete, factual goal. They produce a pro forma bill which is never paid. Johnson, realizing the need for a Biblical explanation here makes a shift at giving us two. These are:

> All we like sheep have gone astray; we have turned every one to his own way; and the Lord hath laid on him the iniquity of us all (Isaiah 53:6).

and

> Christ hath redeemed us from the curse of the law, being made a curse for us (Galatians 3:13).

The latter, Johnson claims, is an exact parallel to what he sees as the imagery of 2 Corinthians 5:21. So Johnson offers us a gospel where a figurative Christ becoming sin has our iniquities laid on Him symbolically, thus exercising a figurative redemption and a figurative curse. So the 'only interpretation possible' for Johnson is that all we have is a bunch of metaphors which remain anybody's guess as to their real meaning. We might dismiss Johnson as the great leg-puller of the age but he is upheld as preaching the truth as it is in Jesus by a militant section of the Reformed party who severely deny the orthodox witness of, say, New Focus Magazine and Go Publications and call us Antinomian and Hyper-Calvinists for disagreeing with them.

Johnson follows Tillich
Johnson's doctrine was one of the main features of Liberal theology, represented by such as Paul Tillich who claimed that all the stages of Christ's work on the cross were merely first century imagery which distorted rather than enhanced the actuality, historicity and thus soteriological effect of the Atonement. Needless to say, Tillich never discovered the actual, historical and soteriological effect of the Atonement or if he did, he kept the knowledge to himself. Contrary to Tillich's and Johnson's phantasmagoria, we believe that the New Testament authors got it right first time!

Keeping to Scripture
The consequences are that if Christ did not bodily become sin for us and sin was not done away with in His life and death, then Christ's mission as outlined in Daniel 9:24, 'to finish the transgression, and to make an end of sin, and to make reconciliation for iniquity, and to bring in everlasting righteousness' failed. The quasi-redeemed are then still in their sins. If sin were not punished in Christ; if Christ were not found guilty and responsible for our sins; if there were no vicarious substitution in Christ; then the Christian faith is in vain. Our faith, Brother Johnson, is based on fact not figurative displays of imagery.

God's 'making' misunderstood
One of the main false arguments for taking 2 Corinthians 5:21 figuratively is that the Greek word poieoo (make) is allegedly used metaphorically in other places in Scripture and thus must be seen metaphorically in this passage. The dubious example invariably given

is Acts 1:36, 'Therefore let all the house of Israel know assuredly, that God hath made the same Jesus, whom ye have crucified, both Lord and Christ'. 'Made', they argue, here is definitely figurative so the same applies to 2 Corinthians 5:21. This is an absolutely groundless argument. There is no conclusive evidence in this verse that 'made' should be understood figuratively at all. The argument is merely presumptive and putative. To convince us that one application of 'made' is figurative, another misapplication of the term is used as 'proof' that the Bible conforms to their alleged Biblical symbolism. This is like producing one dud note to vouch for the validity of another dud note, though the second note is also a forgery. Should not evangelical Reformed believers question such a display of 'reason'? Of course, if all God's works were figurative, one might compare one application of 'made' with another like our critics do but this 'putative' argument gets them nowhere. If we say that Jesus was made Lord and Christ only figuratively, this would be tantamount to denying the very grounds of the Christian faith. Our marriage with the Lamb is no marriage by proxy! Christ needs no substitute.

One blog writer I have had to do with bends the meaning of poieoo to suit his argument, writing,

> Now I don't know of any Sovereign Grace believers that believe Jesus became the Lord. Acts 2:36 is clearly teaching that Jesus was manifested or revealed by God to be Lord and Christ.

However, the basic meaning of poieoo is 'make', 'create', 'construct', 'establish' and 'cause to be' in English which are causative terms. This is the whole doctrine of Biblical Incarnation theology. We read in John 1:14 that 'The Word was made flesh and dwelt amongst us'. He was not merely given a figurative flesh and dwelt figuratively amongst us. I actually met with this way-off theory in a pastors' chat-group. Here the word 'made' is 'egeneto' from 'ginomai' which also means 'to come into existence', 'to be created'. This was the concrete action of the Godhead in the fulness of time so that Christ could actually, not figuratively, take away the sins of the world. Thus we read in the Old Testament that 'with his stripes we are healed'.[2] If there was

---

[2] Isaiah 53:5.

no actual incarnation, there could not have been an actual imputation and thus no atonement. Without real stripes there would be no real healing. The two concrete causal terms poieoo and ginomai thus rule out a figurative meaning. Here we must correct our irate blog-writing friend's Greek. Neither the terms 'manifest' nor 'reveal' are usually used as figurative terms in the Scriptures but as concrete ones. 'Manifest' means to make something clear to someone and 'reveal' means to display or make known. Thus if Christ was clearly displayed as sin, then He must have been 'made sin'. The word 'made' εποιησεν (3rd pers. Sing Aor. 1, ind. Act.) in 2 Corinthians 5:21 is exactly the same word as in Acts 2:36 and the situation in both these passages describes an active, causative feat of God's. In the one passage Christ was made sin, in the other, He was made Lord and Christ.

Christ was smitten with our sin and had none of His own
However, the usual defensive argument against those who take 2 Corinthians 5:21 literally is that they must logically mean that Christ became a sinful creature ready to fulfil the lusts of the flesh. But where is the logic here? The Scriptures make it plain that Christ was made sin but not made to sin and follow evil. Christ was tempted in all things as we are, yet he did not sin. One wise-guy on a pastor's blog-site I frequented (but not for long) said that this was no real temptation for Christ as to tempt someone implies that one can sin. Another ardent present critic of mine tells me that because I believe that Christ took upon Himself my guilt, I believe in what he calls 'a polluted Christ'. At least four contributors to the New Focus Magazine have been condemned recently by so-called Reformed men on blog-sites for teaching that Christ was a sinner because they themselves misunderstand the doctrine of imputation. It is honourable of them to believe in a sinless Christ but hardly fair of them to criticise the very Word of God or explain Christ's imputation away as being merely 'figurative'. However, our accusers are convinced the cap fits because they dwell in the land of imagery and metaphor and not reality. A factual imputation to them is unfeasible.

The decision of the Godhead regarding imputation

The Father in harmony with the Holy Spirit and the Son agreed factually and actually in eternity that Christ should take on Himself not only our punishment but also our guilt. This He did at the Incarnation and throughout His earthly life until His death and resurrection. He was born of a woman, a fallen woman, and had the marks and effects of the fall on Him from birth onwards, though He did not allow them to drive Him to sin. The Roman Catholics get over this difficulty by saying that Mary was also 'immaculate' and thus they elevate her to the Queenship of Heaven. Then why, we must ask, did Christ rebuke her for misunderstanding God's ways? Scripture makes it plain that there is a body of sin[3] which can only be removed through death. This body, Christ took on Himself and destroyed it by His death because He was the only One good enough to pay the price of redemption through His own innocence and obedience. This is a mystery of love outworked through the union saints have with Christ from eternity and it is still beyond our understanding, but to deny it is to deny the Christian faith and our hope of glory. To deny that Christ bore our guilt in the Atonement is to deny the Atonement as we would thus still stand unredeemed before God. To say that Christ was made sin for us does not mean that Christ was made to sin, perish the thought! It means he was made guilty on our behalf. He bore our guilt!

Most of the people who struggle with the difficulties involved in Christ's being made sin, strive to use comparisons to make it a matter of imagery only, but as this was a once and for all time and eternity event, no comparison is adequate as there is nothing with which to compare it.

The difference between Old Testament sin-offerings and Christ's vicarious death

An attempt is made to get over alleged difficulties in interpreting 2 Corinthians 5:21 by turning to the Old Testament Greek translation, used by Christ and the Apostles. It is argued from such as Leviticus 4:3 and other passages that the pictures of sin-offerings there use the term amartia as also in 2 Corinthians 5:21. So the latter passage is not talking about sin at all but of a sin-offering in the OT sense. In his 'Word of

---

[3] Romans 6:6 ff.; Colossians 2:11.

His Grace' website essay, 'Does 2 Corinthians 5:21 mean that Jesus Christ actually became sin?' Peter Ditzel, a New Covenant Theology adherent but with ever-changing doctrines like most of them, argues:

> ... in the Septuagint, the word hamartia is very commonly used to mean a 'sin offering'. That is, it is used where the Hebrew Scriptures are obviously referring to a sin offering and where the English translations also have 'sin offering'.

Ditzel, to prove the figurative nature of Christ's New Testament work binds Christ in his theology to Old Testament types not seeing Christ as the Antitype. Now in Leviticus 4:3, the reference is to a bullock without blemish brought unto the Lord for a sin-offering. Ditzel's comparison fails here because such offerings were merely pointers to Christ and not the real offering itself. So, too, Ditzel does not distinguish between the Greek Bible's use of peri (respecting, concerning, about, regarding) with amartia used in relation to a sin-offering and amartia itself meaning sin, thus he confuses the sin-offering with the sin it was to remove symbolically and which points to Christ who actually removes sin. The bullock was treated as if it were 'made sin', in other words it figuratively pointed to what is actually signified in Christ who became sin. Christ, of course, was not offered on an 'as if', figurative, basis but He was offered as the fulfilment of the reality symbolized by the bullock. 2 Corinthians 5:21 does not tell us that Christ was made as if He were sin, but that he was 'made sin'.

Going back to Leviticus, the whole argument is that a substitution is found concerning sin – for the time being. Thus we find that peri (h)amartia is the usual LXX formula to describe bringing an offering to the Lord to symbolically take away the sin of the people. So here we are really talking about a symbol and not about the real Redeemer Christ who defeated sin in His own body. If Christ were merely a sin-offering in the Old Testament typological sense only, we would still be waiting for the real thing! This is illustrated in the Old Testament by the type of the scapegoat which points to Christ as our Sin-bearer. However, the scapegoat only pointed to Christ and was certainly not Christ. Besides, the life of the scapegoat was spared but Christ combined the types of both bullock and goat and was slaughtered in our stead bearing all our sin and shame for us.

2 Corinthians 5:21 clearly teaches that Christ was made sin itself and the Father condemned that sin in His Son's Person. Amartia as a standalone word means 'sin' in our Greek New Testament in every single case of its appearance, not a sin-offering. This is also its predominant use in the LXX where its meaning is extended to the burden which sin brings and being smitten with sin like a disease. Christ suffered under this deadly disease. This is the very bones and marrow of the atonement. Christ relieved His elect from the burden, disease, penalty and guilt of sin and took it all on Himself as the Federal Head, Mediator, Substitute and Representative of His people. Albeit, amartia is always used of fallen man's sins but when used in connection with Christ, it is to say that Christ Himself never sinned but was made sin in His Bride's stead.

The New Testament writer to the Hebrews clearly distinguishes between the old sin offerings and the one offering to fulfil all former pointers to this act of grace. When Christ offered Himself, He was really and actually, not symbolically, made sin to atone for sin. As the writer says in Hebrews 10:10, Christ was a once-and-for-all 'προσφορας' offering, not the old often repeated sin-offering of Leviticus 6:25, 26, and in order to be made such, our sins were actually transferred to Him and He truly bore the guilt, penalty and shame they brought with them and was made answerable for them. Romans 8:3 tells us that God condemned sin in the flesh and this was surely the flesh of our Lord and not the flesh of bullocks.

As Hebrews 9:12-14 puts it:

Neither by the blood of goats or calves but by his own blood he entered in once into the holy place, having obtained eternal redemption for us. For if the blood of bulls and of goats, and the ashes of an heifer sprinkling the unclean, sanctifieth to the purifying of the flesh: How much more shall the blood of Christ, who through the eternal Spirit offered himself without spot to God, purge your conscience from dead works to serve the living God?

The author goes on to argue that Christ was not the 'pattern' but the real Person Old Testament patterns pointed to.[4] This is perhaps why H. A. Hodges entitled his fine book on the atonement *The Pattern of Atonement* as he argues repeatedly in his book against 'separate theories' of Atonement insisting that:

> ... the Atonement is coextensive with the whole work of Christ. The whole of that work can be seen as a bridging of gulfs, a remover of estrangements, a restoration of unity.[5]

Justification denied

Again we see Grotian Fullerism in the Banner of Truth attack on Biblical justification in the anti-Huntington tirade arising from a book they gullibly read by someone who hardly knew Huntington and was a man of bad reputation. So, too, the 'Banner' also, for good measure, based their evidence on the Murray Publishing House who paid evil gossipers to denigrate Huntington in his day. Should I have to decide between paparazzi journalism and William Huntington, I would choose Huntington any day. I was shocked to find the Banner of Truth also stooped to tabloid press tactics in their affair with Donald MacLeod in which both the former Banner of Truth writer and the Banner of Truth management lost their respectability.

Fuller denied that justification was a decree of God with its origin in what Fuller calls 'the mind of God'. Huntington taught that our full salvation was settled in Christ before the foundation of the world and was objectively secured in the Atonement at the fulness of time which had been God's plan in creating both the world and time. This sound theology is quite foreign to Fullerism. Surprisingly, the Banner of Truth author also objects to the Reformed doctrine that when God sees His elect covered with Christ's righteousness, He looks upon them as being without sin. Surely this was the whole aim and intention of Christ's atoning death. The strange and unfounded argument against Huntington, that to him 'sanctification is no evidence of justification

---

[4] Hebrews 9:23, 24.
[5] *The Pattern of Atonement*, p. 10.

but rather renders it more obscure', only displays the Grotian inability to distinguish between fruits of sanctification and works-righteousness and how God justifies the ungodly. Huntington taught that a believer does not prove his justification by deserving it but because he is justified and sanctified he brings forth fruit unto holiness. This is clearly the teaching of Romans 6:22:

> But now being made free from sin, and become servants to God, ye have your fruit unto holiness, and the end everlasting life.

If Christ's being made sin for our sakes were figurative, our being made free from sin would also be figurative. Thus Johnson and his supporters would rob us both of our gospel and our faith.

The actualities of the gospel

In my book *William Huntington: Pastor of Providence*, I took up this new lapse in sound doctrine on the part of the Banner of Truth to list all the actualities of the gospel, including the imputation of Christ's righteousness. This was set in a framework of the two natures doctrine of man where it belongs, the latter being another vital doctrine dropped by modern pseudo-evangelicals. It was pointed out that there was no make-believe path to holiness and acceptance with God as God's standards of holiness are framed by His own character. Christ actually bore our penalties and His actual death in our stead is a sure and certain actual fact. Christ actually covered our sins with His righteousness which He has imputed to us. Thus God actually sees Christ's righteousness in us. God sees us actually crucified in and with Christ. So this is by no means an 'as if' state. There is practical proof of it as it has practical consequences. The sinner actually becomes a new man (in Christ), clothed in Christ's righteousness though the old man (in Adam) remains until death and resurrection. The actual life we now live is a life actually indwelt by Christ and the Holy Spirit. This is no fairy tale but the practical, concrete, non-metaphorical, factual teaching of Scripture. This atonement, made for man, provides him with an actual eternal life and not with a mere judicial, pro-forma eternal life. Christ has actually created eternal life in Him for those who have 'put on Christ' and are now 'accepted in the beloved'. The Atonement has been actually accomplished not merely figuratively so. A figurative atonement is no atonement whatsoever. One would think this argument was clear enough.[6]

Unless a man has actual righteousness, he cannot approach God. The question, 'With what actual righteousness is the believer endued so that he is accepted in the Beloved?' we answer with full Scriptural backing, 'The Beloved's own'. This is Biblical but also Huntingtonian teaching. If this is called Antinomianism in the Banner of Truth's dictionary, it is time they threw it away and bought a good Bible instead where these facts are clearly outlined.

Some years ago,[7] the Banner of Truth backed David Gay, a notorious hitch-hiker through a galaxy of errors, in calling me a Hyper-Calvinist. Their two reasons seem to have been, judging by their articles criticising my gospel call, that I see the Law as an essential part of the Covenant of Grace and possibly because I believe my justification is entirely in my Saviour's hands, as Huntington also taught according to God's Word. They also backed Gay's unfounded attack that I was of the kind that did not:

> confront their hearers with the immediate responsibility of trusting Christ, directly encouraging them to trust him, and appealing to them to do so now

It is strange that I had been praised by Murray and Roberts for my Banner of Truth articles for taking this very stand before they altered their theology for the worse, shortly after I published my biography of Huntington. This was possibly because I did not appeal to man's agency but Christ's in salvation, as I tell all men everywhere I go to repent and believe the gospel. In Gay's whole book reviewing my small booklet on gospel preaching, Gay quite overlooks this fact and even in his quotes from my book cuts out my references urging the unsaved to place their trust in Christ, thus actually creating falsified quotes to serve his purpose. The fact that the Banner of Truth took Gay's incorrect

---

[6] *William Huntington: Pastor of Providence*, pp. 236, 237.
[7] Banner of Truth Magazine, Issue 497, February 2005.

representations of my work as 'gospel' showed that they had not bothered to check original sources.

Actually, I have been doing what Gay and the Banner of Truth claim I have not been doing for sixty-three years. In my younger days in the fifties when I was, unlike today in my old age, top fit, I preached in the centre of Bradford in the streets, and evangelised from house to house and in trains and buses. Once on a train in Germany in my student days, I was handing out gospel tracks, with little success when the conductor approached me with threats and told me that if I distributed another tract he would throw me off the train. After he had gone, many passengers came to me and asked for tracts so I did not have to either offer them or distribute them. The Lord provides His own hearers and readers of the truth as He did the fish for His disciples to net in. A good friend in England who was also a good friend of a Banner of Truth director who was a fierce critic against my supposed lack of evangelical fervour, asked him if he did such evangelistic work as I did. His answer was negative yet he accused me paranoically, as our mutual friend told me, that I would not witness to the unsaved but only to the saved. Now David Gay has left the Banner of Truth fellowship and become most critical of it and taken up, with a number of former 'Banner' men, the doctrines of the NCT. It must be Gay's sixth or seventh doctrinal U-turn in trying to find a place in which he is really at home in his erroneous theological thinking. I have discussed Gay's new theology and his ridiculous claims to be a superior Bible translator in my book *The Covenant of Grace and the People of God*.[8] What astonishes me is that in Gay's chameleon-like adoption of contrary coloured theologies he always claims that he is proclaiming the truth though every other man be a liar.

Misunderstanding Christ's imputed righteousness

An anonymous Banner of Truth author writing in the July 1988, Issue 298 of the magazine listed on page 8 the five reasons he felt proved that William Huntington was an Antinomian. Apart from the use of inappropriate language and false judgment in the supposed Antinomian attributes in his condemnation of Huntington, the anonymous writer got one feature almost correct, that is Huntington's quite orthodox view of

---

[8] Go Publications, 2020.

imputation but the author interpreted this in a most unorthodox way. He argued that Huntington was an Antinomian because he believed that:

The imputation of our sin to Christ, and of His righteousness to us, was actual, not judicial:

Of course, these two features do not cancel one another out as the unnamed writer supposed. Why did he not say that Huntington believed that Christ's just work on the cross was both? It is clear why. At the time, the Banner of Truth believed that the imputation of sin to Christ and His righteousness to us was a mere legal 'as if' feature of His work and not real. Huntington was, in fact, following Scripture and the Banner of Truth was not. Huntington believed that our sins were actually purged, our debts actually cancelled and Christ's righteousness was actually given us – just as God ordered! To anyone who tells me that Christ's righteousness is not real, I shall with the Holy Spirit's help and that of the Scriptures, Huntington, Bullinger and the host of our Reformers strive to convince him that he is gravely in error.

Imputation of righteousness and the Holy Spirit
Robert Oliver in the January, 1995 issue of the Banner of Truth magazine challenged my reasoning from Scripture in my presentations of Reformed thinking especially in my Bullingerite manner.[9] He protested that in my demonstration of the actualities of the salvation story, I showed that I confuse the imputation of Christ's righteousness with the indwelling of the Holy Spirit in the believer. One might ask, where else does the Holy Spirit dwell but in the one to whom Christ imputes His righteousness? This is what comes of splitting up the doctrine of Atonement 'systematically'. Whom else does the Spirit indwell apart from those who have experienced Christ's saving righteousness? Again, to deny this is typical Governmental thinking

---

[9] My readers are invited to consult Bullinger's many expositions of Christ being made sin for us and our receiving His righteousness, especially in his first sermon in the Fourth Decade when dealing with God justifying the ungodly and how He did it. This is the kind of gospel preaching that the Banner of Truth at that time had lost and indeed called 'Antinomian'. Readers will see that Huntington preached in keeping with one of our very greatest Reformers. Calvin is also worth reading on imputation but his words lack Bullinger's warmth, care and pastoral love for sinners.

which has a very low view of the work of the Spirit and sees Him best as an external aid influencing us from outside. The great question of debate between Governmentalists and Bible-believers is how the benefits of the atonement are made available to the elect. Yes, Governmentalists also speak of an election but mean something quite different than the election in Christ of the Bible. The traditional, evangelical, Reformed faith points to the imputation of Christ's righteousness and the union with Christ which brings with it the justification and sanctification appointed by God, planned before creation and which was the reason for creating all things. This is fiercely rejected by Governmentalists and especially by their modern Fullerite counterparts. They see election as the identification with the benefits of Christ in a two-fold process, which they often wrongly call 'progressive sanctification'. The first stage is the act of belief which they call 'conversion'. This does not settle the matter as afterwards comes the continuing work of the Holy Spirit in the gospel encouraging the believer to follow his obligations to the moral law and his interpretation of the positive law according to right reason. This right reason helps the believer 'infer' (Fuller's word) what is God's will for him. This is the view outlined in Fuller's various works on the Holy Spirit mentioned above and Answers to Objections and Reply to Philanthropos. It would pay Michael Haykin to read these works of Fuller when speaking of Fuller's 'spirituality'. It is a sub-Biblical view. It must be added in all fairness that Fuller repeatedly confessed that he had changed his views here but as we can see from Fuller's reaction to Booth's attack on his pseudo-Calvinism, it was only to become more radically Governmental than ever.[10] Fuller's controversy with Booth is always played down by Fullerites but it was fundamental and embraced the entire Biblical teaching of law and gospel.

The two-natures doctrine ignored

Symptomatic of Oliver's plea for Fullerism rather than Huntington's orthodoxy was that he failed completely to see (or rather ignored) the doctrine of the two natures in the Christian life which is part and parcel of Huntington's view of imputation. Oliver also commented most

---

[10] See especially Fuller's *Works*, Vol. III, Six Letters to Dr Ryland respecting the Controversy with the Rev. A. Booth, p. 699 ff..

negatively on the emphasis Huntington laid on the practical outworking of the indwelling of Christ and the inner guidance of the Holy Spirit in sanctification. It was this that caused him to protest that my defence was a misunderstanding of the work of the Spirit. This is what comes of substituting moral philosophy for the real thing! No alternative interpretation was offered but it would have been interesting to have read a better argument than Huntington's as to how the ungodly can be justified and unholy men made holy.[11] I have had some severe criticisms from Oliver's own denomination during his time of leadership there, though all was mutually well before he took up his pen to harm our relationship. However, I was invited by the Strict Baptist Historical Society to be the speaker at their Annual General Meeting in March 2019, and was asked to make John Gill my subject. I enjoyed the sweetest and warmest reception there possible and was surprised that at the end of my lecture I received a great applause which usually only happens when I lecture in the States. Robert Oliver was not at the meeting. What I was told concerning the present work of the Strict Baptists quite thrilled me and they shall surely reap God's blessing. Indeed, they made me a member of the Society on the spot and I have renewed that membership this year.

The indwelling of Christ in the believer
In Grotianism there is a fundamental lack of teaching concerning the practical outworking of the indwelling of Christ in the believer. This is because it neither holds to the doctrine of man being fallen in the first Adam nor the doctrine of man becoming a new creature in the Second Adam, our Lord and Saviour Jesus Christ. Man is ever in an in-between state of neither being in Adam nor in Christ. He is not in Adam because his natural abilities are not fallen, nor is he strictly speaking in Christ as Christ's influence is not exercised through indwelling him but by providing an external moral deterrent to frighten him into God's arms. Here again, we see the spirit of Aristoteles at work. There is thus no 'two-natures' doctrine in Governmentalism whereby the Old Man remains in conflict with the New Man until death frees the believer from

---

[11] *A Highly Biased Biography*, Issue 376, Banner of Truth magazine, p. 16.

the relics of sin which have burdened him all his life and are part of his lot for being in Adam and born with a corrupt nature. Once this Pauline doctrine is abandoned, it is far easier for Grotianism to find refuge in human rationalism and metaphorical views of salvation. Modern Governmentalists, following Fuller, tend to adhere to the kind of Liberalism made popular by the Tübingen School in seeing several strands of gospel in the New Testament. Baur saw the Pauline and the Petrine strands whereas Fullerites see a Jamesian, Johannine and Petrine teaching with the victory being given James. Pauline teaching is tacitly ignored.[12] It is, however, by the grace of God, that the Pauline epistles, comprising a large section of the New Testament, contain the doctrine of grace taught also in other parts of Scripture but perhaps nowhere else so succinctly put.

Rejecting one Bible doctrine spoils the lot
If we dismiss one part of Scripture, no matter how large or small, there will be a great deficiency left in our doctrines. Over the years, the doctrines of grace have been eased out of much modern quasi-Reformed teaching. The down-grading came slowly, doctrine by doctrine. Its start can be traced to Issue 92 of the Banner of Truth magazine containing the anti-Pauline article by Donald MacLeod entitled Paul's Use of the Term 'The Old Man'. I have combatted this erroneous 'Keswick' doctrine in several New Focus articles and Go Publications books in the past but aired and dealt with the error in my latest book *The Covenant of Grace and the People of God* above mentioned.

As much modern evangelicalism is bent on examining Scriptures as if they were merely figurative and not statements of actual facts, Chapter 11 and further chapters will be occupied in discussing what the Biblical terms for Atonement actually mean.

---

[12] See Alderson's *No Holiness No Heaven*, pp. 100, 101.

Chapter 11

Translating the Biblical Terms for Atonement

Putting the right meaning to the right word

When William Tyndale (1494-1536) began work on his translation of the Bible around 1525, he found the English language at times most inappropriate for the task. There was very little of what might be called the language of Zion in the English of the day. At that time most of the Bibles in circulation were in Latin which was all very well for those who could read it. However, even most monks and priests were as ignorant as the common people in never having learnt the language. It was not that these early Latin translations were wrong in themselves and useless in leading a soul to Christ as I was erroneously told at Bible College. I have found out in my subsequent studies of the Vulgate and Beza's Latin New Testament that they clearly teach us how to partake of the Bread of Life. It was, however, deemed an evil thing by the Roman Catholic hierarchy for the common people to have the Bible in their own language. Nowadays, the opposite is the case. Even theological students in most dumbed down universities do not have to learn Latin, let alone Greek and Hebrew. Protestant pastoral theology has little basic idea of how richly the Bible languages can help us in our walk with God. I am also shocked by modern Christians turning up their noses at Bible work in the Arabic language as some very trustworthy ancient Biblical texts are in Arabic and the Tiberian Hebrew which we use in our universities and Bible Colleges was organised and controlled by the Muslim rulers of Tiberias. It is true that the honest Latin terms used in ancient Roman Catholic Bible versions became highly tainted with Roman superstition just as Jesus showed how the Bible of the Jews had been misinterpreted through the Babylonian philosophies and legalism of the Rabbis. Sadly, most of the Jews in today's world allow themselves to be led astray by Babylonian Kabbala legalistic teaching which places a veil over their faces so that they cannot see that their Messiah has long come.

In my studies dealing with Indian languages, I have often come across claims that the Jesuits in Goa abounded with Bible translators. This is quite true and they turned out much good and helpful work but the subdued Indians were forbidden to read these translations themselves and the grammars and dictionaries were no use to them. Claudius Buchanan (1765-1815)[1] shows from his visits to Goa how the Jesuit city was full of underground prison cells where hundreds of natives and Protestant Europeans were imprisoned, tortured and executed for daring to believe in a Saviour which they had found through the witness of Protestant missionaries and in their secret reading of Scripture. Goa became a centre of 'Exorcism' which lasted hundreds of years.[2] Claudius Buchanan, the Church Mission Society missionary, is well-known for 'holding the ropes' with fellow Church of England missionary David Brown (1763-1812) for William Carey in Calcutta and Serampore when the Baptist Missionary Society broke their promises and cut them loose. This misuse of Latin does not alter the fact that our so-called Textus Receptus is based on multilingual texts including Latin.

Wycliffe's 14th century translation into the English of his day had received the full enmity of the Roman Church. Archbishop Arundel had declared Wycliffe to be a child of the devil and the offspring of Anti-Christ who 'crowned his wickedness by translating the Scriptures into the mother tongue'. Thus a general excommunication against readers of

---

[1] See *The Rev. Dr Buchanan's Notices of the present State of the Inquisition at Goa* in S. Chandler's *The History of Persecution from the Patriarchial Age to the Reign of George II*, Hull, 1813. See also his 1811 work *Christian Researches in Asia*: with notices of the translations of the Scriptures into the oriental languages from which Chandler took the article on Goa. Buchanan is available in numerous reprints today besides free online access.

[2] Portuguese India started in the 16th century and ended in the nineteen sixties of last century. In contrast, British India started in the nineteenth century and ended in 1947.

Wycliffe's Bible and against would-be translators of the Bible into English was proclaimed in 1408. In Scotland Wycliffe's translation was given a longer life through acceptance of Lollard preaching by several Scottish Kings and Dukes. French dominion over Scotland caused, however, several Lollards to be martyred.

William Tyndale's new English translation

By 1525, however, the English language was establishing itself as a language of poetry and prose and had changed radically during the previous hundred years. Wycliffe's language had become archaic and, as it was a mere translation of the Vulgate, it still contained Romanising associations for many which dimmed the full meaning of Scripture for them. Tyndale, working from the original languages, not merely the Latin MSS which he did not ignore, found it particularly difficult to translate words to do with atonement, reconciliation, propitiation, expiation and justification which are all closely linked and overlap in meaning and can often be considered as synonyms. Perhaps Tyndale's eagerness to make the translation really English caused him to reject Latin words which could have been employed usefully. He also might have restored the many Old English and Middle English words which had been previously used to describe the Atonement. It appears, however, that Tyndale did not examine older English translations except Wycliffe's for his vocabulary. Scholars of the day did not use them or perhaps had forgotten them. No Latin words are evil in themselves but must be given fitting meanings. Latin based words like 'justification' and 'reconciliation' can still not be bettered in modern English. Tyndale, however, realised that in his day English had become the poetic language of fable, fantasy and fairy story and looked for words which expressed matters of fact rather than imaginary things. Sadly, even today, much Roman Catholic exegesis is spoilt by their misapplication of Latin terms. However, this can be said, too, of modern English or any other language. Think how we have now changed those beautiful words 'fairy' and 'gay' to mean quite other things. Be this as it may, Tyndale confessed:

I had no man to counterfet neither was holpe with englysshe of eny that had interpreted the same or soche lyke things in the scripture before tyme.

Different loan words for 'Atonement'

Though one initial problem for Tyndale was the paucity of good contemporary words suitable for depicting doctrine, an equal problem was the flood of new words coming into the language to supplement them. As Latin words vied with French, Scandinavian and Saxon words, a whole host of synonyms emerged, many of these quickly taking on new meanings. Of course, English is not a pure language of itself but a mixture of other languages. Our modern English language has to struggle hard with this problem today, especially in a Christian context as we often find numerous words to translate single Hebrew or Greek words but even then, the exact meaning of the original may not be given or understood absolutely correctly. Modern would-be reformers such as Alan Clifford, campaign for a Bible in the language of the streets, not realising that there is no language in the streets capable of expressing Christian truths. We Christians must teach street-dwellers the language of Heaven.

It may thus surprise readers to find that one single Hebrew root word kipper (כפר) which occurs some ninety-five times in the Scriptures and its many derivations such as kofer used for a ransom or kippurim used for sacrifices or kapporet used for the mercy-seat with its Greek equivalents and word-families such as καταλλαγη and ιλαστηριον may be translated by either atonement, cover, washing away, mercy, grace, wiping clean, pardon, reconciliation, appeasement, expiation, propitiation, satisfaction, placation and even, and perhaps especially, ransom. Yet how many of even these terms are common to the non-Christian tongue today? The Septuagint, commonly called the LXX to indicate that 70 translators are said to have worked on it, was the Greek translation of the Old Testament that Jesus and his disciples used. Given the many changes from Ancient or Classical Greek to the Koine Greek of the New Testament, it is quite surprising to find over a dozen ancient Greek words still representing the many meanings of kipper in Old Testament Hebrew in the New Testament Greek text, a copy of which was presented to me by one of my classes after passing their matriculation exams (Abitur). The main term exilaskomai was, however, no longer used by the time of the New Testament. However, in the whole Bible we find some twenty Greek words used for translating kipper. We also find many synonyms indicating Christ's redeeming Atonement in other ancient Bible texts such as Arabic, Coptic, Persian, Chaldee, Samaritan and Syriac. Several of these languages are still spoken today and have good Bible translations. Of course, all the thousands of words expressing 'Atonement' in other languages such as Swedish 'försoning', French 'réconciliation', Romanian 'impacărea' and Hungarian 'engesztelés' can be considered synonyms of the Biblical terms. However, English-speaking Christians quarrel over the meaning of their English equivalents, not understanding the terms.

Modern theologians whether truly 'evangelical' or what was once called 'Liberal'[3] are sometimes at loggerheads over the meaning of the words expiation, propitiation, oblation, placation and especially ransom, but these words are clear expressions of the root biblical meanings and cannot be argued with upon the ground of sound, Biblical exposition and will be dealt with each in turn. It is obvious, however, that these individual synonyms must be used according to the context in which they occur. The Authorized Version translators, I believe, took great care in following this practice, later translators have not been so accurate. Often, the special meanings of words are enhanced by little additions which we would call fixed-prepositions, suffixes and prefixes today. The Hebrew words dealing with Atonement by sacrifice are particularly supported by such tiny additions or the lack of them which determine their true meaning. Thus, merely taking single words out of a dictionary, which sadly many would-be exegetes do, to express a Biblical doctrine is often most unwise.

Older English translators were far freer in their use of very many synonyms for the Atonement than are their modern counterparts as seen in the Anglo-Saxon Bible, the Ormulum, Wycliffe's Bible, Tyndale's

---

[3] 'Evangelicals' were once distinguished from 'Liberals' as the latter followed the philosophy of the Enlightenment and 'Right Reason' which they nigh deified, but now the Liberals claim to be 'evangelical and Reformed'. See my book *The Covenant of Grace and the People of God* for an analysis of this modern phenomenon in the Christian Church.

Bible, Coverdale's Bible, the Geneva Bible and others which are still highly usable and understandable. The Ormulum, a Middle English part translation and paraphrase of the Bible must have been easy at the time for Tyndale to read but his classical education does not seem to have included it. In these older English works we find translations for 'Atonement' such as 'perfitely cleanse', 'taak awaye', 'be don awey', 'be mercifull', 'remitted', 'mercy seate', 'pacifie', 'purge', 'appease', 'disannulled' and many others which can soon be converted into modern English. Most neglected today are the many words in Old and Middle English which have been dropped merely through lack of usage or changes in sentiments. I am all for picking them up, dusting them and setting them back in use so as to counteract the dumbing down of language so typical of today's inexpressiveness. Sadly, our Bible translators today shun practical linguistics and lose much theology into the bargain. I thus feel most strongly, for instance, the enormous exegetical benefits of still using the second person singular pronoun 'thou' which has been removed artificially from the English languages by those who think grammar and syntax are not meaning-carriers. I would also include some ten words and phrases which carry the meaning 'Atonement' which are no longer used for simplicity's sake. Contrary to this, the Psalmist tells us in Psalm 119:129, 130:

Thy testimonies are wonderful: therefore doth my soul keep them. The entrance of thy words giveth light; it giveth understanding unto the simple.

Indeed the Psalms declare time and time again that those who know God's word should not talk down to the simple but lift them up so they might understand and enjoy it. Dumbing down language in theology means also dimming it down from God's full light.

A modern movement of language confusion
Enough has been said to show it is quite impossible to render all the many meanings of Hebrew and Greek synonyms by one single word in English and also that we have really enough English synonyms to fully describe all the aspects of the Atonement if we would but use them. Illustrative of the confusion which arises when one strives to translate on a one word to one word basis is found in modern New Covenant

Theology exegesis. Here, for instance, the NCT denies that the doctrine of 'the Covenant of Grace' is found in the translations they use. Of course, this key doctrine is entirely Scriptural as older exegetes such as Gill show and it occurs often in the Scriptures using synonyms which in Hebrew and Greek mean the same thing and translate the same word or phrase. So we have the Covenant of Mercy and the Covenant of Peace also used in our Authorized Version translation which uses the very words in the original which express the Covenant of Grace. Thus many expositions of the doctrine of the Atonement would be more beneficial and wider applying if all the synonyms of the term 'atonement' were taken into consideration by our pastors and teachers. Too often, we reject essential words which are not to our liking such as 'expiate', 'propitiate' and 'appease' because they are words used by people of other theological convictions. At Bible College I was even told that 'expiate' and 'propitiate' were inventions of the Liberals if not the devil! The good term 'oblation' was said to be Roman Catholic! There are so many different superficial arguments against using each different word that if we took notice of them all, we would be left with no words at all. All the terms which our modern generation find 'old-fashioned' in the Authorized Version are merely 'old-fashioned' because we have rejected them, thinking we are clear enough in our ability to express things in fewer words. A few Bible studies under a qualified pastor would quickly make them re-usable. Yet at a Minister's Conference in Leicester a few years ago, I met pastors clutching all sorts of weird translations and on asking why they did not use the Authorized Version they invariably said that they did not understand it. It is no wonder that someone wrote a book in the sixties asking the question Can the Reconciled be Reconciled? It was Babel that had separated them not theology.

A word for word translation can often be wrong

Most works on the atonement are thus too narrow to be useful. This was made very apparent to me when a dear friend, mentor and editor of mine, criticised another writer for translating a Greek word by different words though its meanings were all contained in the original Greek and the context clearly showed the practicability of using synonyms which fitted into the translation context. Needless to say this editor had never studied either Hebrew or Greek. This may surprise others untrained in linguistics and the original languages of Holy writ but any good Bible dictionary will display all the alternative meanings and their contextual linguistic supports which usually must be synergised to understand the entire meaning of a Greek or Hebrew word. Those Christians, for instance, who insist on translating the Biblical doctrine of baptism either by the single words 'sprinkle' or 'sink' are theologically too narrow-minded for words. Those who drop the word 'baptise' because it is Greek and not English and substitute it by the Latin word 'immerse', thinking they are speaking better 'English' make themselves quite ridiculous. Though not accepting Dillistone's general attitude to Scripture as merely metaphorical, I love some of the expressions used by him to explain the Atonement such as 'perfect integration', 'all-inclusive forgiveness', 'all-embracing compassion' and 'unique redemption'.[4] The Christian Atonement has one teaching which presents Christ as our All in All as recorded in Scripture. It is a factual, historical description of how Christ goes about saving sinners.

God provides an at-one-ment with Himself

The first synonym mentioned above, 'atonement', is of particular interest as it was coined by Tyndale himself to help get over translation difficulties. However there were at least seven good Old English Bible (Anglo-Saxon) words meaning to atone, save, pacify or redeem such as gesybsuma (reconcile) in Matthew 5:24 which he could have fallen back on and updated but perhaps academic Tyndale was unaware of these. William Cowper complained that his classmates could write wonderful Latin but not jot down a few English words to their mums and dads. We theologians are not much better as few of us have been qualified in reading the good old English Bibles of pre-Reformation days. Happily, I was brought up in an area of Yorkshire where we still performed Pask Eggers (Easter Eggs) and, being called George, I was given the role of St. George who challenged Slasher to a duel and said, 'Stand back Slasher an let n'moar be sedd for if tha does, as bahn to strike thi dedd'. Townley and York Morality Plays were still performed in Peel Park, Bradford, and when I studied Middle English in Germany

---

[4] *The Christian Understanding of Atonement*, Nisbet, 1968.

many years later my childhood came back to me. I thus love reading the old pre-King James Bible translations which helps me understand Modern English.

However, we now find the most expressive term 'atonement' in our Authorized Version which was planned and partly translated by King James long before he ever became England's Monarch. Most devastating criticism of James has come from the Neo-Presbyterians of his day who followed Jesuit policies and strove with the French Roman Catholic Humanists to ruin Britain with their totalitarian pseudo-Christian politics. The early Scottish Presbyterians led by the Durie family, praised James' Christian stand, his fine understanding of Christian doctrine and his Christian influence on Scottish worship before the Neo-Presbyterians introduced monarchical elders and institutionalised totalitarian religion. Without James there would have been no Authorized Version and not much of a Reformation in Britain.

Tyndale coins a new word

Tyndale's God-led understanding of the words kipper (כפר) and hilasterion (ιλαστηριον) was that they pointed to God's initiative in salvation, to a full and entire work of the triune God in making a total satisfaction for sin by providing a complete substitution, which was a once-and-for-all act procuring everlasting salvation for the repentant sinner. The Roman Catholic Church viewed the atonement as reconciliation being made to God for man's guilt or original sin but not for the penalty of sin which had to be worked off by works of special merit and penance. This left the reconciled without true union with Christ and with Christ's work only half done. This error led Tyndale to realise that the entire Biblical teaching was concerned with man becoming fully accepted in the Beloved, and thus becoming one with God. This led Tyndale to argue that there was no break between the Two Testaments but the same message throughout.[5] Christ's reconciling death, he therefore viewed as an inter-Testament at-one-ment with God and thus used the word to express both the Old and New

---

[5] This conviction gave rise to Heinrich Bullinger's pioneering work of the Reformation *On the Eternal Covenant* (1534) which is the summary and scope of all Scripture. The true Christian faith as Bullinger sees it is as old as man's need to be saved and God's assurance of such a salvation.

Testament words to do with a man becoming right with God through an expiatory sacrifice at God's initiative which fulfilled His law's demands and cleansed His people from all sin. This word clearly shows what its meaning is and is scarcely open to misinterpretation as too often the other terms are.

Our task is now to view the teaching of the Scriptures on this crucial doctrine and see how it has been assailed by the whims of fashion, rationalism, philosophy and political thought throughout the centuries. Indeed, we find ourselves in the extraordinary situation today where even those who believe they are of the elect, deny the very doctrine and decree which has vouchsafed their election.

Chapter 12

A Redemptive Covering of the Sinner's Shame

Covering sin

The word-family kipper (כפר) and its associate terms is used in the Old Testament in conjunction with offerings to plead for mercy, to appease God, to grant blood money as an equivalent for physical harm done and to renew and keep up the covenant with God by which He has chosen a special people to serve Him and have fellowship with Him.[1] The root meaning of the word here is 'to cover'. The sins of the people are covered over and where this is performed to those given the wherewithal to receive it, God promises to remember their sins no more and grants, as a result of this, reconciliation. Nowhere is this truth so beautifully put as in Ezekiel 16 where the prophet describes the birth of God's people, born in sin and squalor and virtually thrown away as unwanted, yet their nakedness is covered by God's own protective skirt. The cast-away child is washed, cleansed of blood, anointed and clothed in majesty by the grace of God. It will thus come as no surprise to find that kipper also means to wash away and cleanse knowing that 'the blood of the Lord Jesus Christ his Son cleanseth us from all sin'.[2] Zechariah 3 also tells us of Joshua as a type of the Church whose iniquities are put away and new garments given him to cover his

---

[1] See Leviticus 1:4; 4:20; 16:10; Exodus 29:36; Numbers 5:8; Ezekiel 43:20 ff..
[2] 1 John 1:7.

nakedness. Isaiah saw clearly the atoning work of the Messiah with the eye of faith and could exclaim:

> I will greatly rejoice in the Lord, my soul shall be joyful in my God for he hath clothed me with the garments of salvation, he hath covered me with the robe of righteousness (61:10).

Hence David could say, 'Blessed is he whose transgression is forgiven, whose sin is covered'. and go on to say that the Lord is his 'hidingplace'.[3] Here, again, is a preview of the once-and-for-all-time sacrifice of Christ in whom our sinful life is eternally hidden in God and He deals with us as new creatures.[4]

The Old is in the New revealed
Many supposedly evangelical Reformed brethren claim today that such thoughts are all Old Testament and do not apply to the New Testament understanding of Atonement. This thinking is entirely erroneous because these pioneer prophets were preachers of the eternal Covenant of Grace and outlined the teaching of the ever new, ever refreshing and ever reforming Covenant which was the same in Old Testament times as in the New. Times may change but not what happened in the Fulness of Time and God's ever-new Covenant remains the same yesterday, today and forever. I continually turn to Jeremiah for sound New Testament doctrine.

Perhaps the most significant passage in the Old Testament where the word 'atonement' is used is that referring to the Day of Atonement (Yom Kippur). The Hebrew term, however, means 'the Day of Covering' so we see the connection with sin being covered and the Atonement which cleanses the atoned from all sin. After a proscribed ten days of national preparation the High Priest would enter the holy place[5] to make a sin offering for himself and his people. After this was completed, the people's sins were symbolically laid on a scapegoat and sent away:

---

[3] Psalm 32.
[4] Colossians 3:3.
[5] The Temple was not built at the time of the law-giving.

... by the hand of a fit man into the wilderness: and the goat shall bear upon him all their iniquities unto a land not inhabited: and he shall let go the goat in the wilderness.[6]

All this, the writer to the Hebrews tells us, was a pointer to Christ the Coming One and ever present evidence of things to come. It was a forerunner of the day when the veil of the Temple should be rent for ever and Christ would take up his holy work as the Man fit for the task, the God-Man who would bear our sins away in that great and glorious never to be repeated action on the cross in the fulness of time. I take this latter phrase to refer to the purpose of Christ in using created time to bring in the Elect in Christ so that when time's purpose was fulfilled it applied to all time past, present and future. The writer to the Hebrews argues that earthly priests come and go as they must all die but our Great High Priest has gained for us eternal access to God's holy abode and ever makes intercession for us there.[7] This is the meaning of atonement.

Ransoming and Redeeming the Condemned

In the Old Testament presentation of the work of Christ, the ransoming work of sacrificial blood is given pre-eminence. The blood of the sacrificial victim shed is the sign of God's eternal covenant of grace for man to show that He is ever prepared to grant atonement and forgiveness for His people through the blood of the Lord Jesus Christ which is the only sin cleanser. The Old Testament saints were ransomed by sacrifices which were mere pointers to the great sacrifice to come which would be absolute and perfect in its power, working from eternity in the fulness of time both backwards and forwards in history, covering the sins of the elect in all ages. Thus when Christians worship their Saviour, they draw nigh to,

Jesus the mediator of the new covenant, and to the blood of sprinkling, that speaketh better things than that of Abel.[8]

---

[6] Leviticus 16:21, 22.
[7] Hebrews 7.
[8] Hebrews 12:24.

This gives Peter every good reason to write to:

> the elect according to the foreknowledge of God the Father, through sanctification of the Spirit, unto obedience and sprinkling of the blood of Jesus Christ, ... which according to his abundant mercy hath begotten us again unto a lively hope by the resurrection of Jesus Christ from the dead, To an inheritance incorruptible, and undefiled, and that fadeth not away, reserved in heaven for you.[9]

For pastors seeking good Bible information as to what baptism signifies I recommend reading the first three chapters of 1 Peter which presents all the symbolism necessary in the rite. Those who come up with merely one highly restricted symbol and dogmatically insist that it is the only symbol to be used confess their poverty in understanding what baptism really teaches. One cannot say that sprinkling water is not a mode of baptism as baptism signifies the sprinkling of Christ's blood which was the Atonement for our sin and placed us in Christ. If one Biblical mode is rejected, then we reject a true witness to all that Christ has done for us in the Atonement in having our sin covered, cleansed, washed, wiped away, sprinkled by the atoning blood and clothed with righteousness. Surely this knowledge and experience should move all the dipped under, sprinkled on, and poured over to live in peace. Let us in linguistic and doctrinal unity think of baptism in all these terms and more as we shall see in the following chapters. Indeed, one of the basic meanings of Atonement is that which placates, conciliates and brings peace between God and man and between man and man. As we shall see, the doctrine of baptism has a central bearing on the doctrine of the Atonement through Christ's baptism for the dead.

The whole gospel is reflected in 1 Peter 1 verses 2-4. We see that redemption is for the elect of God, otherwise called the Bride of Christ. We note that the blood of Christ atones for the sins of this elect people and sanctifies them. This gives them hope which has been established through Christ's own resurrection. Here we also have a clear testimony of the perseverance of the saints which is incorruptibly and eternally vouchsafed through the Atonement.

---

[9] 1 Peter 1:2-4.

At-one-ment is the work of the Trinity
The passage makes it also plain that salvation is a work of the whole Trinity. The Father sets the operation in action, the Spirit separates the elect from the world and Christ provides not only the victim, His obedient self, but He is the Offering-Provider, giving Himself for His Bride. The fact the entire Trinity was at work in the plan of redemption is very relevant in combating modern views of the Atonement which suggest that either God shows two conflicting wills in the atoning act, or that Christ set his own will against His Father's in redeeming a people for Himself. Exponents also teach in error that Christ merely played the hero's part which was accepted in hindsight by God or that Christ was merely 'offered' by the Father as Abraham was prepared to offer Isaac. Certainly, there is here something most prophetic in Abraham's treatment in faith of Isaac but Isaac did not seem to be a deciding partner in what might have happened but the Father and the Son were equally responsible for what actually happened at Calvary.

The emphasis on Christ's obedience and the blood money (ransom) paid also goes a long way in debunking modern Governmentalists and so-called Evangelical Calvinists who neither see the necessity of a full obedience to the law on Christ's part nor see the relevance of Christ dying for the elect and for none other. If Christ did not give His uttermost in obedience, utterly fulfilling the law on behalf of His Church, then he could not 'save them to the uttermost that come unto God by him'.[10] Such passages show that Christ's atoning sacrifice was entirely successful in obtaining Christ's purpose and goal. Here we have sanctification, obedience, cleansing, grace, undefiled incorruptibility, peace, and an eternal place in God's heavenly mansions, all typical signs of the atoning work of Christ, yet all these terms refer to the one and same Atonement.

God provides a ransom
The basic term kōpher, a derivative of kappa, again with the initial meaning of a covering, this time of covering over a debt with the price of the debt, is used throughout the Bible to illustrate the work of

---

[10] Hebrews 7:25.

179

Atonement. The Bible emphasises time and time again that the atonement was not only a means of releasing man from his sins but it also provided the instrument of this means in terms of ransom. Indeed, our redemption from sin and its consequences was gained by a ransom, otherwise it would not have been a redemption, the two terms being cognate sharing the same meaning. We have this from the mouth of the Saviour Himself recorded in Matthew 20:28 and Mark 10:45,

Even as the Son of man came not to be ministered unto but to minister, and to give his life as a ransom for many.

This truth is often put forward as a New Testament truth only but it was preached as the everlasting gospel of the everlasting Covenant from Genesis to Revelation. Indeed, its basic meaning was preached in the Old Testament and explained by the Christ of both Testaments. Exodus 21:30-36 tells us that if a man has been gored to death by a dangerous ox, the owner of the ox can escape death by paying a ransom. There was, however, no way of ransoming away death itself. Hence we read in Psalm 49:7 that no one can redeem a brother from death, or give God a ransom for him. In Numbers 8:19 we find that the Levites are given to Aaron in order to provide a kōpher for the children of Israel. By the time of the prophets, teaching concerning a ransomed New Covenant people prepared for the New Jerusalem had become widespread as revelation progressed in the face of progressing disbelief. Isaiah could triumphantly say on viewing Christ's kingdom in chapter 35:10,

And the ransomed of the Lord shall return, and come to Zion with songs and everlasting joy upon their heads: and they shall obtain joy and gladness, and sorrow and sighing shall flee away.

This is echoed by Jeremiah in his account of the calling in of the elect Israel in Jeremiah 31:11 and God's promise to Hosea to ransom His people from the grave, saying, 'O death, I will be thy plagues; O grave, I will be thy destruction', reminding us of 1 Corinthians 15:55, the plague of death being sin which is removed from the redeemed. Here, we cannot possibly separate the gospel of Jeremiah from the gospel of Christ, as this is all part of the good news from the New Covenant made between the Father and the Son in contrast to the broken

Covenant with man, shown in Adam but more specifically in the history of Israel through her betrayal of the Covenant in the wilderness journeys. We must also remember that Jeremiah was the great Prophet of the ever New Covenant which was sealed by Christ's shed blood.

All this, of course, as the writer to the Hebrews tells us in great detail throughout chapters 7-10, is only a reflection of and pointer to the 'Lamb slain from the foundation of the world'.[11] This was outworked in the 'fulness of time' at Calvary. Though it happened in time, the Bible teaches that this sacrifice was beyond time, covering the entire history of salvation of the elect from Abel until the gathering in of the saints when Jesus comes in glory. In the Scriptures the New Covenant dawned with its Biblical teaching of a ransom by Atonement as soon as Adam sinned. All Scripture was inspired by God through the Spirit and in Christ to teach us this great truth and blessing.

Christ is our Ransom

In the whole Bible the clear testimony is that Christ paid the ransom for our redemption. Paul, in 1 Timothy 2:5, 6 explains that this is the essential part of Christ's mediatory work of reconciliation 'For there is one God, and one mediator between God and men, the man Christ Jesus; Who gave himself a ransom for sin, to be testified in due time'. The last phrase 'in due time' is not to be taken in its modern alternative meaning of 'in time to come' but in its basic meaning 'in the time that was due', or, 'just at the right time' or as Paul puts it in Galatians 4:4,

> But when the fulness of the time was come, God sent forth his Son, made of a woman, made under the law, To redeem them that were under the law, that we might receive the adoption of sons.

Christ placed Himself under His own Law

Here we see the purpose and benefit of time in which Christ could redeem His Bride, the Church. Again we see emphasised, so strongly, that Christ was not placed above the law as a privileged man and made

---

[11] Revelation 13:8.

a mere symbolic token ransom as such as Hugo Grotius and Andrew Fuller claimed, but emptied Himself so thoroughly for our sakes that he came under the law to redeem those that were under the law.

I am constantly being told by my fellow evangelicals that in teaching that Christ placed Himself under the Law, I am making Christ a sinner, though it is stated clearly that He knew no sin and it would be blasphemy to believe He did. It would also be blasphemy to maintain that Christ did not become sin on our behalf as this was the very purpose of time and of the Atonement. How could anyone misread such a promise and think that this portrays Christ as a sinning man? The clear teaching of Scripture is stated in Galatians 4:4, 5,

> But when the fulness of the time was come, God sent forth his Son, made of a woman, made under the law, to redeem them that were under the law, that we might receive the adoption of sons. And because you are his sons, God hath sent forth the Spirit of his Son into your hearts, crying Abba, Father.

New Covenant Theology tells us that when the Law is mentioned in the New Testament, it merely refers to the Jews and to the Old Testament dispensation. However, here is Paul, the Apostle to the Gentiles speaking to a number of churches in Galatia which are obviously composed of Christians in general, now neither Jew nor Gentile, whom he tells of his old days under an unbelieving Jewish yoke but now he has been made a preacher to the heathen (Gentiles). He tells them that Christ was put under the law to redeem them who are under the law, obviously meaning all people in general. Those who maintain that Paul was only preaching to Jews, when he claims in verse 16 he is preaching to Gentiles ought to wipe the cobwebs from their glasses.

Though many of my Christian friends tell me that Christ was above the law, the very purpose of the Incarnation was that Christ placed Himself under His Law, proclaimed by the Old Testament saints, especially by God's friend Moses, to fulfil its eternal conditions in the fulness of time for the sake of His People.

Bad theology amongst evangelicals

The modern rejection of the redemption doctrine of salvation by those who say Christ's high position and dignity were respected too much by

His Father to place Him under the law, is a great error of judgment as it could never lift the death penalty from man. The teaching that Christ's dignified superiority placed Him higher than the law and this dignity was accepted and given us as an 'as if' status propagated in much modern evangelical theology is very bad theology indeed. Man has no dignity as a sinner and Christ forfeited His 'dignity' and 'emptied himself' and became like a man to save sinners. We are not saved by theoretical imagery but by historical facts. The Biblical way of salvation is that Christ had to become what we were in order to lift us up to be like Him. He voluntarily showed full obedience to the law. No other way was good enough for Him. This transformation was not a mere parable or allegory, nor was it merely judicial but it actually happened for our sakes. We can thus truly say, that we, as the Church of God, have been actually purchased by His blood;[12] this means that we have actually been redeemed by His blood;[13] we have actually been justified by His blood;[14] we are actually sanctified by His blood[15] because our sins have been actually washed away by His blood.[16] This is all thanks to God in Christ who actually bought us with a price.[17]

This ransom was actual and not metaphorical
It is becoming fashionable in so-called 'Moderate Calvinism' to question the doctrine of literal redemption, i.e. that Christ was an actual ransom. The Apostle Peter was familiar with such critics and refers to them plainly and damnably in 2 Peter 2:1 saying:

> But there were false prophets also among the people, even as there shall be false prophets among you, who privily shall bring in damnable heresies, even denying the Lord that bought them, and bring upon themselves swift destruction.

---

[12] Acts 20:28.
[13] Ephesians 1:7.
[14] Romans 5:9.
[15] Hebrews 13:12.
[16] Revelation 1:5.
[17] 1 Corinthians 6:20; 7:23.

183

In view of the modern Neo-evangelical theory, that what they call 'commercial language' is at best to be understood metaphorically, we may quote 1 Peter 1:18-20 for a very matter-of-fact statement,

> For as much as ye know that ye were not redeemed with corruptible things, as silver and gold, from your vain conversation received by tradition from your fathers; But with the precious blood of Christ, as of a lamb without blemish and without spot: Who verily was foreordained before the foundation of the world but was manifest in these last times for you.

Now if Peter had said that God used all the riches, all the gold and silver, at His disposal to save us and gave His last penny to do so, this would be speaking metaphorically. Peter rejects such a symbolic language and comes down to plain honest truth as the Scriptures predicted. Christ was foreordained to be a ransom and a ransom He became. The price was to be paid in blood and, indeed, that is exactly how it was paid. If Christ had not paid the exact price under the obligations freely taken up before time-history began, we would be still in our sins or the slaves of some airy-fairy metaphorical, make-believe alternative.

This is the faith that was secured for Christ's redeemed in the Atonement and if these truths are left out of the gospel then, however it is preached, it will not be preached properly. All this would not have been possible if Christ had not faced and endured His baptism of death for the dead which will be the opening theme of Chapter 13.

Chapter 13

Christ's Baptism, Crucifixion and Resurrection

Christ's Baptism for the Dead

Those interested in Indian Missions will have noticed how the baptism controversy in India in the nineteenth century hampered the work of missionary evangelism and later the evangelism of the Indian Church no end. Instead of concentrating on Christ's baptism, Christian controversialists concentrated on their limited understanding of their own denominational brand of baptism which they felt better indicated what it was supposed to point to. Much destruction has occurred in the churches since the Reformation concerning what our Christian baptism depicts and how Christ's baptism for those dead in trespasses and sins fulfils all that our baptism points to. Perhaps no doctrine has been interpreted by narrow-minded denominationalism as much as that of baptism which is seen as an empty, mechanical rite by some and, as Bunyan warningly pointed out, a god to others. So, too, the pagan doctrine of baptismal regeneration is sadly widespread taught amongst both the dipped and sprinkled. So often baptism was called 'Christening' as if it automatically brought with it the New Birth. Happily, the Church of the English Reformers which led Europe in Elizabethan days and up to the Rebellion distinguished strongly between being baptised as a pointer to Christ's baptism of suffering and the New Birth.

The meaning of baptism is made clear from the start of all four gospels where John the Baptist's preaching is referred to as 'the voice of one crying in the wilderness' to prepare the way for the gospel of Christ's baptism. Luke describes this as a continuation of the Old Testament Covenant of Grace into the New. Right at the beginning of John's ministry the prophet declared, 'I indeed have baptised you with water but he shall baptise you with the Holy Ghost'.[1] When John saw Jesus coming to be baptised, he knew what Christ intended to point to with His baptism and the development it would take and thus greeted Him with the words, 'Behold the Lamb of God which taketh away the sins of the world'.[2] Then Christ declared that His work was to 'fulfil all righteousness',[3] teaching that it was His way of fulfilling righteousness for His Bride, the Church who had no righteousness of her own. The entire Scriptures point out how Christ accomplished His aims in His atoning death which was the real baptism to which all baptisms point. Too often baptism is misused by Christians as a sign of their own piety and not of Christ's fulfilling of all righteousness as he foretold in Matthew 3:15.[4] Some cling sadly to their own brand of baptism as if their salvation hung on it and not on Christ's baptism, truly making their baptism their idol as early Baptists, such as Jessey and not merely Bunyan also pointed out.

Confusing the sacrament with the real thing

Very often the self-efficacy of the sacrament which points to the atoning work of Christ is confused with Christ's work itself. I will not question using the term 'sacrament' here and refrain from using another of the many synonyms some would substitute for it. I take the word at its basic meaning as an ordinance of Christ as also is the Lord's Supper and that it is a solemn engagement between Christians and their Lord. The word sacramentum can also mean a pledge and this fits what is promised in Christian baptism perfectly as also does the equivalent meaning of a 'foretaste'.

Christ's own baptism at the hands of John was significant as a pointer to the procuring of righteousness for His Bride, the Church, through His own crucifixion, atoning death, burial and resurrection so that we might be cleansed from sin and be resurrected also with Him.

---

[1] Mark 1:8.
[2] John 1:29.
[3] Matthew 3:15.
[4] 'Thus it becometh us to fulfil all righteousness.'

The difference between Christ's atoning baptism and our baptism as mentioned in Matthew 28 as a step in Christian teaching and the work of the gospel is clearly stated. Yet we are so often told that Colossians 2:12-14 refers to believer's baptism whereas it refers to what happens to believers in Christ's final baptism for the dead not ours:

> Buried with him in baptism, wherein also ye are risen with him through the faith of the operation of God, who hath raised him from the dead. And you, being dead in your sins and the uncircumcision of the flesh, hath he quickened together with him, having forgiven you all trespasses: blotting out the handwriting of ordinance that was against us, which was contrary to us, and took it out of the way, nailing it to the cross.

One friend of mine who scolded me for not accepting his view of baptism told me how lovely and glorious was his burial with Christ as he sunk under the baptistery waters demonstrating (how?) his faith in Christ. What a false picture of baptism! Christ's baptism of death to which all true baptism points was a horrid slaughter and as inglorious as it could possibly be. By His stripes, not ours, we are healed; by His faith not ours! Being buried with Christ means that He lay in the sepulchre for our sakes, we are not baptised for Christ's sake but He was baptised in death for our sakes. Christ uses the figure of water baptism, (not soil baptism or sepulchre baptism) to declare to us that His blood shed in His baptism of death, proved to be the waters of everlasting life for us.

Objections to the term 'baptism for the dead'
There are those who object to the term 'baptism for the dead' thinking presumably of the Mormons misuse of the term but here we read that we are all dead to God and that Christ in His baptism called us to life eternal. So we note that not only is this a reference to Christ's baptism not ours but the further atoning references to God's faith and God's blotting out of our sins and redemption are also not ours. All these atoning works refer to the one work of Christ's Atonement in which we have no active part. It is an act solely of God's free grace. As John the

Baptist said in John 3:27, 'A man can receive nothing, except it be given him from heaven'. The word used for 'forgiven' in the above quote from Colossians 2:12-14 is charizomonos which means 'graciously remitted'. Remission of sin, faith and the rising from the dead are all wrought out by Christ's baptism not ours. There was only one baptism like Christ's baptism and surely this is the baptism Paul meant when he referred to the Church's 'one body, one Spirit, one hope, one Lord, one faith and one baptism, one God and father of all'.[5] I have met both sprinklers and immersionists who have boasted that Christ meant their baptism! So often I have been told when expounding this passage that it represents the believer's baptism when he sinks under the water and is then lifted out. However, we know that the burial here is of our sins in Christ when Christ paid the ransom for our sins. With His death our sin died and we were given life. There is no reference here to the mere mechanics of a sinner dying and been buried underground. This is clear when we realise that Christ was not buried underground so how can we share in that? He was buried above ground as a step in His redeeming act. I have often been told that having themselves put under water and then drawn out is merely a wet and less risky business of the dry fact of being buried alive under the earth. How they can associate the two, I do not know. At a moment of hopelessness during William Cowper's sufferings which enveloped him at ten year intervals when he felt Christ was dead to him, he confessed he was then in the 'burial above ground' stage himself, longing to be resurrected with Christ.[6]

Thus our baptism which signifies our unity in Christ never depicts our grace, our faith and our rising from the dead as all these are the achievements of Christ alone who worked all this out for His loved ones. It is divine grace, divine faith and Christ's atoning burial and resurrection which all Christians share and to which our baptism is divinely designed to point. It is, however, Christ's baptism which brings us into the Church not our own. It is Christ's faith which is our salvation and not our baptism. So Paul can say in Romans 6:3,

Know ye not, that so many of us as were baptised into Jesus Christ were baptised into his death? Therefore we are buried with

---

[5] Ephesians 4:4-6.
[6] See Cowper's poem *Hatred and Vengeance*.

him by baptism into death: that like as Christ was raised up from the dead by the glory of the Father, even so we also should walk in newness of life.

The baptism of Christ was a baptism for the dead and we who are baptised in His death become partakers of His baptism for the dead. This is how I also understand Paul's remark in 1 Corinthians 15:29. All true baptism which is merged in Christ's baptism through Christ's faith, burial and resurrection is a baptism for the dead. It is the dead in Christ who shall be raised. To put it as plainly as possible, Colossians 2:12 refers to the blood baptism of Christ which the Scriptures plainly teach only He can perform. This is the same baptism that Christ speaks of in Luke 12:50 when He says,

> I have a baptism to be baptised with, and how am I straitened till it be accomplished!

Christ knew how horrible a thing His baptism for the dead was going to be but He alone was worthy of choosing that way for the sake of so many. Spurgeon tells of a child who was compelled to be baptised in a Church of England ceremony which he felt showed the folly of Church of England baptism. I have seen in the USA, repeatedly, little girls of five years of age, dressed in party frocks adorned with lipstick and everyone said, 'Ain't they sweet'. These 'baptisms' occurred in Baptist churches. May he who is innocent throw the first stone.

In Matthew 20:22, 23 and Mark 10:38, 39 we see that we may follow Christ in His baptism. However, this signifies those who are brought to believe they can share in His death at their death. He is talking to people whose baptism looks forward to their own actual bodily death in Christ and their share in His resurrection to glory. The dying, burial and resurrection refers to what happens through Christ's baptism of death only, not our baptism which is a token of what Christ's baptism portrays. No baptism, whether of households in covenant with God or individuals in covenant with God can equal this. So, too, no baptism is backward looking to steps we have taken in 'obedience' or any other pious reason, but forward looking to steps Jesus Christ has taken for us.

I would also say that the idea that Christ's blood baptism makes us members of the 'invisible' Church and our water baptism grants us the right to join a local church destroys fully the meaning of baptism. This doctrine of two baptisms is sadly most prevalent in certain denominations.

What then is the message to which baptism points? It is the one message that Christ has been preaching since the Fall. The blood of the Lord Jesus Christ cleanses us from all sins. Only Christ can shed that cleansing blood in His baptism which was His only, not ours. Mankind cannot shed blood to atone for his own sins so only Christ's baptism is one of atoning bloodshed. Our baptism, whether understood as signifying being washed, cleansed, dipped or sprinkled is a mere pointer, all are valid Biblical interpretations referring to the redeeming blood of Christ in His sacrificial, vicarious and atoning death.[7] 1 Peter 3:18-22 thus teaches,

> For Christ also hath once suffered for sins, the just for the unjust, that he might bring us to God, being put to death in the flesh, but quickened by the Spirit: By which also he went and preached unto the spirits in prison; Which sometime were disobedient, when once the longsuffering of God waited in the days of Noah, while the ark was a preparing, wherein few, that is, eight souls were saved by water. The like figure whereunto even baptism doth also now save us (not the putting away of the filth of the flesh, but the answer of a good conscience toward God,) by the resurrection of Jesus Christ: Who is gone into heaven, and is on the right hand of God; angels and authorities and powers being made subject unto him.

The 'like figure which now saves us' is surely Christ's atoning work and not water baptism which points to it. The 'spirits in prison' certainly do not refer to Christ's preaching to lost sinners in Hell after his resurrection as many in all denominations often relate but to Noah's

---

[7] Some readers will object to this statement but I believe that all the many pointers to baptism in the Old and New Testament use all these indicators. See my book *The Covenant of Grace and Christian Baptism* where I strive to sum up the Biblical teaching on baptism. Baptism is not a stand-alone doctrine but is embedded in the entire Covenant teaching of the Bible. This is centred around Christ's atoning work for our sakes on the cross.

contemporaries before the renewal of God's covenant with Abraham. John the Baptist who stood as the one figure par excellence who continued the Covenant of Grace from the Old Testament to the New thus could say,

> I indeed baptise you with water unto repentance: but he that cometh after me is mightier than I, whose shoes I am not worthy to bear: he shall baptise you in the Holy Ghost and with fire.[8]

This continuation of the gospel from the one Testament to the other was so important that the Holy Spirit started off all the gospels with this good news. The New Testament clearly expounds baptism with reference to Old Testament patterns and types and each evangelist added his own emphasis according to his calling. All link the New Testament news of the Lamb of God's cleansing work with the gospel as preached in the Old Testament. This pan-Biblical teaching on baptism is illustrated by Paul in 1 Corinthians 10:1-4 where he says,

> Moreover, brethren, I would not that ye should be ignorant, how that all our fathers were under the cloud, and all passed through the sea; And were all baptized unto Moses in the cloud and in the sea; And did all eat the same spiritual meat; And did all drink the same spiritual drink: for they drank of that spiritual Rock that followed them: and that Rock was Christ.

Here we have a fine picture of baptism and the Lord's Supper even at the beginning of theology appertaining to the Covenant of Grace.

The atonement and Christ's crucifixion

The way Christ chose to atone for our sins was through crucifixion. This is a barbaric method of ending a condemned criminal's life but it was prophesied of the Messiah in the Old Testament and was actually carried out with all its horror at Calvary. This is of special interest as crucifixion was not the usual Jewish method of ending the life of a

---

[8] Matthew 3:11; Mark 1:8; Luke 3:16; John 1:26.

condemned criminal as this was stoning.[9] Crucifixion came in via the Persians and Romans and was considered an extra shameful death by the Jews as also by the Gentiles. Christ did not die for the sin of the Jews only but for sin as a worldwide phenomenon. However, it was already foretold in the internationally-minded Old Testament that Christ would suffer under the worst form of punishment imaginable, the shame of the cross, for the whole Bride of Christ in whichever country they might be. Thus the Scribes and the Pharisees who wanted Christ to die by crucifixion to increase His shame, and not by stoning, were only agents in God's outworking of the Atonement.

Today we might think how barbaric the ancient world was but it was hardly more barbaric than our modern times concerning capital punishment where those found guilty, at least in the U.S.A. are imprisoned for years, undergo severe stress and mobbing before poison is injected into their veins amidst public viewing. This is accompanied by tortuous physical and mental pains and sometimes 'works' but at times does not. Another alternative in Europe is to lock up criminals in lunatic asylums and keep them sedated for life. In Christ day's crucifixion was not only a means of execution but provided entertainment in a public show as at the time of the French Revolution when the guillotine was used. Some countries are even base enough to keep up the tradition which France has happily eliminated and choreograph the death of a criminal for public viewing.

The 'tree' in Biblical prophecy and fulfilment
However, we have to do with prophecy and fulfilment here and the Old Testament had taught that the accursed are hung on a tree as in Deuteronomy 21:22, 23,

> And if a man have committed a sin worthy of death, and he be to be put to death, and thou hang him on a tree: His body shall not remain all night upon the tree, but thou shalt in any wise bury him that day; (for he that is hanged is accursed of God;) that thy land be not defiled, which the LORD thy God giveth thee for an inheritance.

---

[9] Leviticus 20:2; Deuteronomy 13:10.

Paul takes up this central Biblical theme in Acts 13:24-30, recorded by Luke, equating the 'tree' with the wooden cross on which Christ was crucified. Speaking of John the Baptist's testimony to Christ, he says,

> Men and brethren, children of the stock of Abraham, and whosoever among you feareth God, to you is the word of this salvation sent. For they that dwell at Jerusalem, and their rulers, because they knew him not, nor yet the voices of the prophets which are read every sabbath day, they have fulfilled them in condemning him. And though they found no cause of death in him, yet desired they Pilate that he should be slain. And when they had fulfilled all that was written of him, they took him down from the tree, and laid him in a sepulchre. But God raised him from the dead:

Here we note again, Paul differentiates between the true children of Abraham and the 'righteous-over-much' religious rogues in Jerusalem. The Apostle Paul affirms this blessed truth again in Galatians 3:13,

> Christ hath redeemed us from the curse of the law, being made a curse for us: for it is written, Cursed is every one that hangeth on a tree.

We note that the authorities who had Christ crucified had found no sin in Him but the prophecies of which they were ignorant, although they were publicly declared every Sabbath, were designed to be fulfilled to the letter.

Many refer to 'Pauline Theology' as if Paul's gospel differed from that of the other New Testament authors but the Apostle Peter says in Acts 10:39, 40, as recorded by Luke who was not an apostle,

> And we are witnesses of all things which he did both in the land of the Jews, and in Jerusalem; whom they slew and hanged on a tree. Him God raised up on the third day and shewed him openly.

193

This is of great significance to the worldwide proclamation of the gospel as it was the custom of the Old Testament prophets to distinguish between the Jews as a people and Jerusalem. The prophets all along viewed Jerusalem as an international type of the New Jerusalem to come which would be peopled by believers from all over the world before the coming of the Messiah. It was thus at Jerusalem where the eternal gospel of the eternal Covenant of Grace was ratified to the world in Christ's atoning crucifixion.[10]

Again we have Peter in 1 Peter 2:24, 25 of his epistle referring to Christ's crucifixion in similar terms, applicable to all peoples everywhere, saying of Christ,

> Who his own self bare our sins in his own body on the tree, that we, being dead to sins, should live unto righteousness: by whose stripes we were healed. For ye were as sheep going astray; but are now returned unto the Shepherd and Bishop of your souls.

Here we see again how the vicarious death of Christ on the Cross granted us reconciliation and atonement. This is the heart of the worldwide gospel displaying the power of God as 1 Corinthians 1, verses 18 and 24 puts it and this is why every Christian is an ambassador for Christ to all the world and can say 'we preach Christ crucified' as indicated in verse 23,

> For the preaching of the cross is to them that perish foolishness; but unto us which are saved it is the power of God … But we preach Christ crucified, unto the Jews a stumbling block, and unto the Greeks foolishness. But unto them which are called, both Jews and Greeks, Christ the power of God, and the wisdom of God.

We have hitherto seen when dealing with Romans 5:12-17 that it is by one man's offence that death passed to all men. The Second Adam, Christ, also died in an offensive way through the fallen eyes of many, but with a difference. The offence caused by Adam is seen by believers to point to a need for Atonement but the offence caused by Christ is

---

[10] See my book *The Covenant of Grace and the People of God* where I major on this theme.

only offensive to unbelievers and is the very counter offence which they need for their Atonement. We thus read of the 'offence of the cross' to the thinking of fallen man. This 'offence' is seen as such through the eyes of men without faith who have felt that law-duties are the way to saving themselves and not pointers to Christ the only Saviour. Thus Paul says in Romans 9:31-33:

> But Israel, which followed after the law of righteousness, hath not attained to the law of righteousness. Wherefore? Because they sought it not by faith, but as it were by the works of the law. For they stumbled at that stumblingstone; As it is written, Behold, I lay in Sion a stumbling stone and rock of offence: and whosoever believeth on him shall not be ashamed.

It is all too easy for non-Jews and even professing Christians to say, 'Yes, that was the Jews but we are not Jews'. Paul's remarks to the Church in Rome, however, were to people of New Testament times as a warning of the mistakes made amongst Old Testament peoples. Those mistakes, of course, did not cease to be made after Christ's days on earth. All have sinned and fallen short of the glory of God and Christ is still an offence to all those who have not bowed their knees before Him. Because they ridicule His atoning work on the Cross. We thus read in Galatians 5:10, 11; 'But if I, brothers, still preach circumcision, why am I still being persecuted? In that case the offence of the cross has been removed'.

Here Paul is criticising the trend in the Church to stick to outward signs such as circumcision and law duties for their salvation as being part of the Christian faith. The offence of the Cross to the law-bound is not removed by trying to find salvation under both Law and Grace but it is all of Grace. It is this that offends 'law-Christians' who are ruled by carrying out duties as a faith substitute.

The Messianic meaning of the Cross
When David refers to the lovingkindness of God to His people in Psalm 89:32-34, he refers to the great sin of David's people,

Then will I visit their transgressions with the rod, and their iniquity with stripes. Nevertheless my lovingkindness will I not utterly take from him, nor suffer my faithfulness to fail. My covenant will I not break, nor alter the thing that is gone out of my lips.

The whole chapter speaks of God's covenant promises to David and how God will protect his own. The entire chapter here is Messianic and there is far more than just a wee hint that God has appointed David as a type of the Messiah, Christ. The rest of the Old Testament, especially the Book of Isaiah as we have seen, points to the fact that the visiting of the rod and stripes, dealing with the punishment God's people deserved, will be laid on Christ. The whole Bible knows only one Atonement and that is through the death of the Suffering Servant so vividly described in Isaiah 53:3-5,

He is despised and rejected of men; a man of sorrows, and acquainted with grief: and we hid as it were our faces from him; he was despised, and we esteemed him not. Surely he hath borne our griefs, and carried our sorrows: yet we did esteem him stricken, smitten of God, and afflicted. But he was wounded for our transgressions, he was bruised for our iniquities: the chastisement of our peace was upon him; and with his stripes we are healed.

The Resurrection of Christ ratifies and seals Christ's Atonement
The crucifixion of Christ is an essential event leading to the resurrection of Christ, thus in Acts 5:30, Peter says, 'The God of our fathers raised up Jesus, whom ye slew and hanged on a tree'. We read in Acts 13:24 that 'they took him down from the tree, and laid him in a sepulchre. But God raised him from the dead'.

Indeed, every single book in the New Testament builds its gospel on the fact that our Christ is risen from the dead and in Him we shall also be raised. The Scribes and Pharisees, whom Christ forgave because they were doing God's will, looked for a different, worldly, national and political Messiah. So, after crucifying Christ, they were fearful Christ's prediction He would be resurrected on the third day might, after all, be fulfilled. They begged Pilate to seal the grave as if that could stop Christ from carrying out His work. Their fears were justified and we read,

> And behold, there was a great earthquake: for the angel of the Lord descended from heaven, and came and rolled back the stone from the door and sat upon it.[11]

I like especially those last words, 'and sat upon it'. Here is the finality of the Atonement. When an angel sits on the rolled-away stone, no man can put it back! The angel gave the faithful women the good news of the glorious gospel, 'he is risen as he said'. Then we read:

> Go quickly, and tell his disciples that he is risen from the dead; and, behold, he goeth before you into Galilee; there shall ye see him: lo, I have told you. And they departed quickly from the sepulchre with fear and great joy.[12]

Before they reached the disciples, however, Jesus met the women on the way and they came and bowed down to His feet and worshipped Him. The good news the women brought was received with mixed feelings by the disciples and Jesus had to scold them for their unbelief and hardness of heart as we read in Mark 16:14. However, their fears and doubts were overcome through the Lord's patience with them and we read further in Mark,

> They went forth, and preached everywhere, the Lord working with them, and confirming the word with signs following.[13]

Luke extends this wonderful story after verifying the words of Christ telling them of His crucifixion and resurrection[14] and adds the account of the two disciples on the way to Emmaus who were so slow to believe the Old Testament's teaching. There was more than one Doubting

---

[11] Matthew 28:2.
[12] Matthew 28:7.
[13] Mark 16:20.
[14] Luke 24:6.

Thomas amongst the Apostles. The Christ goes through all the teaching of Old Testament times, saying,

> O fools, and slow of heart to believe all that the prophets hath spoken: Ought not Christ to have suffered these things, and to enter into his glory? And beginning at Moses and all the prophets, he expounded unto them in all the scriptures the things concerning himself.

We then read after Christ broke bread with them, their eyes were opened and they knew him and could then say, 'The Lord is risen indeed'. Here is the message of the Old Testament which brought salvation to those at its continuation in the New. This is the full gospel of the Lord Jesus Christ which is worthy of all acceptation. Only by preaching the whole gospel from the whole Bible can we open the eyes of the spiritually blind and the ears of the spiritually deaf. This gospel culminates in the crucifixion and resurrection of Christ's atoning work and is the only gospel to be preached.

John goes into great detail regarding Christ's resurrection in chapters 20 and 21 and deals with both the physical and spiritual truth of Christ's been raised from the dead and so bringing life to His own as illustrated in the gospel,

> But these are written, that ye might believe that Jesus is the Christ, the Son of God; and that believing ye might have life through his name.[15]

We will now deal with some neglected terms regarding Atonement.

---

[15] John 20:31.

Chapter 14

Propitiation, Expiation, Appeasement and Oblation

Here we have to do with four terms which seem to be less used for various reasons, mostly unsound, in evangelical jargon than in Scripture. Indeed, I learnt at Bible College that these were Liberal terms and ought therefore not to be used in preaching. This Liberal theology, as I found out, was made popular in the 12th century through Abelard's Moral Influence Theory, but was already there when he brought it into vogue. There is nothing new under the sun and sadly this error continues still today in evangelicalism, as demonstrated in the earlier chapters, amongst those who deny the penal and ransoming aspect of Christ's death. Obviously, if we think that God would seek no propitiation or appeasement for our breaking His holy standards, we can forget the historical nature of Christ's redeeming death.

At Bible College they were thinking more of the Welshman Charles Harold Dodd (1884-1973) who felt that propitiation was a pagan idea of man trying to pacify angry gods. Oddly enough, Dodd claimed that propitiation should be replaced by the word 'expiation' in the Bible and so great was his influence that later major translators followed his unbiblical view of propitiation and opted for 'expiation'. Dodd seemed to think that 'to expiate' merely meant to remove sin and thus did not apply to ideas of appeasing God. This was wrong Biblical and grammatical thinking. R. W. Dale says in his work *The Atonement*, pages 479, 480 concerning misunderstandings of 'expiation' and 'propitiation' that:

> Dr Bushnell,[1] in his *Vicarious Sacrifice*, tries very hard to eliminate the idea of Expiation from the Old Testament as well as the New ... he objects that 'the original of the word atone, or make atonement, in the Hebrew Scriptures, carries no such idea of expiation.

Dale explains how the words mean simply 'to cover' and in relation to expiating sin 'it always means to cover it as to avert the penalty due to it, and that this covering is almost always effected by atonement'.

To 'expiate' is thus an exact synonym of 'propitiate' and is a transitive verb which needs both a subject who acts and an object which is acted upon. Furthermore, it is a causative word with the basic meaning of appeasing, paying the penalty for or making amends for, which is, of course, again, propitiating. Obviously our subject is our God in Christ and the purpose is to eliminate what stands between Him and His People. Every breach of the Law is an insult to God's Holy character and thus must be done away with. So, before Horace Bushnell (1802-1876) or Dodd changed the meaning, the terms were looked on as synonyms and still are by educated users of the English language. Those with a firm Biblical background, who accept 'propitiation' as a Biblical term, find nothing 'pagan' in the way the Godhead was propitiated through the sacrificial, vicarious death of the Son. Again, a look at the original Greek removes all problems. Here again we have words to do with ἱλάσκομαι (ilaskomai) which can mean to render propitious, to expiate, to be gracious, to show mercy, to atone, and to make expiation, etc.. There is perhaps no better word in the New Testament to describe Christ's saving work. Sadly, what is simple Hebrew or Greek has led to much confusion with the English languages. One of the reasons why English speaking Bible expositors have so many theological problems that other language speakers do not have is the host of different words they have for the same thing.

---

[1] Horace Bushnell (1802-76) was an American Congregational minister and theologian.

Another main reason why some Christians are reluctant to use such terms as propitiation, expiation and appeasement is that their preaching has become so 'well-meant' in persuading sinners of the loving-kindness, tender-mercies and forgiving nature of God in salvation and the emphasis on duty-faith on the part of fallen man that we tend to overlook the enormous scale of the sinner's antagonism to God and his horrible rebellion. Here our hot-gospellers who merely repeat 'Jesus loves you' like some pagan mantra join hands with the Liberals in denying God's wrath against sin and His method of allaying this wrath against His People. There is thus a great divide between man's fallen nature and God's holy righteousness. We must not forget the wrath of God against sin which was His motivation for dealing with it and the Saviour's labour of love in procuring freedom from it. To deny this is to deny the gospel.

Especially nowadays in times of 'duty' preaching, we evangelical, Reformed, Bible-believing Christians have a hard time witnessing to the wrath of God and the need for deliverance from it. 'Ban that from your preaching', our brethren say, 'and you will have more success!' One brave minister in Bremen who has been persecuted for many months now for preaching the sinner's need to repent is currently being disciplined by his church authorities for insulting his hearers by calling them sinners. His own church, who hear the bulk of his preaching, stand unanimously behind their pastor and praise God for his testimony. They believe that the Word of God rules our preaching and not those who preach flowery beds of ease for those at enmity with God.

God's wrath against sin

The word ὀργή (orgé) is used widely in the New Testament for God's wrath against sin and is even used to indicate punishment for sin. It is also used in its verb form (orgizoo) for provoking to wrath. This goes also for the word thumos as used in Revelation 14:10 ff. to show the destruction that will come to those in fallen Babylon who have the mark of the beast on their forehead.

Thus, the fairy tale amongst modern evangelicals that the Old Testament depicts a wrathful God and the New Testament a merciful Father is a great error. The Scriptures speak with one voice.

Does not the Old Testament depict David saying 'surely goodness and mercy shall follow me all the days of my life and I will dwell in the House of the Lord for ever',[2] yet Romans 1:18 in the New Testament says:

> For the wrath of God is revealed from heaven against all ungodliness and unrighteousness of men, who hold the truth in unrighteousness.

Similarly, we read in Deuteronomy 9:7 in the Old Testament how Israel had broken covenant with God on the way to the Promised Land and provoked Him to wrath which led to their destruction and the annulling of the old covenant they had promised to keep but had quickly broken. Happily, those who were not punished so lethally (there was always a faithful rest of true believers in Old Testament times) were then instructed by Moses and the Prophets who pointed to a Messiah who would keep all covenant conditions for them.

We see this grace preached in the New Testament in such passages as John 3:16 and how the Apostles were full of joy on finding 'the Messias which is, being interpreted, the Christ'.[3] The clear truth is that the entire Scriptures teach that God is wrathful against sin but in Christ has condemned sin in the flesh so that we may live in the spirit in Him and He in us.[4] Greater love hath no man but this.[5] This is the goal of Christ's atoning incarnation.

The cause of God's wrath is sinful man with his broken covenant. However, the preaching of the gospel ministers grace against man's bitterness, anger, clamour and malice.[6] Such ambassadors for Christ have put on the new man, which after God is created in righteousness and true holiness. They must demonstrate this in being kind one to another, tender-hearted, forgiving one another, even as God for Christ's sake has forgiven us.[7]

---

[2] Psalm 23:6.
[3] John 1:41.
[4] Romans 8:1-17.
[5] John 15:13.
[6] Ephesians 4:29-31.
[7] Ephesians 4:21-32.

John Ball on propitiation, expiation and appeasement

This does not mean that preachers must ignore the dark side of fallen human nature. After being told by my brethren in Christ for many decades that the so-called dark and secret side of God's will concerning election and predestination and His wrath against both sin and the sinner should not be preached but duty-faith, it has always been a blessing for me to turn to the more level-headed evangelists of yesteryear who knew their Bibles. John Ball in his *Treatise of the Covenant of Grace* of 1645 is a case in point here and I will try to summarise his teaching on atonement via propitiation, appeasement and satisfaction because of man's fall and his law-breaking.[8] Where I quote Ball verbatim, I shall update his language a little. Ball teaches clearly the wrath of God on sin because of man's fall but tells us:

> God will not execute the severity of his Law, because he is merciful, slow to anger, and ready to forgive. His free and everlasting love, and infinite delight which he hath in mercy, disposes him abundantly to pardon, and exercise loving kindness on the earth.[9] And if the Lord should utterly destroy all men, there should be no religion upon earth, as man should everlastingly lose the fruition of God, so he should likewise lose the voluntary service and subjection of his creature;[10] For these reasons God purposed not utterly to cast man off, and pour upon him deserved vengeance: but withal he purposed not to let sin go unrevenged.

Ball, however, still maintains that there must be a propitiation, appeasement and satisfaction because of the Nature of God and the authority of His Law and lists the reasons 'why God would not pardon sin without satisfaction for his truth and the Law which he had established against sin, which he will in not wise abolish'.[11] Ball points

---

[8] For those familiar with 17th century English I would heartily recommend reading Ball's *A Treatise of the Covenant of Grace*, here p. 288 ff., which has been reprinted in an inexpensive facsimile edition by Peter and Rachel Reynolds.

[9] Exodus 34:7; Micah 7:18; Jonah 4:2; 2 Chronicles 30:9; Psalm 86:5; Psalm 103:8; Isaiah 55:7; Jeremiah 9:34 and 31:20; Luke 6:36; Romans 2:4.

[10] John 15:8; Ezekiel 33:11.

[11] Matthew 5:18.

out that God hates sin and it provokes abhorrence in Him,[12] but the punishment must fit the crime and the authority of the Law must be observed, obedience demanded and men deterred from sinning.[13] He then says:

> Also God will have men always to tremble before him, and by his terror to be persuaded from sinning,[14] and therefore he reserves to himself entirely the punishment of sin, that man might always fear before him.[15] The omission of punishment after the publication of the Law, does detract somewhat from the authority of the Law, with the subjects' God therefore willing to show mercy to the creature fallen, and with all to maintain the authority of the Law, took such a course as might best manifest his clemency and severity, his hatred of sin, care to stablish the Law, and tender compassion towards them that are spared is the more illustrious, that he spared them, who rather that he would not punish sin, would give his only begotten Son to die for sin.

It is objected again, that God doth freely remit and pardon sin, therefore he willed not that Christ should make manifest satisfaction: because free remission will not stand with satisfaction. And most sure it is, that God is favourable to our iniquities[16] but God hath set forth Christ to be a propitiation through faith in his blood.[17]

The gospel according to Jeremiah

It is significant that Ball cites Jeremiah 31 here as Jeremiah was the great prophet of the New Covenant and lived it out hundreds of years before the Redeeming Messiah entered into his Incarnation, and in whom he already trusted in faith. Such faith being his evidence of things to come. Even our so-called 'secular' poets knew this. How thrilled I

---

[12] Habakkuk 1:13; Psalm 5:6; Zechariah 8:17; Revelation 3:6; Amos 5:21, 22; Isaiah 1:13, 14.
[13] Exodus 32:10, 11; Numbers 11:1; 16:22; John 3:36.
[14] 2 Corinthians 5:10, 11.
[15] Matthew 10:28; Luke 12:4.
[16] Jeremiah 31:34.
[17] Romans 3:25; Acts 10:43; Luke 1:68, 70.

was in my youth to read that great poem from the pen of Alfred Lord Tennyson (1809-1892) In Memoriam, especially the verse:

> We have but faith: we cannot know;
> For knowledge is of things we see
> And yet we trust it comes from thee,
> A beam in darkness: let it grow.

Tennyson was obviously influenced here by the Author of Hebrews who put the truth even more poetically and correctly in Chapter 11:1, 'Now faith is the substance of things hoped for, the evidence of things not seen'.

This was the great difference between the pansophy of John Durie and that of John Amos Comenius. The latter sought for an encyclopaedic knowledge of all elements of knowledge whereas Durie looked for that synergism of knowledge which was found by faith in God-Only-Wise (Romans 16:27). Modern science, education and theological training has profited greatly from Durie's works but Comenius was much misused by communist powers, especially in the Czech Republic, the home of Comenius' youth. It is through Durie's God-given discerning powers and divine knowledge engineering that we have our best definitions of the all-embracing covenant of grace.

The vain idea that Biblical prophecy is merely prognostic
The idea propagated by some modern NCT followers that Jeremiah said what he said without realising the future purport of his words is refuted by the many chapters Jeremiah writes concerning his gospel with its historical and timeless truths. So, too, Jeremiah shows how the wrath of God came upon those who had changed God's covenant into a legal covenant of works or keeping to the letter which brought slaughter on the pre-Law covenant breakers and on most of the post-Law Children of Israel before the Promised Land was reached. There is no Promised Land for those who ridicule or even ignore God's gracious Law which points to forgiveness in Christ and reconciliation with God.

Our debt to the Law is paid

Ball goes on to explain that our debt to the Law is paid in a two-fold way: first by Christ becoming our surety in lieu of the true 'delinquents' as Ball calls his fellow-sinners. Then God's full remission in pardoning our sin. This is what the Bible means by 'satisfaction'. God was completely satisfied with the work of Christ. This is the message of the Old Testament which Isaiah taught and which our New Testament writers faithfully preached:

> Surely he hath borne our griefs, and carried our sorrows: yet we did esteem him stricken, smitten of God, and afflicted. But he was wounded for our transgressions, he was bruised for our iniquities: the chastisement of our peace was upon him; and with his stripes we are healed.
>
> All we like sheep have gone astray; we have turned every one to his own way; and the Lord hath laid on him the iniquity of us all.
>
> He was oppressed, and he was afflicted, yet he opened not his mouth: he is brought as a lamb to the slaughter, and as a sheep before her shearers is dumb, so he openeth not his mouth.
>
> He was taken from prison and from judgment: and who shall declare his generation? for he was cut off out of the land of the living: for the transgression of my people was he stricken.
>
> And he made his grave with the wicked, and with the rich in his death; because he had done no violence, neither was any deceit in his mouth.
>
> Yet it pleased the Lord to bruise him; he hath put him to grief: when thou shalt make his soul an offering for sin, he shall see his seed, he shall prolong his days, and the pleasure of the Lord shall prosper in his hand.
>
> He shall see of the travail of his soul, and shall be satisfied.[18]

We marvel at the clarity of the revelation given to Isaiah which described Christ's sufferings to satisfy the Law on our account but shake our heads over professing Christians of today who blindly write,

---

[18] Isaiah 53:4-11.

As long as we insist upon holding tightly to the rigid inerrancy of the Old Testament scriptures, we will forever be kept from fully embracing the clearest and most accurate portrayal of who God really is.

Until we relax our grip on the idea that the Old Testament prophets were truly seeing God clearly and recognize that the Abba Father we see revealed in Christ overrides those limited and flawed perspectives of God, we will remain confused about who God really is.

I found this statement on the web written by a Keith Giles who was doing an advertising campaign for his books *Jesus Untangled; Jesus Unbound* and *Jesus Undefeated* which his website claims are 'best sellers'. He writes apparently claiming to be a 'progressive Christian' against God's wrath and believes we are already ruled by the Anti-Christ. In his spare time he sells 'Wild Food' which even his team claim that they have no proof of any beneficiary effects. All Giles' arguments are based on a Bible robbed of the Atonement and the Christian gospel. He views himself as a prophet born to lead the NCT into new fantasies.

To get back to clear-headed Ball, who teaches that Christ's mind and will in procuring satisfaction is,

> … that grace might justify herself in pardoning offences, and not that pardon should be given of justice. And lo the satisfaction of Christ is full and perfect and our pardon is every way free and gracious.

Ball has much more gospel gold on this subject and I heartily recommend him for further studies in satisfaction.

God's wrath against sin is part of His love for His People
So we see that the wrath of God against sin is an irremovable part of His love for sinners but the offence of sinful man towards God and his stubborn attitude to all that is holy must be rectified before full reconciliation with God is attained. A further difficulty put forward by Bible scholars is that they have difficulty in translating the four Greek

words we usually translate by 'propitiation' leaving them with the problem, does 'propitiate' mean, expiation, appeasement, satisfaction, reconciliation or what? The truthful answer here, which is not dodging the issue but looking the facts in the eye, is that the term 'propitiation' means the lot and much more.

Oblation

This is another word fought shy of by today's evangelicals who seem to associate it with some Roman Catholic sacerdotal function. Yet we find the word used most positively and meaningfully some 25 times in our English Bible but also we read of Isaiah's warning that no 'vain' oblations should be linked with faith in God.[19] Indeed, where Isaiah speaks of pure oblations in comparison to the majority of Jews (not the remnant of believing Jews) whose oblations were vain, he is referring to the work of the gospel on behalf of a 'very small remnant' (v. 9).

So that the Messiah's flock can be gathered in he sends out a general call to faith in verse 18,

> Come now, and let us reason together saith the Lord: though your sins be as scarlet, they shall be as white as snow, though they be red like crimson, they shall be as wool.

Isaiah claims Jerusalem is a harlot of vain oblations instead of a faithful city and teaches the appearing of the New Jerusalem which will be formed by a remnant of believers worldwide. Isaiah is the Prophet of the New Testament and the New Jerusalem which will culminate Christ's work. It is thus no wonder that when Christ started his ministry he claimed that He was the fulfilment of Isaiah's hope and faith.[20] Indeed, we find the gospel right up to the so-called Minor Prophets, building on Isaiah to proclaim Christ's work in a seamless continuation in the New Testament.

All these synonyms point to the work of reconciliation which Christ undertook for his Bride which will be the subject of Chapter 15.

---

[19] Isaiah 1:13.

[20] See Luke 4:17 and the very many references of Christ in the Gospels to His fulfilling Isaiah's prophesies besides being announced as such by John the Baptist.

Chapter 15

Atonement as Reconciliation

Since my earliest Christian days, I have realised that the way of the Godhead to keep up the internal Covenant of Grace with Christ between Father, Son and Holy Spirit was to create reconciliation through atonement. Here we have the cause and effect of the central theme of Covenant Theology. It was Christ's sacrificial and vicarious work of love in dying to save His Bride, the Church. So it comes as no surprise to find that the Biblical words for Atonement are synonymous with those for reconciliation. Just as seeing means the opening of the eyes, so reconciliation means the outworking of Atonement.

It must be admitted, however, that many evangelicals as well as those far from the evangelical, Reformed fold today are smitten with Roman Catholic dogmas and question this understanding which many of us would think, according to such beautiful passages as Romans 5:6-11 was the natural meaning of the Atonement:

> For when we were yet without strength, in due time Christ died for the ungodly. For scarcely for a righteous man will one die: yet peradventure for a good man some would even dare to die. But God commendeth his love toward us, in that, while we were yet sinners, Christ died for us. Much more then, being now justified by his blood, we shall be saved from wrath through him. For if, when we were enemies, we were reconciled to God by the death of his Son, much more, being reconciled, we shall be saved

by his life. And not only so, but we also joy in God through our Lord Jesus Christ, by whom we have now received the atonement.

Here, we see that the full scope of being united in Christ through the Atonement entails also the work of justification, delivery from sin, freedom from condemnation, reconciliation, salvation and joy in God through our Redeemer Christ. Yet A. Dalzell, who otherwise says a good deal of good things about the Atonement yet feels free to call his book written in 1900 *Atonement is not Reconciliation*.

The Summerhill experiment

When I was a young trainee teacher in the early nineteen sixties, one special kind of educational discipline was rubbed under our noses week after week. It was the example of Summerhill, a boarding school near Ipswich, in England, founded in 1924 by Scotsman A. S. Neill. This educator ran his school on extraordinary lines. If his pupils were naughty in any way, whether it was by fighting, lying, breaking windows or whatever, Neill would call them into his study for discipline. And here was the surprise. They did not get a telling off; they did not get a whipping; they did not have to stay in after classes and were not given detention work to do. They were patted on the head; told what good children they were and given a silver sixpence out of the Headmaster's own pocket. This was to be our disciplinary goal and our teaching pattern. The idea was that if you showered naughty little boys and girls with goodness, you would make them good. During our teacher-training 'post-grad' course at Hull University there was one misguided tutor who made donating silver sixpences to naughty children his life's ambition.

Thousands of years ago, God showered His creation with goodness. All that He made was good. He created Adam as monarch of all he surveyed, the Lord of the birds and the beasts and the land. But Adam fell. Good as he was, he wanted to be better. His own natural goodness was derived from His Creator and could only be maintained in harmony with his Creator. But Adam did not want derived goodness, given Him by the God who loved him. He wanted to be a god himself by fair means or foul. He chose the foul means. To his surprise, God gave him no silver sixpence though He provided a way back to Him.

Summerhill was like a shooting star that blazed through the pedagogic heavens for a generation or two and then fizzled out. All it created was selfish, arrogant, snobbish prigs who never learnt the difference between right and wrong but thought they themselves were gods who could do what they liked with impunity. The word 'impunity' means 'without punishment'. Nowadays, we can only laugh at the deceivers who built and financed Summerhill and feel sorry for the thousands of victims who were duped by Neill. The man was quite oblivious to the main ingredient of true education and discipline which is to know human nature and to introduce the child to our God-Only-Wise. Wisdom begins with God. It is to be found nowhere else.

Really, Summerhill was no surprise to those wishing to bring atoning reconciliation to a fallen world and Neill was no exception to the normal fallen human rule. Neill behaved as we all behave. We rebel against our God. We sin a multitude of sins, far worse than Neill's problems of fighting in the playground and breaking windows. Then we feel we can go to God who is morally bound to pat us on the head and give us a silver sixpence. Is not God the God of love and has He not promised us to be at our beck and call?

This view of God is, of course, pure fiction. God is not what we think He is and we are not what we imagine we are. Let us look at the situation from God's side. What was it like after the Fall in Eden when man was shown his rebellion against his Creator, Friend, Judge and Teacher? We read of God:

> So he drove out the man; and he placed at the east of the garden of Eden Cherubims, and a flaming sword which turned every way, to keep the way of the tree of life.[1]

No silver sixpences there! What about Adam's offspring, whom God longingly in love suffered to come unto Him? We read:

> Because that, when they knew God, they glorified him not as God, neither were thankful; but became vain in their

---

[1] Genesis 3:24.

imaginations, and their foolish heart was darkened. Professing themselves to be wise, they became fools, And changed the glory of the uncorruptible God into an image made like to corruptible man, and to birds, and four-footed beasts, and creeping things. Wherefore God also gave them up to uncleanness through the lusts of their own hearts, to dishonour their own bodies between themselves: Who changed the truth of God into a lie, and worshipped and served the creature more than the Creator, who is blessed for ever. Amen. For this cause God gave them up unto vile affections: for even their women did change the natural use into that which is against nature: And likewise also the men, leaving the natural use of the woman, burned in their lust one toward another; men with men working that which is unseemly, and receiving in themselves that recompence of their error which was meet. And even as they did not like to retain God in their knowledge, God gave them over to a reprobate mind, to do those things which are not convenient; Being filled with all unrighteousness, fornication, wickedness, covetousness, maliciousness; full of envy, murder, debate, deceit, malignity; whisperers, Backbiters, haters of God, despiteful, proud, boasters, inventors of evil things, disobedient to parents, Without understanding, covenantbreakers, without natural affection, implacable, unmerciful: Who knowing the judgment of God, that they which commit such things are worthy of death, not only do the same, but have pleasure in them that do them.[2]

There is little chance shown here that man would ever be able to reconcile himself to God. Sadly, we hear much anti-semitic thinking here in some modern covenant teaching which blames the Jews for everything and boasts that Gentiles have a special revelation from God which excludes the Old Testament as part of God's Covenant with man. They being under a separate Covenant of Law which knows no grace. Of course, the Jews as a united nation rather than a religious body covered only a small part of the world's history or even the Palestinian area before Paul made, under the Spirit, this astonishing condemnation of all men. We must face the fact that Paul is writing about you and me

---

[2] Romans 1:21-32.

and every one of us, not just unbelieving Jews. We cannot claim that we in our modern culture are quite different. Paul's description of a life without God is still up-to-date but it is not the life Summerhill and our humanistic wisdom has to offer. Even if modern teachers of a covenant without the history of the Jews in it do believe in a *tabula rasa* and new beginning with the death of Christ irrespective of all God's covenantal dealings in Old Testament times Paul tells both Jews and Gentiles:

> For if God spared not the natural branches, take heed lest he also spare not thee. Behold therefore the goodness and severity of God: on them which fell, severity; but toward thee, goodness, if thou continue in his goodness: otherwise thou also shalt be cut off. Therefore thou art inexcusable, O man, whosoever thou art that judgest: for wherein thou judgest another, thou condemnest thyself; for thou that judgest doest the same things.[3]

This is why Paul in Romans 8:5, 6 tells us:

> For they that are after the flesh do mind the things of the flesh; but they that are after the Spirit the things of the Spirit. For to be carnally minded is death; but to be spiritually minded is life and peace.

The Bible makes it quite clear there is no true life and true peace unless God initiates it. Man neither will nor can accomplish such a necessary task. However, there is grace and spiritual renewal for both Jews and Gentiles and always was.

Arguments against equating Atonement with Reconciliation
Naturally (concerning natural fallen man), there are those who would reject an Atonement through Christ altogether. Indeed, the day before writing this I read a published article by a wrongly informed man who protested there is no passage in Scripture which refers to Christ dying to atone for our sins. Be this as it may, there are a number of evangelical,

---

[3] Romans 11:21, 22.

Reformed writers, pastors and teachers besides a number of less evangelical writers who will not hear of the Atonement being described in terms of reconciliation or sin-cleansing and restitution with God.

Arthur Pink on reconciliation

Arthur Pink is one 20th century man of God who is highly respected as an evangelical teacher. He spent all his adult life expounding the Scriptures and making his findings public through books and magazines. His massive tome *An Exposition of Hebrews* has opened many an eye to covenant blessings, his Elijah has shown us how God is still working his purpose out in this modern world and his *The Sovereignty of God* fills us with awe before our great and glorious Heavenly Father. Pink's *Profiting from the Word* is a very handy tool for young Christians. I confess I have been greatly influenced by this Bible expositor and have even had the pleasure of examining and reading through a number of his hand-written manuscripts sent for publication. Though freshly sent by Mr Pink, they looked yellow with age but this was because Pink had written them in a tobacco-smoke filled room the smell of which was so strong and lasting that it filled the room in which I was examining the documents with my mentor Sydney Houghton. Sadly, Pink spent his last years as a recluse without church fellowship believing no church came up to his standards of Christianity. So, too, the following statement found in one of Pink's works leads me to utter a phrase I picked up from Iain Murray 'The best of men are but men at best'. Concerning the Atonement, Pink penned the following words:

> A pertinent example of what we have just said (i.e., that people are jumbled in their minds about the atonement) is seen in the now almost current idea that the Atonement of Christ signifies 'at-one-ment', the bringing of God and the sinner together. But that is not the meaning of the term at all, either as used in Scripture or as employed in sound theology. Reconciliation is one of the many effects or fruits of Christ's Atonement but was not part of the work He did. Many others have failed to distinguish between the Atonement of Christ and the Redemption which is one of its fruits. It is vitally important

to distinguish between what Christ did and that which has resulted therefrom.

These words are found in Pink's book *The Satisfaction of Christ: Studies in Atonement* which grew out of the instalments of his Studies in Scripture written between 1930 and 1931.

Two conflicting theologies advocated in one book

I found the first chapters of this book heavy going indeed as Pink deals closely with metaphysical and philosophical problems in his attempt to portray the sovereignty of God in salvation which I found quite superfluous. After some 200 pages, however, Pink gives us some of the best theological writing I have ever read and shows up the weaknesses of the conditional and universal views of the atonement, one would think, in an irrefutable way. However, I could not reconcile these first 200 pages with the good material that came after them as Pink had removed from his subsequent thoughts the Biblical basis on which they ought to have stood. Indeed, there is much in the early chapters which totally contradict Pink's conclusions in subsequent chapters. So, too, Pink displays here a most unsympathetic way of boasting he knows better than almost anyone else in analysing a topic though he fails completely to get to the bottom of many an argument which the ordinary man in the pew often understands immediately. This is especially the case in his inadequate handling of righteousness and sanctification.

It appears that Pink's first thoughts on coming to an understanding of God before having an experience of salvation and his later, mature, experience of Christ and knowledge of the Scriptures have been shaken together and laid out in one work. I truly wonder whether this book is an original and complete work of Pink's or is it a collection of works moulded into one by editors who were not skilled enough to know what they were doing. Pink admittedly has often suffered very badly from editors. The work therefore seems to have been written by two men with two conflicting theologies.

Atonement versus Satisfaction

Pink starts off by arguing that the word 'atonement' is too limited to express the full Biblical meaning but rules out all the wider meanings of redemption and reconciliation which one would think are contained in the Biblical words used. Indeed, Pink's view does not tie up with the Hebrew and Greek words expressing Atonement at all. If we use the kipper/kōpher group of words for the basis of an understanding of 'atonement', which are Scriptural words but not the only words dealing with Atonement, we find that the ideas of ransom, redemption and reconciliation are central to them. Atonement is a covering of sin, a ransoming of the sinner, a redemptive act and the means of reconciling a sinner to God. Satisfaction is only one of the elements Pink brings up appertaining to Atonement. Pink first empties the term Atonement of its true meaning and then complains it is inadequate to express redemption and reconciliation!

An unnecessary atonement

When speaking of the necessity of the atonement, Pink now argues for it with great dogmatism and then turns tail and argues severely against it. He seems to want to eat his cake and keep it. Some of his statements just beg to be criticised! On page 33, he says, 'To say that the all-wise God Himself could find no other way of saving sinners, consistent with His holiness and justice, than the one He has, is highly presumptuous'. This approaches the theory of Andrew Fuller who argues that the way in which God allowed His will to be enacted was solely arbitrary and not an actual but a token demonstration of justice, mercy, etc.. One might equally add that to say that the all-wise God Himself could have found a better way of saving sinners, consistent with His holiness and justice than the way He chose as the best way, is highly presumptuous.' It is highly presumptuous indeed to speculate on whether God could behave differently than he does. We do not speculate concerning an alternative or better method of atonement than that recorded in Scripture. We base our theology on what Atonement is, not what it might have been.

What is odd is that that Pink on the one hand denies the necessity of God's act in Atonement but then on the other hand goes on to talk of its necessities, admitting that the reader will probably think he is contradicting himself, which is, of course just what Pink compels his readers to think. However, Pink goes on in this strange fashion arguing that 'To declare that Omniscience was helpless, that God was obliged to adopt the means which He did, is perilous nigh unto blasphemy'. But surely the speculation that God might have used another way and even spared His Son and even spared us the Fall would be truly outrageous blasphemy for a Christian. The Biblical truth is aired in the hymn we sing: 'There was no other good enough to pay the price of sin. He only could unlock the door of Heaven and let us in!' Surely it is blasphemous to say that Christ did not think it absolutely necessary to do what He did. This is obviously what Pink is suggesting. The fact that God in His love for His people chose the way of salvation which was alone necessary should close our mouths against silly utterances to the contrary.

Reconciliation not part of Christ's work on the cross!
Pink is entirely mixed up in his theology of ransom, reconciliation, expiation and salvation in general. Those Reformed men who see the *kipper* family of words referring to a means of establishing unity with God, do not teach that God must be reconciled to man but that man must be reconciled to God. The root meaning 'at-one-ment' thus still holds. They also believe that the atonement effects this. Here the word 'effects' does not mean 'causes later effects to ensue at, say, the act of believing. It means that the Atonement *activates* reconciliation. This is the root meaning of the word. Reconciliation is not activated through the act of believing on the sinner's side. God's purpose in the Atonement is secured in its activation and its activation is not when I decide to believe and thus activate what was dormant until then. The activation is the will of God before the foundation of the world, worked out in Christ's redeeming death on the Cross. Just as when God says 'Let there be light', there is light. Just as God atones, atonement is accomplished. There is not an Atonement on the one side and its accomplishment on the other separating cause from effect in two different theologies. When Christ atoned for our sins, our sins were covered and the Atonement accomplished.

217

Separating the inseparable

Pink seeks to separate the activities of the atonement from its action on the Cross. He severs the effects from the cause by removing the attributes of the atonement, placing them somewhere in the future after man expresses faith. It is on the Cross that we are reconciled to Christ, there and then, and when Pink says that the work of reconciliation is, 'not part of the work He did', in the atonement, then this is at best idle speculation, but at worst, and coming from such an enlightened man, a most unguarded criticism of the work of our Lord in Salvation. Such sentences as 'It is vitally important to distinguish between what Christ did and that which has resulted therefrom' can only confuse sinners. It is vitally important not to separate them as the results which Pink refers to are what Christ did on the Cross in His atoning work. There is no Atonement void of its outcome. One cannot remove the attributes of a saving act from the act itself as the act is the substance and composition of the saving factors. The glorious Scriptural truth is that in the Atonement 'God was in Christ reconciling the world to Himself'.[4]

Like Wesley and Fuller, Pink seeks to separate the attributes of the saving act from the act itself. Pink sees the act as being performed by Christ but the attributes as being activated when the believer grasps out and takes them. He does not accept Christ's act on the Cross as the once and for all time securing activity of the saving element in the atonement. Indeed, Pink teaches that the work of reconciliation has nothing 'really' or 'actually' to do with the Atonement. He leaves us with two quite different historical understandings of the Atonement: 1. Reconciliation being made possible at Calvary and 2. Reconciliation being made actual on the act of believing.

Up to the writing of this book Pink had been constantly attacked as a Hyper-Calvinist who believed that reconciliation, redemption, ransom, sanctification and imputation of righteousness were all accomplished on the Cross. Was this now Pink's way of shaking off such criticism? However, our union with Christ is secured and vouchsafed in the Atonement. It is not a by-product, nor a possibility awaiting fruition at some future date.

---

[4] 2 Corinthians 5:19.

Difficulties with Old Testament teaching
Page 62 also causes concern as Pink deals with what he feels is the Old Testament view of Jewish sacrifices implying that Christ's sufferings were merely identical with those of the OT sacrificial animals. If this were so, the Jews might well ask why they should need Christ and we must ask what need have we of a New Testament.

Pink's emphasis that he knows better than all other Christians
On page 76 Pink informs his readers that he knows of some vital doctrine which is 'completely unknown to almost all of our readers' – readers, we presume, who are mostly established Christians and Reformed men. This page should certainly have been edited out.

Ransomed or redeemed?
On page 100, we find Pink again separating the inseparable. He insists on a basic difference in meaning between 'ransom' and 'redemption' building different theologies on each. Again, he is distinguishing between the act and its attributes. To pay a ransom is to redeem. In the nineteen forties and early fifties we were very poor and our best clothes and my uncle's medals were frequently pawned on Mondays and redeemed on Fridays (pay-day). 'Redeemed' was the word we used. To ransom is to redeem. If one analyses the Hebrew, Greek or even Latin, French and English translations of it, one comes to the result that Christ's ransom is our redemption. There is no ransom without redemption. There is no redemption without ransom. Both terms derive from the one meaning to free from captivity or punishment by paying a price. In many languages, the one word describes both terms as in Hebrew and German and the only reason we have two words in English is that possibly one has come down through French and one through Latin. What is, then, this 'important distinction' between the terms that Pink tells us about on page after page but never really explains?

Pardon in stages
The theology aired on Page 182 on 'Application' contradicts totally what comes after Chapter 15. Pink's ideas of 'application' really gives cause for confusion. Pink seems to be arguing that the atonement brings

pardon for all pre-conversion sins but not for those committed after conversion because there can be no pardon before sin is committed. Against such an odd idea, the Bible clearly teaches that Christ died for all the elect who were also born after His death and died to pardon all their sins, though they were not yet committed! Christ's pardon embraces all time backwards and forwards from time's fulfilment on the cross. Pardon, for Pink, means there is only pardon for sins when each sin is confessed. There is no absolute pardon for sin in Christ's Bride. Pink later takes this all back (perhaps not realising that he has said it), but he should not have given it to us in the first place.

An Atonement in three stages two of which are post-Calvary
What can we say to Pink's view of atonement in three stages? He writes of Atonement as shed, as pleaded, as sprinkled. Only one stage is fulfilled at Calvary and two stages are accomplished with human agency. To plead that the efficacy of the blood (the shedding) lies dormant until grasped by believers (the sprinkling) is a mockery of Christ's Atonement. To further argue, as Pink does, that Christ's blood is only sprinkled equal to the believer's prayer for pardon for individual sins confessed, denies the once and for all time nature of the Atonement. Pink, however, quotes Hebrews 12:24 as if it refers to a post-atonement repetition of the shedding of Christ's blood. His argument that there is a difference between Christ's blood as shed and as sprinkled is merely playing with words.

Hebrews 12 refers to the New Covenant situation we find ourselves in through the mediation of Christ. The author is not talking to sinners who have still to find salvation but to 'the general assembly and church of the firstborn, which are written in heaven'. He is talking about those who are already in – of just men made perfect. Pink's obvious trouble here is that he has wandered through several different theologies through his numerous denominational try-outs and collected a confusing amount of different, contradictory ideas which have obviously become part and parcel of his thinking.

Pink criticises others harshly for using non-Biblical examples to illustrate Biblical points, yet he is always appealing to the non-Biblical to describe the Biblical. His story of the heir who died before coming into his inheritance thus prematurely forfeiting it is a strange comparison indeed with an atoned-for soul who has not yet come to faith and thus might be eventually lost. Is Pink suggesting that God would allow a soul for whom Christ died to perish before receiving the gift of faith?

When was redemption accomplished?
A question must also be raised against Pink's argument that it is the resurrection which ensures the vicarious remission of sin and not the time of the renting of the veil. It is widely taught in Liberal theology that the Christian's view of redemption is based on what they call 'the resurrection myth'. Pink does not think the resurrection is a myth, of course, but is he not rather casting doubt on the historicity of the atonement itself? The essential part of the historicity of the atonement is its effectiveness which was activated before the resurrection, the resurrection ensuing because of this finished work. It was not the resurrection that sparks-off atonement but the atonement which moved a propitiated God to give His Son and all those who are in Him, the rewards of Christ's work. Christ claimed that the saving work was over in the death He died. He did not proclaim 'It is finished' on the resurrection morning. I was told at Bible College not to use the word 'propitiation' because it smacked of 'Liberalism'. However, to deny that propitiation was accomplished in the Atonement reconciling God's People to Himself is 'liberal' indeed.

Separating synonyms again
The next few chapters are much clearer theologically but waste much time distinguishing between words for the apparent sake of the exercise only. Pink seems not to have consulted his Hebrew dictionary and grammar in any way. On page 189 Pink has obviously forgotten about Hebrew parallelism i.e., the Hebrew love of saying the same thing in two different ways. His exposition of Jeremiah 31:11, 'For the Lord hath redeemed Jacob, and ransomed him from the hand of him that was stronger than he', and Hosea 13:14, 'I will ransom them from the power of the grave; I will redeem them from death', just cannot stand. If he had only looked up the words for ransom and redemption in a good dictionary or in the original text, he would have found that where he quotes a word to mean ransom, the same word means redeemed and

vice-versa elsewhere. Hosea 13:14 illustrates this well where 'redeem' in Hebrew is the very word translated as 'ransom' in Jeremiah 31:11. Here we see the folly of building two different theologies on two different words which mean the same thing. Pink's alleged differences in meanings would demand two different terms in the Hebrew texts whereas they use but one.

Had Pink had his *novum* and his *vets* in his hands, he would not have made such mistakes. If he did not have the required learning, he should not have posed as a Bible translator. Not understanding English usage correctly and not understanding Hebrew or Greek at all has led many NCT writers to tell us that the OT Prophets contradicted each other and therefore the Old Testament is unreliable. A typical example is the case of Keith Giles of the 'Heretic Happy Hour Podcasts' who continually speaks about Bible characters who contradict others therefore making the Bible unreliable. He tells us not to look at the Bible but Christ. How he knows Christ without the Bible, including Christ's testimony of Himself, I do not know.

Page 190 ff. continues with what is either linguistically untrue or exegetically impossible and again contradicts what Pink says on page 58. The Biblical and historical atonement produced final and absolute pardon and at-one-ment. Pink's doctrine of purchased but unforgiven saints cries out to be worked over and put on a more Biblical basis.

In spite of many good features in this book, I would hesitate to place it in a person's hand who was not firmly established in the faith. Pink's slogans 'No Reconciliation in Atonement', 'No Reconciliation on the Cross' leaves us with an atonement void of contents which therefore does not atone and a reconciliation which has nothing to do with Christ's work. It is no wonder Pink preaches that the atonement only brings pardon for pre-conversion sins. It is a wonder that it does even that as no actual reconciliation has ensued according to Pink.

These doctrinal issues remind me of the controversy between John Wesley and James Hervey reflected in the former's *Preservative against Unsettled Notions in Religion* and the latter's *Aspasio Vindicated*. The problems were the contents of atonement, the timing and scope of reconciliation and the means of pardon, freedom from guilt, righteousness and justification. Wesley had a similar view to Pink's conception of pardon in stages, depending on the atonement for pre-conversion pardon and for repentance and faith concerning post-conversion pardon. Hervey taught Wesley that pardon was fully obtained for us in Christ's atoning work. Hervey thus points Wesley to Hebrews 10:14, 'By one offering, he hath perfected for ever them that are sanctified.' Believers, Hervey explains, are not reconciled for one day or one year, according to how they fall in and out of grace; they are reconciled for ever. 'The pardon is irrevocable; the blessing inalienable.' Hervey believed pardon was full because reconciliation was complete. Pink denies both these factors. Reconciliation, he maintains, is not the work of Christ in the atonement and full pardon is conditional to the behaviour of the believer.

Here Daniel 9:24, a favourite verse of Hervey's, helps us. The work of the Redeemer is 'to finish the transgression, and to make an end of sins, and to make reconciliation for iniquity, and to bring in everlasting righteousness.' This was the complete work of the atonement and a clear refutation of Pink's extraordinary theory.

Finally, perhaps the clearest refutation comes from Paul as he says in Romans 5:10:

> For if, when we were enemies, we were reconciled to God by the death of his Son, much more, being reconciled, we shall be saved by his life.

How hollow is the sound of Pink's words on page 58. He writes, 'Reconciliation is one of the many effects or fruits of Christ's Atonement, but was not part of the work He did.' What Christian could refrain from condemning such a false view of our Lord's perfect and finished work?

When viewed in the light of Scripture, Pink's doctrine of delayed-action pardon and reconciliation is seen to be totally erroneous. It must be thus condemned as such and seen as dangerous in the hands of those who have, up to now, known Pink as an orthodox man and will thus accept anything new from him in trust and dependency on his good standing. It must be shown that whether Pink, Gill, Spurgeon or Bavinck, these men are only good guides to us as long as they have their eyes on Scripture and their gaze on Christ. I feel my readers must be warned about this strange teaching of Pink's regarding the Atonement. The Christian's duty as a watchman must not be neglected.

Pink tells how 'painful'[5] it is for him to find the bulk of Christians disagreeing with him and he is upset they even ridicule his view. I do not want to join in this ridicule but I suggest that anyone who feels he has a private interpretation and finds no one to share it with him, must become suspicious of himself. Especially when that strange view moves Pink to write, '*The work of Christ, of itself, never did, never will, and never can, save a single soul.*'[6] I suggest that Pink's view not only goes against traditional reformed interpretation but it is neither linguistically true nor exegetically possible. This is why the Baptist theologian P. T. Forsyth said in his book *The Work of Christ*, 'Reconciliation was finished in Christ's death. Paul did not preach a gradual reconciliation. He preached what the old divines used to call the finished work … He preached something done once for all – a reconciliation which is the base of every soul's reconcilement, not an invitation only.'

Refreshing, comforting words from Scripture
How much different it is from Pink's theological tangle to turn to the plain, uncomplicated Word of God. In 2 Corinthians 5:18-20, we read:

> And all things are of God, who hath reconciled us to himself by Jesus Christ, and hath given to us the ministry of reconciliation; To wit, that God was in Christ, reconciling the world unto himself, not imputing their trespasses unto them; and hath committed unto us the word of reconciliation. Now then we are ambassadors for Christ, as though God did beseech you by us: we pray you in Christ's stead, be ye reconciled to God.

Ephesians 2:14-22 backs this up in teaching us:

> For he is our peace, who hath made both one, and hath broken down the middle wall of partition between us; Having abolished in his flesh the enmity, even the law of commandments contained in ordinances; for to make in himself of twain one new man, so

---

[5] P. 200.
[6] My emphasis, p.128.

making peace; And that he might reconcile both unto God in one body by the cross, having slain the enmity thereby: And came and preached peace to you which were afar off, and to them that were nigh. For through him we both have access by one Spirit unto the Father. Now therefore ye are no more strangers and foreigners, but fellow citizens with the saints, and of the household of God; And are built upon the foundation of the apostles and prophets, Jesus Christ himself being the chief corner stone; In whom all the building fitly framed together groweth unto an holy temple in the Lord: In whom ye also are builded together for an habitation of God through the Spirit.

Reconciliation an essential part of the Atonement

Our reconciliation is an essential part of the work of Christ on the cross. It was His work, not ours. Thus, the Bible teaches that the purpose of the atonement is the work of reconciliation. The means and the cause, are inseparable from the effect or result. What once was estranged is brought together by Christ's Atonement and by this act of grace we are saved.

Chapter 16

Looking Back and Summing Up

The purpose of this book has been to show that the term 'Atonement' covers the entire work of the Sinless Christ leading up to and finding its goal in His triumphant, vicarious death on the cross and glorious resurrection. Hereby Christ enabled His Bride the Church to follow Him and share His eternal inheritance with Him. Whether we see the Atonement as the righting of man's wrongs, the deliverance from sin, the justifying of the ungodly or the imputation of Christ's righteousness to us, it is all one to us as all this was accomplished on Calvary for our sakes. Thus, the Bible tells us from Genesis to Revelation that believers are ransomed, redeemed, healed, restored and forgiven. They are made children of God and Christ's death propitiated the sentence of death raised against them by their own fault, thus expiating them from all sin. Christ's Atonement gained for all believers peace with the Father through Christ's oblational work of reconciliation. This is all summed up in the New Testament's favourite group of words centred around 'katalassoo'[1] which basically mean 'to make other' or 'to exchange.' Where one thing was, another thing takes its place. Where once sin reigned, Christ's atoning love has taken over. Through man's fallen nature sin excluded him from God's purpose for him. Christ removed

---

[1] The double 'o' pronounced as a long 'o'.

this sin and unrighteousness in man and exchanged it vicariously for His own sinlessness and righteousness through His atoning death. The Just dies for the unjust.

Preaching hope for sinners
At a bible study I led for some years in the local Reformed Church, I sought to emphasise this great exchange to the twenty or so who gathered weekly around the Word. One elderly lady stopped coming. I met her in the street some weeks afterwards and we conversed briefly. The lady was eager to tell me that my teaching was wrong. I asked her to explain what she meant. The lady told me that she felt she had been addressed by my words as a sinner though she strove to lead an upright life. This she believed would gain for her God's mercy when she died. She told me that she did her best and the Lord would do the rest.

I told this dear lady, who had often eaten at our house, that our best was not enough to cover our sins but only Christ's atoning shed blood could do that. I told her of the sinner's shame before God and the need for Christ's righteousness to replace it. She would not accept that all we have is our sin and shame so we have nothing with which to bargain before God. The good lady did not return to the bible study and happily no one else left. Two members visited me for further tuition, one the mother of our Church Superintendent who was well anchored in the Word. These believers were ashamed of their own sinful state but rejoiced in God's holiness and mercy for humanity in its separation from God. This Great Exchange has happily been believed by the saints throughout all time. On the one side we read in Habakkuk 1:13 concerning our Creator:

> Thou art of purer eyes than to behold evil, and canst not look on iniquity: wherefore lookest thou upon them that deal treacherously, and holdest thy tongue when the wicked devoureth the man that is more righteous than he?

On the other side we read in 1 John 2:1, 2:

> My little children, these things write I unto you, that ye sin not. And if any man sin, we have an advocate with the Father, Jesus Christ the righteous: And He is the propitiation for our sins.

It is spiritually healthy to know one is a sinner and to experience the Balm in Gilead given by the Great Physician as we read in the Gospel as preached by Jeremiah.[2] To be reconciled is to find peace where there was disruption. God, the Holy Other, reconciles us to Himself so that we become other than we were and we are made partakers of the Divine Nature.

If there had been no enmity of God against sin, there would have been no Atonement. Man would have remained lost. Then God would not have been a God of love who longed for a holy people like Himself. He knew a better way to elect a People of His choice. In the Great Tribunal of the Trinity regarding the elect, we know that Christ offered Himself to save His Bride, the Church. To quench that enmity Christ identified Himself fully with man except for his sin and offered Himself as a once and for all time sinless, vicarious and substitutionary sacrifice to reconcile His elect. Christ Himself is proof that God hates sin and punishes the sinner. Romans 5:9 tells us that we shall be saved from wrath, so there must be wrath on God's side from which we are to be saved. Furthermore, the preaching of the gospel is not only a preaching of salvation but also a preaching to show that God's wrath might be taken away just as man's wrath against God can be taken away. This is the at-one-ment of the gospel.

Fallen man's disposition can never be holy unless God's holiness subdues man's wrath against Him. The difference between God's wrath and that of man is that God's wrath is righteous but man's wrath is unrighteous. James points this out in Chapter 1:19, 20:

> Wherefore, my beloved brethren, let every man be swift to hear, slow to speak, slow to wrath: For the wrath of man worketh not the righteousness of God.

The question here is how is man enabled to be redeemed and justified by God so that he is right with God? There are two conflicting ideas about this.

---

[2] Jeremiah 8:22.

Reach out and grasp it

Many a modern preacher, even those who call themselves Calvinists tell us that reconciliation is there for the asking. There is a feast spread before us and all we need to do is to sit at God's table, reach out and grasp it.[3] There is nothing so simple, they argue. This method, which has become known as Easy-Believism, is most flattering to human nature but it is belief in a faulty gospel. We are told everything is within our reach. Everything is served on a plate. God's sovereignty is shown by His preparing the dish. Man's agency is shown in his eating of it. Thus, so-called moderate Calvinists such as Geoff Thomas and Iain Murray were teaching us, at least until a few years ago, that their 'good news' was that salvation is all of God and all of man.[4] God offers and man accepts.

This 'moderate Calvinism' all sounds wonderful but how truthful, or rather how treacherous, is it? We have just seen above that man is at enmity with God. If you have an enemy, you do not go to him and ask for a favour unless you wish to ruin him by it. If you have a real enemy, you are not even on speaking terms with him. You would never accept an invitation to eat at the same table. You would think he wanted to poison you. This is fallen man's attitude to God and he knows of no duties to believe otherwise even if he hears the gospel which he by nature hates. That fallen man has a known duty to exercise a faith he does not possess is one of the greatest humanistic heresies prevalent in modern so-called evangelism.

This attitude is not only confirmed by Scripture, it is portrayed in much more hopeless and concrete terms. Not only has the sinner nothing in common with God, he has lost all means of communication with Him. 2 Corinthians 4:3, 4 tells us:

> But if our gospel be hid, it is hid to them that are lost: In whom the god of this world hath blinded the minds of them which believe not, lest the light of the glorious gospel of Christ, who is the image of God, should shine unto them.

---

[3] See Fuller's *Works*, Vol. 11, p. 338.
[4] See Thomas' review of Iain Murray's *Spurgeon and Hyper-Calvinism* in the July, 1995 issue of the *Evangelical Times*.

In 1 Corinthians 2:14, we read:

> But the natural man receiveth not the things of the Spirit of God: for they are foolishness unto him: neither can he know them, because they are spiritually discerned.

How on earth then, can we be reconciled to God? The very question is futile as there are no means on earth whereby we can be reconciled to God. All motivations for reconciliation are outside of mankind. They are not of this world. They are fully independent of us. We need an atonement for our situation which can only come from God alone.

Man has no corresponding agency in the Atonement

Leon Morris in his fine book called *The Apostolic Preaching of the Cross* tells us, 'The New Testament view is that reconciliation was wrought on the cross before there was anything in man's heart to correspond.' Strange as it might appear to our logic, reconciliation was secured on Calvary one-sidedly in the Atonement. This is the difference between the empty gospel of the Arminians and the full gospel of the Scriptures. Arminians teach that Christ opened the way at Calvary for anyone to be reconciled, should they wish. Faith comes when the sinner grasps out for it. The Atonement placed all mankind in a reconcilable state but did not Atone for any man solely by its own virtue. Thus, the Atonement is only as efficacious as human reception makes it. Actually, this view is one of absolute scepticism for two reasons.

Man left alone has no will to be saved

First: We know from Scripture that man, left on his own, has neither the will, nor the ability to be reconciled to God. I mention both these aspects as modern Fullerites tell us that although man has not the will, he has the natural ability and could even have the will if he wanted to. Or as Arthur Kirkby sums up Fuller's gospel, 'man could if he would'. This is in stark contrast to Scripture which tells us that man has neither the will not the ability.[5] People dead in trespasses and sins have no spiritual life whatsoever. Salvation is not a matter of free-willing. Grasping out for salvation by a moral act of the fallen mind is a useless substitute for being given spiritual faith which can only come as a gift from God. A natural man is dead. A spiritual man is one made alive by God's gift of grace.

God demands no holy disposition from man before saving him
Second: Arminians teach that reconciliation is determined by the spiritual state of the believer through a fallen man's supposed holy disposition. Natural man has no spiritual state but what God gives him. For the Arminian a person can thus be a child of God today but a child of the devil tomorrow. I am quoting John Wesley verbatim. Thus, there is no such thing as a permanently reconciled person. Indeed, Wesley taught that if we do not become perfect in this life, there will be no eternal life to come as the reward of our perfection. This, to me, is like saying that there is no reconciliation leading to future hope for anyone at all as all have sinned and fallen short of the glory of God. As long as we are in this body of sin, we will not take on perfection until we stand before the throne of grace and receive an incorruptible body.

How then can we ever be Atoned for by God?
Here we may turn to Romans 5:6-11 for spiritual enlightenment. We read:

> For when we were yet without strength, in due time Christ died for the ungodly. For scarcely for a righteous man will one die: yet peradventure for a good man some would even dare to die. But God commendeth his love toward us, in that, while we were yet sinners, Christ died for us. Much more then, being now justified by his blood, we shall be saved from wrath through him. For if, when we were enemies, we were reconciled to God by the death of his Son, much more, being reconciled, we shall be saved by his life. And not only *so*, but we also joy in God through our

---

[5] I had this from Kirkby personally but he emphasises this in his PhD Dissertation *The Theology of Andrew Fuller and its Relationship to Calvinism*, p. 160.

Lord Jesus Christ, by whom we have now received the atonement.

Here it is obvious that justification was wrought out through the Atonement. We notice six things from this Bible teaching:
1. God loves His Elect as sinners; therefore, He is reconciled to us already. We need to be reconciled to Him.
2. Christ died to reconcile us to God whilst we were in an irreconcilable state from our side.
3. We were already reconciled to God whilst at enmity with God by the death of His Son.
4. Reconciliation in the plan of God is anchored in the Atonement, salvation in the life of Christ is anchored in us by Christ's indwelling nature. Christ in us our hope of glory!
5. We do not obtain the benefits of the Atonement by the choosing of them. We receive reconciliation by God's outworking of the Atonement for our sakes. The benefits are a free gift of grace and have nothing to do with our deserving or choosing.
6. The word translated 'atonement' in the Bible is the same word used for translating 'reconciliation.' Atonement is reconciliation and this has already taken place. These points must be further outlined below:

1. God loves us as sinners
We see this doctrine illustrated in Leviticus 8:14, 15:

And he brought the bullock for the sin offering: and Aaron and his sons laid their hands upon the head of the bullock for the sin offering. And he slew it; and Moses took the blood, and put it upon the horns of the altar round about with his finger, and purified the altar, and poured the blood at the bottom of the altar, and sanctified it, to make reconciliation upon it.

Our sin-forgiving God is also illustrated in 2 Chronicles 29:20-24:

Then Hezekiah the king rose early, and gathered the rulers of the city, and went up to the house of the LORD. And they brought seven bullocks, and seven rams, and seven lambs, and seven he goats, for a sin offering for the kingdom, and for the sanctuary, and for Judah. And he commanded the priests the sons of Aaron to offer them on the altar of the LORD. So they killed the bullocks, and the priests received the blood, and sprinkled it on the altar: likewise, when they had killed the rams, they sprinkled the blood upon the altar: they killed also the lambs, and they sprinkled the blood upon the altar. And they brought forth the he goats for the sin offering before the king and the congregation; and they laid their hands upon them: And the priests killed them, and they made reconciliation with their blood upon the altar, to make an atonement for all Israel: for the king commanded that the burnt offering and the sin offering should be made for all Israel.

The New Testament continues this truth in Romans 5:19:

For as by one man's disobedience many were made sinners, so by the obedience of one shall many be made righteous.

2. Christ died to reconcile us whilst we were in an irreconcilable state from our side

The Scriptures clearly state that we were dead in trespasses and sins. The soul that sinneth shall die. But our 'Moderate Calvinists', 'Fullerites' and 'Arminians' demand a new interpretation and tell us that we are taking Scripture too literally. They tell us that Scripture is only there to give us broad principles of conduct which we have received as laws of behaviour and moral action in our search for personal happiness. These people quote Fuller correctly as saying that all men, even in their fallen state, have a natural desire to find happiness in God and the preaching of the gospel is to awake this natural desire which all men possess.[6] Thus when the gospel comes, it does not come to satisfy spiritual longings or an awareness of sin and need of salvation but to satisfy the human search for happiness. Once this happiness is obtained, they say, the soul will love God and begin to grow spiritually.

---

[6] *Gospel Worthy of All Acceptation*, Vol. II, p. 344.

Thus, it is an essential feature in the gospel preacher that he tells people they can open their hearts to God otherwise they believe no evangelism is possible. What kills evangelism, they say, is the false doctrine that man is by nature dead to the gospel and is not aware of his moral duty to accept the gospel. In his *The Gospel Worthy of All Acceptation*, Fuller clearly teaches:

Or if the inability of sinners to believe in Christ were of the same nature as that of a dead body in a grave to rise up and walk, it were absurd to suppose that they would on this account fall under the Divine censure. No man is reproved for not doing that which is naturally impossible; but sinners are reproved for not believing, and given to understand that it is solely owing to their criminal ignorance, pride, dishonesty of heart, and aversion from God.[7]

Notable here is Fuller's de-theologisation of sin which he sees as 'criminal ignorance'. Calvin looked on such teaching as Platonism.[8] All these symptoms, Fuller reasons, do not point to physical and spiritual death, nor even moral inability, but merely an 'unwillingness to believe'. This is his mock fall. The *real* fall, according to Fuller, comes when Christ is rejected on hearing the gospel because man then refuses to use his inherent capabilities to believe in Christ savingly.

Fullerites do sometimes stop and think that if man is not truly fallen in all respects, then salvation cannot be all of grace and from God in all respects. However, instead of concluding that Fuller must be wrong they come to the weird but logical conclusion, for them, that salvation is a co-production of man's work with God. God provides the means and human agency the application of those means. God invites all to a feast and those who take the raisins of salvation out of the cake of invitation are saved.

The Scriptural view of man in his sin and in his salvation is quite different. We read in Ephesians 2:1-3:

---

[7] *Works*, Vol. II, p. 355.
[8] *Institutes I.* 242, Eerdmans' two volume edition.

And you hath he quickened, who were dead in trespasses and sins; Wherein in time past ye walked according to the course of this world, according to the prince of the power of the air, the spirit that now worketh in the children of disobedience: Among whom also we all had our conversation in times past in the lusts of our flesh, fulfilling the desires of the flesh and of the mind; and were by nature the children of wrath, even as others.

There is no talk of a man being an agent in his own salvation here.

We read also in Colossians 2:13, 14:

And you, being dead in your sins and the uncircumcision of your flesh, hath he quickened together with him, having forgiven you all trespasses; Blotting out the handwriting of ordinances that was against us, which was contrary to us, and took it out of the way, nailing it to his cross.

3. We were already reconciled to God whilst at enmity with God by the death of His Son

Nothing speaks more against the fond idea that we can get ourselves reconciled than the Biblical fact that all those to be reconciled are already reconciled. They have their names in the Lamb's Book of Life. The work of reconciliation in the Bible is a work which is already done, already finished before ever the gospel was preached. One of the many purposes of this gospel is to announce this fact. A gospel depending on man's agency to accomplish it would merely be man's own gospel. But fallen man cannot atone for his own sin. When we bring the gospel to people to whom God has sent us as preacher, pastor, personal friend or whatever, to bring them the good news, He is sending us to those for whose reconciliation He has already provided. This he is clearly illustrated by 2 Corinthians 5:18-20:

And all things are of God, who hath reconciled us to himself by Jesus Christ, and hath given to us the ministry of reconciliation; To wit, that God was in Christ, reconciling the world unto himself, not imputing their trespasses unto them; and hath committed unto us the word of reconciliation. Now then we are ambassadors for Christ, as though God did beseech you by us: we pray you in Christ's stead, be ye reconciled to God.

The Scriptures tell us that there are two essential parts to the Covenant of Grace outlined in the Bible which make up the one great Covenant of Salvation. The one, the law part, is for natural man outlining his natural duties to obey God's standards. These are eternal standards which spell out God's eternal, never-changing righteousness. The other is with spiritual man who is placed under forgiveness and grace. This entire covenant was with one Man alone as the only One worthy of keeping it. It was solely with Christ and all those who seek and find their righteousness in Him. When in the Council of God, it was debated how natural man was to be made spiritual, we read that Christ offered Himself to redeem his elect by doing all that they ought to do as natural men and giving them all they need as spiritual men. The Old Testament pointed to this fact in the sacrificial offerings which pointed to Christ's sacrifice to come. Here we might compare Psalm 40:7 with Hebrews 10:3-18, the latter explaining these pointers to Christ as:

But in those sacrifices there is a remembrance again made of sins every year. For it is not possible that the blood of bulls and of goats should take away sins. Wherefore when he cometh into the world, he saith, Sacrifice and offering thou wouldest not, but a body hast thou prepared me: In burnt offerings and sacrifices for sin thou hast had no pleasure.

Then said I, Lo, I come (in the volume of the book it is written of me,) to do thy will, O God. Above when he said, Sacrifice and offering and burnt offerings and offering for sin thou wouldest not, neither hadst pleasure therein; which are offered by the law; Then said he, Lo, I come to do thy will, O God. He taketh away the first, that he may establish the second. By the which will we are sanctified through the offering of the body of Jesus Christ once for all. And every priest standeth daily ministering and offering oftentimes the same sacrifices, which can never take away sins: But this man, after he had offered one sacrifice for sins for ever, sat down on the right hand of God; From henceforth expecting till his enemies be made his footstool. For by one offering he hath perfected for ever them that are sanctified. Whereof the Holy Ghost also is a witness to us: for after that he had said before, This is the covenant that I will make with them after those days, saith the Lord, I will put my laws into their hearts, and in their minds will I write them; And their sins and iniquities will I remember no more. Now where remission of these is, there is no more offering for sin.

This is why the author to the Hebrews (12:24) calls Jesus the *Mediator of a New Covenant.* A covenant in which Christ does all. The Old Testament word for Covenant refers to a bilateral enactment between the Father and the Son. As far as man is concerned it is not a 'You do this and I will do that' agreement with man because no man can keep to such terms. It refers to a unilateral enactment in which Christ says to man, 'You cannot do this so I will do it for you'. This Covenant, Testimony or Will however, only comes into effect when the testator dies. It is the death of Christ which opens covenant blessings for us as Christ has provided the means for the fulfilling of the Covenant of Grace.

4. Reconciliation is the entering of Christ's life in us and His faith in us
This truth is clearly taught in Romans 5:6-11where we read:

> For when we were yet without strength, in due time Christ died for the ungodly. For scarcely for a righteous man will one die: yet peradventure for a good man some would even dare to die. But God commendeth his love toward us, in that, while we were yet sinners, Christ died for us. Much more then, being now justified by his blood, we shall be saved from wrath through him. For if, when we were enemies, we were reconciled to God by the death of his Son, much more, being reconciled, we shall be saved by his life. And not only so, but we also joy in God through our Lord Jesus Christ, by whom we have received the atonement.

It is especially important to know that not only did Christ reconcile His Bride to God but His vicarious work went so far as to give us His very own atoning faith which was the impetus behind the Incarnation in the first place. This wonderful truth is emphasized three times in the one verse of Galatians 2:16-21:

Knowing that a man is not justified by the works of the law, but by the faith of Jesus Christ, even we have believed in Jesus Christ, that we might be justified by the faith of Christ, and not by the works of the law: for by the works of the law shall no flesh be justified. But if, while we seek to be justified by Christ, we ourselves also are found sinners, is therefore Christ the minister of sin? God forbid. For if I build again the things which I destroyed, I make myself a transgressor. For I through the law am dead to the law, that I might live unto God. I am crucified with Christ: nevertheless I live; yet not I, but Christ liveth in me: and the life which I now live in the flesh I live by the faith of the Son of God, who loved me, and gave himself for me. I do not frustrate the grace of God: for if righteousness come by the law, then Christ is dead in vain.

Christ's faith was in the fact that through all His sufferings, He would conquer and this faith He has given to all those who have been drawn to Him. So we may bask in that great Biblical blessing pronounced over us in Hebrews 13:20, 21:

Now the God of peace, that brought again from the dead our Lord Jesus, that great shepherd of the sheep, through the blood of the everlasting covenant, Make you perfect in every good work to do his will, working in you that which is well pleasing in his sight, through Jesus Christ; to whom be glory for ever and ever. Amen.

5. We do not obtain the benefits of the Atonement by the choosing of them
I love to read Ephesians Chapter Two. Verses 1 to 9 read:

And you have he quickened, who were dead in trespasses and
sins; Wherein in times past ye walked according to the course of
this world, according to the prince of the power of the air, the
spirit that now worketh in the children of disobedience: Among
whom also we all had our conversation in times past in the lusts
of our flesh, fulfilling the desires of the flesh and of the mind;
and were by nature the children of wrath, even as others. But
God, who is rich in mercy, for his great love wherewith he loved
us, even when we were dead in sins, hath quickened us together
with Christ, (by grace ye are saved;) and hath raised us up
together, and made us sit together in heavenly places in Christ
Jesus: That in the ages to come he might show the exceeding
riches of his grace in his kindness towards us through Christ
Jesus. For by grace are ye saved through faith; and that not of
yourselves: it is the gift of God: Not of works, lest any man
should boast.

I take the term 'quicken' here to refer to life given to spiritually dead
men not life appropriated by spiritually dead men. This life was given
those who were beguiled by the devil to live in disobedience to God.
Yet God, in His boundless mercy gives them life and that in eternal
abundance. Here we see that the mind of unsaved man belongs to his
nature of flesh and thus cannot be activated spiritually from its carnal
embodiment until God works on such a sinner from the outside by
undeserved mercy and from the inside by the work of the Holy Spirit.
All in Adam must die unless they are made alive in the Lord Jesus
Christ.

This means that the Atonement was purchased for us by Christ alone
and it is impossible for man to atone for himself through any religious
merit-earning duties. Christ makes it clear that such attempts only show
that we are still unprofitable servants should we have the cheek to stand
before our Lord and say, 'We have done that which was our duty to
do.'[9] No duty ever saved anyone except those self-given duties
exercised by Christ on the Cross. Sinners need a new life in Christ
before they can perform religious duties such as loving the Lord with

---

[9] Luke 17:10 ff.

all their hearts. The results of salvation from God's side are not the cause of salvation affected by man.

James Hervey, as a very young man, was much taken up with his old righteousness. He had, however, a very good friend by the name of George Whitfield who had preached a rousing sermon against reliance on one's own filthy rags of righteousness. This sermon reached the heart of Hervey and he realised his own wretchedness and the fact Christ had chosen him to be an ambassador for Christ and preach Christ's righteousness alone in salvation. He confessed to his Arminian friends that he had now found the righteousness of Another which really worked in salvation. He was very quick to write to Whitfield explaining what a change Christ's righteousness had made in him through his sermon and wrote:

I now desire to work in my blessed Master's service, not *for*, but *from* salvation. I believe that Jesus Christ, the incarnate God, is my Saviour; that he has done all which I was bound to perform; and suffered all I was condemned to sustain; and so has procured a full, final and everlasting salvation for a poor damnable sinner. I would now fain *serve* him who has *saved* me. I would glorify Him before *men*, who has justified me before *God*. I would study to please him in holiness and righteousness all the days of my life. I seek this blessing, not as a condition but as a part – a choice and inestimable part – of that complete salvation, which Jesus has purchased for me.[10]

From then on, Hervey preached to the thousands and very soon became known as 'The Preacher of Righteousness'. Yet modern Fullerites rank Hervey with the Antinomians. Is this because their adherence to Natural Law provides a loop-hole to let one's own righteousness in?

---

[10] *Evangelical Magazine*, 1794, p. 503.

6. The word translated 'atonement' in the Bible is the same word used for translating 'reconciliation'

I was converted in Sweden in the winter of 1956 and grew very fond of the Swedish Bible, especially the edition printed by the Evang. Fosterlands-Stiftelsen which added the Old Testament translation of 1903 to the New Testament translation of 1883 to make a complete version. I had the privilege of sitting under Professors Helmer Ringren (Hebrew and Aramaic) and Harald Riesenfeld (Greek), faithful men of God at Uppsala, who were working on a revision of the older work which kept as close to the originals as linguistically possible. In this 1905 version the word 'Atonement' in Romans 5:11, is rendered 'försoningen' in the Swedish version. When we look at 2 Corinthians 5:18, 19 which refers twice to Christ's work of reconciliation in the English text, the same term 'försoning' is used in Swedish as in Romans 5:11. The English text, however, refers in Romans 5 to an Atonement and in 2 Corinthians 5 to reconciliation. Where the Swedes have a theology built on one Greek word to express it, the English languages uses the synonyms at hand in that language for reasons of style and variety. Swedish has also a number of synonyms at her disposal but translates almost everything referring to the Atonement by one term only. Thus, we do not have the theological quarrels in Swedish and other languages which have opted for the same solution as the Swedish Bible translators as are sadly present in English. Most of the modern theological problems in the English-speaking world are caused by the English language and not by the Greek and Hebrew as we have seen in the case of Arthur Pink.

The Atonement was in the fulness of time

Atonement for the Christian is not a thing of the future to which we strive, it is a thing of the 'the fulness of time' for all time, past, present and future.[11] Thus, if we argue as the Arminians and Fullerites, we are leaving Christ and his ransoming, redeeming, propitiating and reconciling death out of our plan of salvation. This is very important for us to grasp, otherwise we will be led astray by modern teaching that sees reconciliation as either a work of man or as a second Atonement.

---

[11] Galatians 4:4.

Experimental salvation is not separating the work of the Father, Son and Holy Spirit in the atonement but believing in the covenant work of the Trinity in providing a ransom for our sins. It is faith in what Christ has done for us and is doing in us. This is the work of the Spirit, to reveal Christ to our hearts as our Saviour. Seeing reconciliation as the delayed action of the cross in our lives wrought out by our wilful participation '*in memoriam*', as it were, of what was there provided but not secured is not reconciliation in any way at all.

My indebtedness in the Lord to James Hervey

During the early 1990s, a number of friends approached me requesting a book from my pen outlining my theology. I said this was not necessary as James Hervey had already written some nine volumes outlining his theology which was also mine. I then promised that I would write a book about the life and works of James Hervey instead. This was graciously published by my dear friend and brother Peter Meney of Go Publications in 1997 under the title *James Hervey: Preacher of Righteousness*. For, me, Hervey stands almost alone as a great expounder of the Word of God yet one who felt the strongest of calls to preach the whole gospel to the whole man as the Spirit leads. Then the Holy Spirit led Hervey constantly into places and to people hitherto shut out from the pure gospel of Covenant Grace. It is true that Hervey wrote mainly for the learned and much of his work presents tough eggs to crack for those not up to his spiritual and intellectual standard. His aim, however, was to fit out the educated Christians of his day so that they could devote their time and talents to the spiritual education of all ranks of society. So, after expounding his theology to those whom he believed would pass on the good news, he ended with the rousing admonition to them to wake up, stand up and go into the world and preach the gospel, writing:

> Most of all, ye ministers of the sanctuary, heralds commissioned from above; lift everyone his voice like a trumpet, and loudly proclaim the Redeemer. Get ye up, ye ambassadors of peace, get ye up into the high mountains; and spread far and wide the honours of the Lamb 'that was slain, but is alive for

evermore.' Teach every sacred roof to resound with his fame, and every human heart to glow with his love. Declare as far as the force of words will go, declare the inexhaustible fulness of that great Atonement, whose merits are commensurate with the glories of the Divinity. Tell the sinful wretch, what pity yearns in Immanuel's bowels; what blood he has spilt, what agonies he has endured, what wonders he has wrought, for the salvation of his enemies. Invite the indigent to become rich; entreat the guilty to accept of pardon; because, with the crucified Jesus is plenteous redemption, and all-sufficiency to save.

While you, placed in conspicuous stations, pour the joyful sound; may I, as I steal through the vale of human life, catch the pleasing accents! For *me*, the Author of all blessings became a curse: for *me* his bones were dislocated, and his flesh was torn: He hung, with streaming veins, and an agonizing soul, on the cross for *me*. O! may I, in my little sphere, and amidst the scanty circle of my acquaintance, at least whisper these glad transporting tidings, whisper them from my own Heart, that they may surely reach, and sweetly penetrate theirs.

May we not turn a deaf ear to such admonitions
Let us not turn a deaf ear to Hervey's gospel mission according to the Scriptures and may we teach and preach the same gospel as the Lord gives us strength and directs our ways. We who have been reconciled to God by Jesus Christ have also been given a ministry of reconciliation by God. We do not perform this ministry because of any desires of works righteousness. As Hervey made it clear to Wesley, we do not need such a pseudo-righteousness as we have the perfect righteousness of Another, Jesus Christ which is all that we need and all that those who hear our witness need. However, it is a great comfort to know through the parable of the lost sheep[12] that when a soul is led to Christ, even the angels in Heaven rejoice. So, when fruit for our labours come, let us rejoice with the angels!

---

[12] Luke 15:1-7

Appendix I

A letter to the English Churchman defending the term 'atonement' as being descriptive of Christ's full work on the cross.

Sir,
The News & Comment article on the atonement (No. 7686) needs etymological and theological correction. The assertions that 'at-one-ment' is a breaking up of 'atonement'; is only '*a* result of atonement' (that is, not atonement itself); and this is merely a 'marvellous coincidence'; are false.

The word 'atonement' was intentionally coined from the three particles 'at', 'one' and 'ment'. Thus the term 'atonement' is meaningless if made to stand outside of its individual parts and semantic content. The word was a Reformation neologism, used to translate the Hebrew and the Greek, there being no English word of exact equivalence at the time for the At-one-ment.

William Tyndale probably coined the word. In his *A Pathway into the Holy Scriptures*, he speaks of sinners through the work of Christ being, 'loosed, justified, restored to life and saved, brought to liberty and reconciled unto the favour of God, and set *at one* with him again.' Fellow-martyr Philpot uses the term in his translation of Caelius Secundus Curio's *Defence of Christ's Church* where the author is arguing that there cannot be any unity between a false and true church. 'What concord', he says, 'either what atonement (as very well speaketh Paul), is there betwixt light and darkness, betwixt Christ and Belial, betwixt the faithful and unfaithful?' Curione is saying that one cannot reconcile light with darkness. This meaning is echoed in the Homily for Good Friday which reads, 'Without payment God the Father would never be *at one* with us'. An early A.V. example of this usage is Acts 5:26: 'And the next day he showed himself unto them as they strove, and would have set them *at one* again, saying, Sirs, ye are brethren; why do ye wrong one to another?' This is also the meaning behind John 17:21-23. Tyndale and the early Reformers knew that to be reconciled to God and to be atoned (made at one) were the same thing. See Daniel 9:24, where Christ's work is described as 'to finish the transgression, and to make an end of sin, and to make reconciliation for iniquity and to bring in everlasting righteousness.'

One does not limit the meaning of 'atonement' by reading 'at-one-ment' into the term. Understanding where the word comes from shows that the limitations are on the side of critics who view 'at-one-ment' as separate from justification, forgiveness of sins, redemption, adoption and sanctification. This was foreign to our Reformers' faith. They saw Christ's at-one-ment as bringing into being all that Christ has wrought out in salvation. Thus to be for penal substitution is also to be for at-one-ment.

Appendix II

The Banner of Truth Trust alters Bunyan's gospel.
A letter to the English Churchman

Sir:

Bunyan's *Come and Welcome to Jesus Christ* based on John 6:37 is beset with the finest jewels of Christian preaching, infusing hope and joy into the hearts of sorrowing sinners. The BOT's 1991 reprint of Bunyan's original version was a most welcome evangelistic venture as Bunyan's elegant, pithy language speaks as clearly today as it did in the 17th century.

So why has the BOT now published a new, badly edited and altered version with an introduction and blurb containing irrelevant and misleading New Divinity propaganda? Paul Austen (Nr. 7652) rightly challenges the suitability of a publisher's preface which presents Andrew Fuller as freeing the churches from the grip of Gill's alleged Hyper-Calvinism, thus misusing Bunyan to promote Fullerism. In *Come and Welcome*, Bunyan reveals the fallacy of Fullerism regarding atonement, reconciliation, imputed righteousness, law, gospel, justification and eternal security.

The Banner of Truth's 'counterfeit Bunyan' is said to practise 'the free offer of salvation to sinners without distinction' but the real Bunyan specifically denies this, arguing that 'no rational man in the world will conclude' that John 6 refers to all and not some. Bunyan explains that a conditional call would entail God saying 'I will if you will' but here

God is saying 'I will and you shall'. Thus Bunyan stresses the discriminating work of the gospel, writing, 'The gift intended in the text must be restrained to some, to a gift that is given by way of speciality by the Father to the Son'. He teaches that all those who God turns to himself are all those whom He has given to his Son and for whom He died. Bunyan explains that when the call to the sheep comes, they are made sensible and it is these 'coming sinners', drawn by God who will be received. Christ gives these sensible sinners 'a glimpse of Himself' and they 'receive a kiss of the sweet lips of Jesus Christ' and feel 'the very warmth of His wings overshadowing' their souls.

Besides perverting Bunyan's theology, the publishers' arbitrary alterations to the sweet music of Bunyan's language, and his AV text are also baffling. Why, for instance, is 'cometh' accepted but 'saith' altered to 'says'? Why is 'design' dumbed down to 'show'? To alter Bunyan's language and teaching in this amateur way is inexcusable and deceptive. *Come and Welcome to Jesus Christ* is Christian literature at its best and it can happily be obtained in its original form elsewhere.

Appendix III

A letter to the Foundation Journal concerning their mass-distribution of Iain Murray's Spurgeon v. Hyper-Calvinism

Dear Brethren,

I waited until I received a copy of Murray's book Spurgeon versus Hyper-Calvinism before replying to your strictures. Up to now, I had only the chapter on Gill, published in the Banner magazine to go on. Usually Banner books arrive after five days but I had to wait five weeks this time to receive the ordered books.

What a terrible book S. v. H-C is! I wish for Murray's sake that he had never written it. It is far, far below the standard of most of his other works especially his Puritan Hope. However, Murray, as usually, shoots over the mark when employed in controversy. The cheek of his sub-title The Battle for Gospel Preaching! This is obviously written in the face of strong criticism that the Banner is watering down the gospel so that it is hardly discernible from Finneyism. Murray has, indeed, made all the major mistakes a historian could possibly make. He has back-projected a modern controversy with modern terminology into the past and pretended it was there all along. This is the method of many a historical novel writer but ought to be limited to that guild. Although Murray says there is no sign of Hyper-Calvinism reviving, he yet does his very best to awaken the sleeping dog. It cannot be thought an exaggeration to say that he is provoking Hyper-Calvinism, whatever it is, and wherever it is, to show its ugly face. Murray throws terms into the arena without defining them and pastes labels on people without either saying what the title entails or why the person ought to have it. He suggests that Fullerism is an antidote for Hyper-Calvinism but neither adequately defines the one nor the other. What Murray says about Fullerism shows even more fantasy than what he says about Hyper-Calvinism. To argue that Spurgeon thought Fuller a man of God, in no way suggests that he thought Gill was no such being. Gill had the benefit of being a man of God without going into Fuller's Latitudinarian and New Divinity extremes. Murray says that Spurgeon stopped hanging Hyper-Calvinist labels on people but Murray is loath to follow Spurgeon's excellent advice. Indeed, Murray is misusing a bulldozer (Spurgeon) to crush a hypothetical gnat (Hyper-Calvinism) whereas the bull-dozer in question (Spurgeon) very rarely used his powers for such a dubious enterprise. Where he has allegedly done, according to Murray, this is more in Murray's imaginative reconstructions than in fact. Note, for instance, Spurgeon's supposed fourfold appeal to Scripture against modern theoretical Hyper-Calvinism. Murray tells us with whom Spurgeon would agree or disagree, giving us his own word for it which he believes no one ought to doubt. Primary evidence is, however, not forthcoming. On the contrary, Murray backs up what he says about Spurgeon merely by quoting Toon as a most dubious authority, and rarely allows Spurgeon to have a say in the matter. When Spurgeon is quoted, apart from in one quote where numerous dots between words confuse the issue, it is not difficult at all to find parallels in Gill and Huntington who are supposed to be modern Hypers. Huntington, as always, is completely misrepresented by Murray and made to say what he categorically denies. Huntington was certainly less a Hyper in his view of the law than Murray himself as I have informed him with evidence from both the men's writings.

Throughout the book, Murray never proves his case because he never states it clearly. He has some fossil bone to pick but we must have flesh on identifiable bones to know what animal they belong to. It is difficult to agree or disagree with Murray in his theological testimony as agreement stands or falls on definitions used. When, for instance, Murray speaks of a 'warrant' in relation to salvation, he argues that this means a guarantee of salvation ought to go out to all unconditionally as a gospel call. Spurgeon, however, contradicts Murray here as he clearly says in Murray's quote that the warrant of faith is to the truly penitent, just like Gill and Huntington do. I cannot possibly imagine any of Murray's supposed Hypers quarrelling with Spurgeon here. The use of a nebulous word like 'warrant', a favourite of Murray's, cannot but be confusing. As a noun it can mean anything from a necessity to a safeguard or guarantee and as a verb means to put in a position of safety or security. Murray seems to now use the one meaning and now the other. The gospel obviously offers security in Christ but, in the wisdom and mercy of God, only to those for whom Christ is made a security through His ransoming and redeeming salvation.

The way Murray argues to build up his own argument is quite unfair. He is only able to find one contemporary of Spurgeon's who comes anywhere near his idea of a Hyper-Calvinist. This was a man who stood almost alone in his age and in history. Yet Murray misuses his own trump card. He builds up an exaggerated case against Wells,[1] and therefore against Hyper-Calvinism, which he later admits was one-sided and artificial. As Murray's attempted argument progresses we find that even Wells was not the man Murray first made him out to be. It seems odd to me that Murray acknowledges how Wells drew the crowds and I know from my own reading that many conversions took place, but Murray seems to argue that this was in spite of his gospel preaching!

Murray is equally confusing and careless with most of his quotes. He refers to John Rippon as disagreeing with Gill in his Brief Memoir but this is a sheer misrepresentation. Rippon is not emphasising where he personally differs from Gill, who is not even named in the context, but that the two sides on the Modern Question are united in the essentials of the gospel. Where Gill is named, as 'our author', it is where Rippon agrees with him (p. 46). Rippon is emphasising agreements not disagreements between the two sides. Why then seek to drive a wedge in where there is no gap? Murray does not fellowship with his hypothetical Hyper-Calvinists on the essentials of the gospel and does

---

[1] James Wells (1803-1872) Pastor of Surrey Tabernacle, Southwark, London

not agree with Gill, as Rippon did. He has no business to bend Rippon out of his position of one who can view both sides generously and with understanding. Murray has not Rippon's gift, here. Notice, too, how Murray misuses Kenneth Dix (p. 108). What Dix sees as objective, Murray depicts as if Dix were sorry about the fact. Dix's view of the Modern Question differs radically from Murray's. Dix points out how co-operative and brotherly both sides of the Modern Question were with each other – Murray will have war! Dix shows how 'Historically, SBs have consistently maintained that "saving faith is not a legal duty imposed on unregenerate men".' (p. 15, SBHSB, No. 13). Murray maintains the very opposite. Note, too, how Dix affirms that the roots of the SBs are in the PBs.[2] Since 1976, the SBHS has moved radically from this position. I believe you will know why. (Happily, the bulk of the SB's though now less numerous as in the seventies and even eighties, are moving back as I have found at first-hand experience).

Murray shows such a lack of knowledge of Baptist history that it is quite painful to read what he says. He obviously does not know the 17th century Particular Baptist creeds. See my criticism of this point in my Focus article enclosed last. To make the Gospel Standard such fierce opponents of Spurgeon is quite unfair. One must understand here, however, that the name Gospel Standard is being used as an umbrella term by Murray and Erroll Hulse for those whose Calvinism differs from their new Grotian interpretation of it. Erroll Hulse called me a Gospel Standard man at a time when I had no idea who they were. I wrote to him several times, asking him to justify his continued accusation but he chose to snub me. When I found out who the GS were, I wrote to them concerning their Declaration of Faith, suggesting that Scriptural evidence was lacking on the 'added' points and received very gracious, brotherly replies. I am still not a Gospel Standard man but I know they are not the demons Murray, Erroll and Co. made and make them. I am now corresponding with a number of their pastors and people and find they know far more about both law and grace than most Christians. I am thankful to Erroll for forcing me to compare views with them. Through them, I have been introduced to those fine men of God that Murray says were used for the gospel's sake in spite of their system.

---

[2] SB-Strict Baptist, PB-Particular Baptist, SBHS-Strict Baptist Historical Society, SBHSB-Strict Baptist Historical Society Bulletin.

What a silly comment! Murray's accusations concerning the GS and their declaration is greatly at fault. He seems to believe that what he calls the 1689 Confession contained what the 1878 GS Declaration denied. This is not the case. The GS action was to show clearly that pro-duty-faith additions made to the old Baptist confession by succeeding liberals were not part of the traditional Particular Baptist faith. This is confirmed by SB older publications (see Dix again) besides PB publications. This is why the GS cannot accept Andrew Fuller as a Particular Baptist. Though not a Particular Baptist denomination-wise, I agree with their concern but I can live with Fullerites providing they do not insist on my substituting their cut-down gospel for the real thing. Actually, I find most modern Fullerites are orthodox but they call themselves such because Murray and Erroll have re-coined the word Fullerite, to mean orthodox. These two now see Gill and Co. as 'Hyper-Orthodox'. I have recently received two letters from a convinced Fullerite who had never read Fuller. The first letter was to tell me off for being critical of Fullerism. I advised the gentleman to read Fuller's major works. In his second letter the brother thanked me for opening his eyes as he found Fuller a wolf in sheep's clothing.

Actually, I find myself clearly agreeing with Murray only on one point as it is difficult to get beyond his smoke-screens to his faith. This is on the matter of open communion, which has really nothing to do with the subject matter of the book and there were those for and against this matter on all sides, in all denominations. I am used to being frank with my brethren and do confess that it is the question of church government and the ordinances which deny me full fellowship with many Particular Baptist churches who seem, to me, to be very popish in these things and practise what goes clean against their sound theology. I certainly, however, find that the main 18th century Baptist Creeds which I have referred to and commented on in my Gill biography are more in tune with Christian faith and practice than with the Westminster Confession, wonderfully good as it is. My own favourites remains the 39 Articles and the 1729 Particular Baptist Declaration, however. Contrary to what Murray says, Rippon used the latter until well into the 19th century.

I need not dwell on Chapter 8 of Iain Murray's book as I have already recorded my views. Murray needs to do his homework on the relationship between Hussey, Skepp and Gill. I think he is in for some surprises. Of course, nearly everything Murray says in this chapter has little foundation in historical fact and is prejudice run loose. I would like to challenge him on almost every line. Murray's army continually quotes Hussey as the founder of Hyper-Calvinism, forgetting that he came to his 'none offer' position quite late in life after he had spent years of arguing with other people who held to the doctrines he later assumed. I cannot help feeling that Hussey is being set up as an Aunt Sally, merely because he is an easy target for the coco-nut throwers. It is odd that Murray leaves out Richard Davis in this connection. Davis is the stumbling block of all Bannerites. A High Calvinist with an enormous evangelistic outreach. I suppose Murray will put Davis down to 'Revivalism' and not 'Revival'. (I am not referring to Samuel Davis).

Now to the promised subject of using quotes from Spurgeon (Chapter 11) as a weapon against hypothetical Antinomianism. By way of introduction, I would like to suggest the obvious, namely that a man will say one thing and mean one thing but a second person will understand that one thing in another way. A third ear or eye is tuned differently and will receive a different impression. On reading Spurgeon, I have been tempted to think of him now as a 'high' Calvinist and now as a free-willer, until I realised that the latter instances were very few and spoken in very special circumstances and I must accept Spurgeon's whole testimony, not force it to represent now one, now another point of view. It is most important in understanding Spurgeon to find the Sitz-im-Leben not only of his text under scrutiny but also of the circumstances under which he expounded it. We must also bear in mind, as Spurgeon so graciously admitted, that we fallen humans are notoriously inconsistent in our thoughts, words and deeds. This is also very much true of John Gill, who is flanked against Spurgeon so often by Banner men these days. It is rather sickening, for instance, to find the best of Spurgeon so often compared with what many think the worst of Gill in order to score a point against Gill. Spurgeon would have given such critics a severe dressing down as we know from his history. Personally, I find no man as consistent as Gill in theology, though, in my opinion, he is inconsistent at times in his work on the covenants, the ordinances, church government and eschatology. This may reflect negatively on me but I presume I am inconsistent in certain matters, too. You will remember that although Gill is depicted nowadays as a Hyper of Hypers, he was accused of Antinomianism by contemporaries. This is because of his great fervency in preaching and his obvious evangelical approach and emphasis on combining faith with duties. John Rippon gave such critics of Gill a good telling off! Murray's criticism of Rippon for being too moderate in his evaluation of Gill's life and ministry is quite unbalanced.

I believe you will agree with me that Spurgeon invariably speaks of Gill with great respect and even awe. Murray finds Spurgeon here 'too generous'. Spurgeon exercises the usual fond criticism against Gill that a pupil makes against his favourite teacher but who will take such banter amiss? Where his mild criticism comes, it is in Gill's sermon construction and academic work. We know that Spurgeon ordered Gill's books for the education of his own children, affirming that they had been the best of the best for him. He even affirms that his doctrines are those of Gill and of Christ and we wonder why Christ is put last! When, therefore, men who should know better, make Spurgeon Gill's most prominent and sometimes fiercest critic, we are suspicious. Especially when words are forced into Spurgeon's mouth against Gill which the Prince of Preachers never uttered and evidence which Spurgeon used for other matters is picked up and used as if Spurgeon were fighting Gill. This is the situation in Murray's latest extravagances against Gill in which this man, who has blessed many, has suddenly become most glaringly inconsistent with himself. I believe in such a case as this, we will be forgiven for protesting loudly.

Now let us turn to the passage taken from Spurgeon's exposition of 1 Timothy 2:3, 4 which Brother Reisinger, following Murray uses. It is obvious that this passage is chosen to illustrate Spurgeon's polemics against the modern Hyper-Calvinist controversy of which he was fully unaware. As an illustration of this unawareness, we may take the example of Robert Hawker. This great preacher of righteousness was even thought to be an Antinomian in his day by Arminians and even a few professing Calvinists. John Kitto's first theological essay in the days of his youth was to 'prove' that Hawker was an Antinomian. Yet, read Spurgeon on Hawker. He finds him all sweetness and recommends

255

him warmly. The only criticism Spurgeon has of Hawker is that he sometimes finds Christ in the Bible where others would not see Him. Would to God that this were my only 'fault'! Note, too, Spurgeon's comments on the man he called the 'prince of divines', John Owen. Today I received an American magazine in which a Brother Passerello (unknown to me) points out the now obvious. The Banner of Truth has discarded Owen's theology. He suggests, which is equally plain, that they have rejected Witsius. I would also add Louis Berkhof.

It is very dubious whether Spurgeon is attacking any form of Hyper-Calvinism at all as his criticisms are directed against then commonly held opinions expounded by those who had nothing to do with Hyper-Calvinism. I spent some 12 years as a pupil in a Methodist Sunday School and two years as a teacher there. I studied theology at a most 'moderate' Bible College before further studies at Hull, Uppsala, Hamburg, Essen, Duisburg and Marburg. I never came across a single $17^{th}-18^{th}$ century Hyper-Calvinist commentary but I did come across a number of non-Calvinist and 'mild' or 'moderate' Calvinist commentators who took the very side with which Spurgeon seems to be disagreeing. Those who disagree with Spurgeon's exegesis of 1 Timothy 2:3, 4, 'Who will have all men to be saved' do so mainly because they believe that the covenant of works is binding on Christians even in post New Testament times without seeing it as part of the Covenant of Grace and the gospel they see as a mere legal matter (following their 'moral law'). Furthermore, Paul in the entire book is certainly thinking of God's world rule, the rule of the Church as also how Christian families are to be governed here and not giving a general call in preaching. This is also continued in the second epistle. (Here we note, too, that those who helped change the theology of the Banner of Truth in former years such as Tom Wells, now reject Paul's dealings with Timothy as being 'Jewish' and thus not 'Christian').

Furthermore the problems Spurgeon discussed put forward by Murray as being against Hyper-Calvinism has little to do with the problems of present day critics of Hyper-Calvinism. The whole construction and contents denies such thought. Spurgeon wished merely to emphasise God's love for mankind and the world He had created. So did Gill, Huntington and Hawker.

Furthermore, it is obvious that this passage is not quoted by Murray so that we might be addressed and edified as Spurgeon's hearers undoubtedly were. It is used as a hammer to knock in a nail of Murray's own forging. Nor can we imagine that Spurgeon expected posterity to weigh every one of his words on a goldsmith's scales. To use quotes from Spurgeon as a touch-stone to test Hypers is a preposterous endeavour and demands more of the text than it can possibly give. Such attempts would have us believe that Spurgeon's words have a theological, exegetical and text-critical level for which they never intended. They certainly cannot be used as the best comprehensive analysis of the dangers of Hyper-Calvinism. This is no fault of Spurgeon's, the fault lies entirely with Murray and with yourselves. Spurgeon's gospel sermon will stand when your misuse of it falls.

Murray sees John Gill as the Proto-Hyper, though he was obviously nothing of the kind. Not only do Gill's works speak for him, so does a massive amount of contemporary witness. It would seem that Murray chose the passage because it refers playfully to the follies of 'a doctor', whom he nevertheless views as 'very able'. Could it be that Murray takes this to be Dr John Gill? Evidence in Murray's book points to this. Spurgeon, however, always called Gill by his name and title or used the epithets 'good' or 'eminent' or even 'glorious' with the definite article. He never thought of Gill in terms of 'some doctor or another', no matter how able. I have read all that Spurgeon clearly says about Gill, including Murray's quotes in his works but cannot ever find Spurgeon referring to his predecessor as 'a doctor' but as the doctor. Rather this is a name which Spurgeon gave to not only academics but clergymen in general. This was the custom of the day. Spurgeon also gave Gill's sermons three stars, which was his way of saying 'the very best' and used words such as 'precious' and 'ever green' to describe them and says of those who are not moved by his sermons that they are 'incapable of elevated feelings'. He bemoans the fact that his contemporaries have been so prejudiced by Arminians that they have no eyes for Gill's beauties.

It is depressing indeed to see how Murray, over the years, has worked himself into an increased criticism of Gill at Spurgeon's expense. I have watched this developments since around 1959. Note that in 1962 Murray enthusiastically presents Spurgeon as the loving pupil and successor of a 'glorious' Gill with no shade of criticism. Four years later, we find Murray casting doubt on Spurgeon's allegiance to Gill, without new evidence being forthcoming. The doubt concerning Gill was obvious in Murray's eyes, not in Spurgeon's. Now, with the introduction of Murray's controversy, we have the 1995 Banner of Truth article followed by Murray's work on Spurgeon as a weapon against Hyper-Calvinism and though, Murray still has to affirm that Spurgeon loved Gill, he makes it quite obvious that he, himself, has no love for the man and obviously bends Spurgeon's arm to make him agree. Again, Murray brings no further evidence to back up his case but must revert to historical juggling as referred to in my Focus article. If you look at what Spurgeon actually says about Hypers, you will find that he uses the term to describe those who reject theological and exegetical works, i.e. he is talking about those who are the opposite to Gill and Co.! He points out, however, that even they cannot do without such works completely and they must look into Gill's 'invaluable' commentaries 'on the sly' and if they do so, even these perverters of the truth 'will not go far wrong'. In other words, he sees Gill as helping to curb Hyper-Calvinism, not spread it!

But back to the text under discussion and to evidence of Gill being the butt of Spurgeon's criticism. It is furthermore unlikely that Gill is referred to by Spurgeon because, if we look at Spurgeon's sermon, in his introduction, he makes much of the different interpretations of 'all', criticising 'a doctor's' laborious explanations about what the word means before expounding a text containing the word. Although such an introduction is obviously necessary, given the different applications of 'all', in Gill's preaching on the same text, there is no such introduction. To extend the meaning of 'all' savingly to every single person in history and relate this to God's will (to save), is a risky business indeed, especially in the Pastoral Epistles and can only be argued on the basis of speculation. 2 Thessalonians 2:11, 12 must serve as a warning here. If the Banner had to reject all their authors who believe that 'all' has a different reference in different contexts, they would soon have to declare themselves bankrupt. Again, I shall not mention particular names through fear that the Banner will indeed put them on their index.

You will find that Gill sticks closer to the text than Spurgeon who has Matthew Henry against him in his 'asides' and diversions at times. I mention Henry on second thought as no one, we hope, will call him a Hyper. But I have seen strange things!

Gill and Spurgeon on 1 Timothy 2:3, 4

If we look at Gill's and Spurgeon's exegesis of 1 Timothy 2:3, 4, we see at once that they thwart any comparison. Spurgeon is speaking informally, teasingly, chattily and in a most friendly way, obviously because this was most suited to his hearers. Gill is expounding closely, meticulously, scientifically and in the wider context. To compare the two methods and the different aims of these men and use the criteria of one as a yardstick for the criteria of the other would be like using a piece of entertaining, though uplifting, poetry as a standard for news broadcasts. What would be the point?

In his sermon, Spurgeon emphasises that he is not wishing to stir up controversy but he is dealing with a side of the gospel which he feels is neglected. This is a legitimate stand. He is now being used, however, by Murray to thwart his own wishes. He is being misused as a controversial figure. Nevertheless, we notice that Gill does not qualify, excuse and fill out his exegesis in this way but gets down to the text at once. There is no 'beating about the bush'. His people were already interested in the subject. Gill's hearers were a very well-schooled congregation. From 1719 on to 1771, Gill dealt out deep theology. Perhaps he was more a teacher than a preacher but he was amazingly well-equipped didactically and what he said went home. Spurgeon had the difficult business of gaining the interest of his hearers before preaching to them. This is the only explanation I can find as to why at least half of the passage you give against Gill are not taken up with direct exegesis whereas Gill's handling of the text is.

Next we notice that Spurgeon does not centre his text in the context as Gill does. Again this is legitimate in certain kinds of evangelical preaching but it cannot be then used as a standard for establishing the meaning of a text. Here Gill is more careful. Of course, when preaching in an open-air market etc., one cannot give the people 'the whole works' but Gill always came very near to it.

Now Spurgeon adopts a daring and critical stand to the Scriptures, testing what they mean. This often interests preaching to unbelievers but just as often puts believers, who know their Bibles, off. Surprisingly, Spurgeon tells the people that when God wills that someone will be saved, as in this passage, He does not mean this is the divine purpose. Note that Gill does. He takes the text at its face value.

To will is not to wish
In order to justify his statement, Spurgeon says 'will' means 'wish'. This it might do sometimes as perhaps in Galatians 4:20, but it is only a 'perhaps'. Normally speaking the word used here means to choose, to will into being, to intend or to design. Spurgeon's is, therefore, a questionable exposition but he is preparing his hearers to understand that God's will in salvation must be translated into deed, whereas His wish need not. This is superfluous metaphysics, though prompting interesting thought processes. Talking about God's unfulfilled wishes is a red herring and is not in the text. Gill finds the text means what it says and keeps to the meaning of 'will' which he only finds conditional according to the conditions God has set and not according to conditions of response set up by man. Here Henry and our Lutheran evangelical friends keep to the meaning of 'will' as Gill but believe that this will applies to putting everyone in a saveable state. Gill cannot accept this because, like Spurgeon (I quote from Murray's 1962 work) he believes: 'Some persons love the doctrine of universal atonement because they say, "It is so beautiful. It is a lovely idea that Christ should have died for all men; it commends itself", they say, "to the instincts of humanity; there is something in it full of joy and beauty." I admit there is, but beauty may be often associated with falsehood. There is much which I might admire in the theory of universal redemption, but I will just show what the supposition necessarily involves. If Christ on His cross intended to save every man, then He intended to save those who were lost before He died. If the doctrine be true, that He died for all men, then He died for some who were in hell before He came into this world, for doubtless there were even then myriads there who had been cast away because of their sins. Once again, if it was Christ's intention to save all men, how deplorably has He been disappointed, for we have His own testimony that there is a lake which burneth with fire and brimstone, and into that pit of woe have been cast some of the very persons who, according to the theory of universal redemption, were bought with His blood. That seems to me a conception a thousand times more repulsive than any of those consequences which are said to be associated with the Calvinistic and Christian doctrine of special and

particular redemption. To think that my Saviour died for men who were or are in hell, seems a supposition too horrible for me to entertain. To imagine for a moment that He was the Substitute for all the sons of men, and that God, having first punished the Substitute, afterwards punished the sinners themselves, seems to conflict with all my ideas of Divine justice. That Christ should offer an atonement and satisfaction for the sins of all men, and that afterwards some of those very men should be punished for the sins for which Christ had already atoned, appears to me to be the most monstrous iniquity that could ever have been imputed to Saturn, to Janus, to the goddess of the Thugs, or to the most diabolical heathen deities. God forbid that we should ever think thus of Jehovah, the just and wise and good!'

Now Spurgeon, in order to maintain his Calvinistic doctrine that God wills the salvation of the elect, (but he is not willing, for the sake of his general metaphysical speculation, to use the word 'all' to describe this number), gets himself into extraordinary difficulties. He extends his speculation. We cannot blame him, here, as even Witsius and Owen speculated about what would have happened if man had not fallen or Christ had atoned for all. I have thought about it much myself and it has filled me with shame that myself and my fellow men have so fallen from Adam's original state. In the pressure of the moment, however, Spurgeon does not pay enough attention to his expression and grammar in the text and removes the word he is speculating on from its sense content. His speculations have made themselves independent. A mistake Spurgeon rarely made. He now, however, tells his hearers that it is God's 'wish that every man should be saved'.

Is there hope of salvation outside of election in Christ?
Giving the language of the time, and knowing Spurgeon's theology as a whole, it seems that he is merely saying 'Mankind has been given the chance of salvation but lost it at the fall'. Nowadays, however, with the emphasis on man's retained ability to believe which has not been lost by the fall, Spurgeon's words could be interpreted as indicating, 'There is still a chance for the non-elect to be saved and if they do not get themselves saved, it is their own fault. They ought to be saved, according to God's wish'. Condemnation, to them, lies in rejecting

Christ rather than in the Fall, but the Scriptures state clearly that Christ came to save His elect from the consequences of the Fall not from the consequences of not being elected! Even in Spurgeon's days, however, to say that God wishes that man should be saved must have left many puzzled. If God thought that all men should be saved, why did He not save them? Spurgeon raises this question but confuses the answer which lies in God's will by diverting too much and speculating on God's imaginary wish. Gill does not speculate for a moment on what might have been if ... and keeps to the plan of God's will as revealed in Scripture. We may not agree with him, but what is the use salvation-wise in agreeing with Spurgeon that 'God wishes that we should be saved'. If this really were our gospel to all men, surely we are deceiving them if we do not preach an atoning solution which gives man a chance to comply with the conditions, using his own abilities. We would also be taking away man's responsibility for not complying with them if he was not intended to do so. The modern Banner movement get over this problem by following Fuller who maintained that man's responsibility lay in his not following his natural abilities to believe. He is thus damned for rejecting Christ according to his abilities and responsibilities. Spurgeon would not accept that for a moment. He believed that man was responsible for his lost state because of the Fall which left all his abilities to comprehend his spiritual state marred, indeed, lost. He is, however, clearly responsible for this state. This is what Gill, Hervey, Huntington, Hawker, Philpot, Kershaw etc. also believed, i.e. men whom Bannerites claim are Antinomians.[3]

Causing readers to misunderstand Spurgeon

We do find Spurgeon here rather weak exegetically, but this does not warrant Murray to see his weakness as the very strength of his own questionable theological position. The odds are, if it were not for the Banner's new theology, few would misunderstand Spurgeon at all! Thankfully, I read Spurgeon through my own glasses of the blossoming fifties rather than through Murray's glasses of the decadent 90s. Believe me, Spurgeon free makes much better reading than Spurgeon

---

[3] When Fuller was going through a strong Hyper-Calvinistic phase he learnt from Gill what human responsibility really meant. Gill, however meant the responsibility and condemnation of man as man whereas Fuller, following Grotius and the New Divinity, felt that man was not by nature fallen but only fallen in his will. He could therefore believe if he wanted to.

capsulated in Murray's tight system, portrayed with such an exclusive spirit!

Responsibility, ability and will

By the way, Brother Reisinger, you speak of 'responsibility', 'ability' and 'will'. You will find most certainly, that the people you are backing have completely different interpretations of these words to yours. Indeed if you collect their various views of these matters, you will find they are all keenly anti-Gill etc. but differ from one another far greater than they differ from Gill. Bannerites have views on these terms which extend from Baxterism to crass Hyper-Calvinism. Could it be that you confuse Hyper-Calvinism with Fullerism? It was Fuller who maintained that 'If a man is to be held responsible for something, then he must have the ability to do it. On the other hand, if a man does not have the ability to perform it, he cannot be obliged to do it'. Surely this is his main argument in *The Gospel Worthy of All Acceptation*. He will not accept the reformed view that man cannot comprehend his spiritual state because he argues this would mean he could not be held responsible. Reformed teaching has always been that man has been condemned for not carrying out his responsibilities. Fuller also teaches that God demands gospel faith from sinners, though He has made no provision for such for them (*Letter to Philanthropos*). He also argues that the proper gospel is only for believers (ditto). This all smacks of Hyper-Calvinism at its worst to me but the Banner is promoting Fuller as if he were the answer to all our theological problems, including Hyper-Calvinism! I have become a very cautious person as I have been duped by pseudo-reformed men many times. Could I be forgiven for confessing that I see more Hyperism in Bannerism than I have ever seen in Gillism or Huntingtonianism? I also see much Latitudinarianism and not a little Socinianism. It seems that the devil is throwing all he has got at the reformed faith now that the Banner of Truth has been lowered!

Respect for Spurgeon's gospel lowered

When I read Murray's Banner article on the Prince of Preachers and heard immediate comments, I was fearful that the Banner would provoke criticism of Spurgeon as they have unwittingly provoked criticism of other good men, not forgetting Dr Martyn Lloyd-Jones. This would be a back-firing, indeed. Recently, I received an article from a British Reformed magazine that did not so much criticise Murray for using Spurgeon as the soap with which to wash his dirty linen, but instead made an all-out criticism of Spurgeon as if this one-off sermon was typical of him and he accepted Murray's misrepresentation of Spurgeon. As Murray back-projected a modern controversy on Spurgeon, the writer in question, whom I believe belongs to Murray's denomination, back-projected further modern ideas which have arisen as a reaction against the new Bannerism. Though I am much in sympathy with this magazine, I was sad that they had allowed Murray to provoke them in such a way that they worked off their frustration on Spurgeon instead of Murray.

Murray's Second Down-Grade Controversy
Iain Murray will certainly go down in history as the man who instigated the Second Downgrade Controversy. There are, indications, however, that the second controversy is more dangerous than the first as it is within evangelicalism and the Reformed faith and does not attack from the outside.

To start with, it was mainly a British affair which, backed by the Banner of Truth's large financial resources was propagated worldwide. Now extremism in the English-speaking world is being nurtured by Murray and Co. to a degree far more serious than over a hundred years ago. We see this in the present down-grading going on in the Banner of Truth, Foundation Journal and Reformation Today. Five point men, on the whole are now regarded as Hypers and the trend is towards Arminianism, Baxterism and Socinianism in an effort to appear innocent of Hyperism. This is encouraged by the Banner's condemnation of such people as Gill and their modern counterparts and by their rejection of the Biblical doctrine of the Atonement in place of a satisfaction through application, reconciliation through repentance and sincere obedience and election through reception. Erroll Hulse and Robert Oliver must be named as Murray's right and left hands in this 'enterprise'. The result is a rejection of the Old Testament Law as in Wesley's teaching, a rejection of Christ's necessary obedience to the whole Law as per Baxter and a Socinian usage of the Word of God. During the First Downgrade Controversy, there were orthodox men still on both sides. In the Second Downgrade Controversy there are no orthodox men on either side. The Hypers do not really exist but Five Point men are automatically ruled out by their now bad reputation and the other side is ruled out because of its liberal theology. The sides are separating at a hellish speed, or rather orthodoxy is going over to heresy. We are left with an old Tohuwabohu (and a new Babel).

The tragedy here is that Spurgeon relied on Gill to help him through the first Downgrading Controversy. It is in conjunction with this that Spurgeon affirms that he has taken up Gill's mantle and Gill's doctrine. Murray, in ruining Gill's doctrinal and personal reputation is undermining the defence of any opposition which might come up against him. This is very cunning. I find it very evil.

This must suffice for now. I shall await your replies before proceeding further. If I have been unfairly critical or too heated in my argument, please point this out to me. If I have said anything which you feel I could not verify, please inform me. If I have accused anyone wrongly, then please fall on me like a ton of bricks, I will have deserved it!

Bibliography

Anonymous, *The Voice of Years*, A. Maxwell, 1814, reprinted by John Crowter, Coventry, England.

Anselm, *Cur Deus Homo*. Written between 1094-1098.

Aristotle, *Nicomachean Ethics*, Oxford World's Classics, ed, Leslie Brown, 2009, also Public Domain.

Ball, John, *A Treatise of the Covenant of Grace*, 1645, facsimile reprint by Peter and Rachel Reynolds, 2012.

Booth, William, *Glad Tidings to Perishing Sinners or, the Genuine Gospel a Complete Warrant for the Ungodly to Believe in Jesus*, W. Button, Paternoster Row, 1796

Bunyan, John, *Come and Welcome to Jesus Christ*, London, 1681, also Public Domain.

Button, William, *Remarks on a Treatise, entitled The Gospel of Christ Worthy of All Acceptation, Wherein the Nature of Special Faith in Christ is Considered*, J. Buckland, 1785.

Bullinger, Heinrich, *The Decades of Henry Bullinger*, Reformation Heritage Reprint with Introduction by Joel Beeke and George Ella, 2004.

Calvin, John, *Institutes of Christian Religion*, 2 vols, Eerdmans, 1979.

Carey, William, *An Enquiry into the Obligations of Christians to Use Means for the Conversion of the Heathen*, facsimile reprint, the Carey Kingsgate Press Ltd, 1961.

Chandler, Samuel, *The History of Persecution from the Patriarchial Age to the Reign of George II to which are added, The Rev. Dr*

Buchanan's Notices of the present State of the Inquisition at Goa, Hull, 1813.

Chun, Chris, *The Legacy of Jonathan Edwards in the Theology of Andrew Fuller*, Brill, Leiden, 2012.

Cowper, William, *Hatred and Vengeance*, Public Domain.

Crisp, Tobias, *Christ the Only Way*, Christian Bookshop, Ossett, 1995.

Dale, R. W., *The Atonement*, Congregational Union of England and Wales, 1898.

Dalzell, A., *Atonement is Not Reconciliation*, Lucas Collins, 1900.

Denney, James, *The Death of Christ*, Tyndale Press, 1960.

Dillistone, F. W., *The Christian Understanding of Atonement*, James Nisbet, 1968.

Edwards, Jonathan, *A Treatise on Religious Affections*, 1746. Most of Edwards' works are now available free online or in cheap reprints.

Edwards, Jonathan, *An Enquiry into Modern Prevailing Notions of the Freedom of the Will which is Supposed to be Essential to the Moral Agency, Virtue, and Vice, Reward and Punishment, Praise and Blame*, 1754.

Edwards, Jonathan, *Miscellaneous Observations On the Medium of Moral Government*, Edwards' Works, B.O.T., 1979.

Ella, G. M., *A Gospel Unworthy of Any Acceptation*, Focus, No. 8, Winter 1993/94, pp. 4-6.

Ella, G. M., *History of the English Calvinistic Baptists 1771-1892: from John Gill to C. H. Spurgeon*, Robert W. Oliver, Banner of Truth. Review, New Focus

Ella, G. M., *Robert Oliver and the Twists and Turns of Historical Revisionism*, Focus, No. 14, Summer, 1995, pp. 8-11.

Ella, G. M., *The Atonement in Evangelical Thought I-VI*, NF, Vol. 1, No. 01 onwards.

Ella, George M., *The Free Offer and the Call of the Gospel*, Go Publications, 2001.

Ella, George Melvyn, *John Gill and the Cause of God and Truth*, Go Publications, 1995.

Ella, George Melvyn, *John Gill: Justification from Eternity*, Go Publications, 1998.

Ella, George Melvyn, *Law and Gospel in the Theology of Andrew Fuller* (second edit.), Go Publications, 2011.

Ella, George Melvyn, *The Covenant of Grace and Christian Baptism*, VKV/RVB, Bonn, 2007.

Ella, George Melvyn, *The Covenant of Grace and the People of God*, Go Publications, 2019.

Ella, George Melvyn, *William Huntington, Pastor of Providence*, Go Publications, 1994.

Ella, George M., *Common Grace and the Call of the Gospel*, Go Publications, 2004.

Ella, George M., *The History of Christian Evangelism in India: From the First Century A. D. to William Carey (1761-1833): A Revaluation*, Go-Publications, scheduled for 2022.

Forsyth, P. T., *The Work of Christ*, Wipf and Stock Reprint, 1996.

Forsyth, P. T., *The Cruciality of the Cross*, Lightning Source, 2018.

Fuller, Andrew, *The Complete Works of the Rev. Andrew Fuller with a Memoir of his Life by Andrew Gunten Fuller*, 3 vols, Sprinkle Publications 1831 reprint, 1988. Also printed by the B.O.T. in one volume, 2007.

Gill, John, *The Cause of God and Truth*, Baker Bookhouse, 1980.

Gill, John, *Sermons and Tracts*, 3 vols, Primitive Baptist Library, 1981.

Gill, John, *Body of Divinity*, 3 vols, Subscription, 1769.

Goadby, J. J., *Bye-Paths in Baptist History*, Elliot Stock, London, 1871.

Gordon, Bruce and Campi Emidio, *Architect of Reformation: and Introduction to Heinrich Bullinger, 1504-1575*, Baker Academic, 2004.

Grau, Alexander, *Hypermoral: Die neue Lust an der Empörung*, Claudiu Verlag, 2018.

Grotius, Hugo, *de iure belli ac pacis*, 1625, German translation by J. H. V. Kirchmann, Berlin, 1869.

Grotius, Hugo, *opera omnia theologica*, 3 vols, Amsterdam, 1679, Faksimile-Neudruck, Friedrich Frommann Verlag, 1972.

Grotius, Hugo, *The Truth of the Christian Religion in Six Books*, translated by John Clarke, Le Clerk edition, James and John Knapton, 1729.

Grotius, Hugo, *Defensio Fidei Catholicae de Satisfactione Christi*, 1617.

Haykin, Michael, *Armies of the Lamb: The Spirituality of Andrew Fuller*, Sola Scriptura, 2002.

Haykin, Michael, *Andrew Fuller and the Promise of the Spirit*, B.O.T. Magazine, Issue 278, p. 1 ff.

Haykin, Michael, *Andrew Fuller, Life and Legacy*, B.O.T. Magazine, Issue 533, p. 22 ff.

Haykin, Michael, *One Heart and One Soul*, Evangelical Press, 1995.

Haykin, Michael, *The Early Life of Andrew Fuller*, Reformation Today, November, 1995.

Headlam, Arthur C., *The Atonement*, Hodder and Stoughton, 1935.

Hervey, James, *The Works of the Rev. James Hervey*, Thomas Nelson, 1837.

Hodges, H. A., *The Pattern of the Atonement*, SCM Press, 1957.

Jones, J. A., *A Sketch of the Rise and Progress of Fullerism, or Duty Faith, That Gangrene now rapidly Spreading in Many Baptist Churches*, Earthen Vessel, 1861.

Kirkby, A. H., *Andrew Fuller: Evangelical Calvinism*, Baptist Quarterly, XV, 1954, pp. 111-112.

Kirkby, A. H., *The Theology of Andrew Fuller and its relation to Calvinism*, Ph,D, Edinburgh, 1956.

Kuiper, E.J., *Hugo de Groot en de Remonstranten*, Nederlands Theologisch Tijdschrift, 38 (2), 1984, pp. 111-125,.

MacGregor, James, *The Free Offer in the Westminster Confession*, Banner of Truth Magazine, 82, 83, 1970, pp. 51-58.

Morris, Leon, *The Apostolic Preaching of the Cross*, Eerdmans, 1965.

Murray, Iain, *John Gill and C. H. Spurgeon*, Banner of Truth Magazine, November, 1995.

Murray, Iain, *Spurgeon v. Hyper-Calvinism*: The Battle for Gospel Preaching, Banner of Truth, 2001.

Murray, John; *The Free Offer of the Gospel*, Banner of Truth, 2001.

Nettles, Thomas J., *Andrew Fuller and Free Grace*, Reformation Today, January, 1984, pp. 6-14.

Nettles, Thomas J., *By His Grace and For His Glory*, Baker Book House, 1990.

Nettles, Thomas J., *Teaching Truth, Training Hearts*, Calvary Press Publishing, 1998.

Nettles, Thomas J., *Why Andrew Fuller?*, Reformation Today, January, 1984, pp. 1984.

Nuttall, G. F., *Northamptonshire and the Modern Question*, Journal of Theological Studies, NS, XVI, 1965, pp. 101-23.

Oliver, R. W., *Historical Survey of English Hyper-Calvinism*, Foundations (Engl), 7, 1981, pp. 8-18

Oliver, R. W., *Significance of Strict Baptists Attitudes to Duty-Faith*, SBHSB, 20, 1993, pp. 3-26

Parker, T. H. L., *Calvin's Doctrine of Justification*, Evangelical Quarterly, , XXIV, 1952

Peski, A. M. van, *Waarom Grotius als Oecumenisch Theoloog Mislukken Moest*, NTT, 38 (4), 1984, pp. 290-297

Pink, Arthur, *An Exposition of Hebrews*, 3 vols, Grace E-Books. Com, Public Domain.

Pink, Arthur, *The Satisfaction of Christ: Studies in Atonement*, Amazon Books, 2001.

Pink, Arthur, *Studies in the Scriptures*, 17 vols, 1922 onwards.

Remensnyder, Junius Benjamin, *The Atonement and Modern Thought with an Introduction by B.B. Warfield*, Lutheran Publishing Society, 1905.

Roberts, Maurice, *The Free Offer of the Gospel*, Banner of Truth, Issue 503, 4, 2005, pp. 39-46.

Rushton, William, *A Defence of Particular Redemption Wherein the Doctrine of Andrew Fuller Relative to the Atonement of Christ is Tried by the Word of God*, Liverpool 1831, reprinted in 2007 by Go Publications with an Introduction by G. M. Ella.

Ryland, John, *The Work of Faith, the Labour of Love, and the Patience of Hope, illustrated in the Life and Death of the Rev. Andrew Fuller, Late Pastor of the Baptist Church at Kettering and Secretary to the Baptist Missionary Society from its Commencement in 1792*, Button & Son, 1818.

Sant, Henry; Ella George M., *William Huntington: The Sinner Saved*, undated, Focus Christian Ministries Trust, (Essays published courtesy of the Bible League Quarterly).

Sant, Henry, *William Huntington: Pastor of Providence*, Review Article, Focus, No. 14, Summer, 1995, pp. 15-16.

Sell, Alan, *The Great Debate: Calvinism, Arminianism and Salvation*, H. E. Walter Ltd., 1982.

Sheehan, Robert J., *The Presentation of the Gospel Amongst Hyper-Calvinists: A Critique, (Part One)*. Foundations (Engl), 8, 1982, pp. 28-39

Sheehan, Robert J., *The Presentation of the Gospel amongst Hyper-Calvinists: A Critique, (Part Two)*. Foundations (Engl.), 9, 1982, pp. 42-46

Smith, C. Ryder, *The Bible Doctrine of the Atonement*, Epworth Press, 1941.

Stanley, Brian C. H., *C. H. Spurgeon and the Baptist Missionary Society*, BQ, 29 (7), 1982, pp. 319-328

Stevens, John, *Help for the True Disciples of Immanuel: being and Answer to a Book Published by the Late Rev. Andrew Fuller, entitled The Gospel Worthy of All Acceptation, or the Duty of Sinners to Believe in Christ*, Simkin and Marshall, London, 1841.

Stevens, John, *The Pleasure of God in the Salvation of His People*, Simkin and Marshall, 3rd edit., 1844.

Stevens, John, *Thoughts on God in the Salvation of His People*, Simkin and Marshall, London, 1844.

Stevens, John, *Thoughts on Sanctification and a Glance at Strict Communion*, Sherwood, Neely, and Jones, 1816.

Sunkler, Bengt, *Missionens värld, Svenska Bokverlaget*, Stockholm, 1963.

Tyndale, William, *A Pathway into the Holy Scriptures*, 1530.

Van Valen, L. J., *Van kolendrager tot predikant: Het Leven van William Huntington*, Den Hertog, 1996.

Venema, Cornelis P., *Heinrich Bullinger and the Doctrine of Predestination*, Baker Academic, 2002.

Warfield, Benjamin, *Modern Theories of the Atonement*, 1902.

Warfield, Benjamin, *Jonathan Edwards and the New England Theology*, 1912.

Whitfield, George, *What Think ye of Christ*, sermon Public Domain.

Williams, H. L., and North, J. E. (eds), *Calvin v. Hyper-Spurgeonism: The Battle for the Preaching of the One Scriptural and Reformation Gospel*, Berith Publications, 1997.

Wright, George, *Fullerism*, Gospel Magazine, Vol. XII, 1877, p. 343.

Wright, Thomas, *The Life of William Huntington*, Farncombe & Son, 1909.

Young, Doyle L., *Andrew Fuller and the Modern Missionary Movement*, Baptist History and Heritage, 17 (4), 1982, pp. 17-27
Zaspel, Fred G., *Divine Law: A New Covenant Perspective*, Word of Life Baptist Church, 1997.
Zaspel, Fred G., *New Covenant Theology and the Mosaic Law*, World of Life Baptist Church, 1994.
Zaspel, Fred. C., *The Theology of Fulfillment*, Interdisciplinary Biblical Research Institute, 1993.
Zwaag K., *Afwachten of verwachten' De toe-eigningdes heils in historisch en theologisch perspectief*, Uitgeverij Groen, 2003.

Index of Scriptural Passages

Old Testament

New Testament

Index of Names, Places and Institutions

Hezekiah	138, 233
Hindu	21, 23
Hodges, H. A.	157
Holy Spirit	15, 17, 28, 32, 88, 105-107, 129, 134, 154, 158, 161-163, 191, 209, 240, 243
Hopkins, Samuel	40, 57, 61, 83, 85
Hull University	210
Huntington, William	50, 63, 64, 64fn., 71, 89-93, 95-116, 105fn., 111fn., 112fn., 157-162, 159fn., 161fn., 250, 251, 262, 263
Hyper-Calvinism	26, 51fn., 61-63, 70, 93, 96, 104fn., 151, 159, 218, 230fn., 247, 249, 250, 251, 254-258, 262fn., 263
Imputed righteousness	90, 92, 99, 105fn., 106, 107, 124, 160, 247
Imputed sin	124
Jebusites	138
Jews	37, 43, 64, 65, 75, 76, 100, 138, 139, 143-146, 166, 182, 192-195, 208, 212, 213, 219
Jezebel	65, 74
John the Baptist	185, 187, 191, 193
Jones, J. A.	40, 55
Kiel	16
Kirkby, Arthur	231, 232fn.
Lamb's Book of Life	236
Lambert, Francois	62
Latitudinarians	25, 38, 39, 53, 108, 250, 263
Lefevre, Jacques	62
Lessing, Gotthold Ephraim	57fn.
Lewis, C. S.	59
Lollards	167
London Baptist College	27
London Missionary Society	20
MacLeod, Donald	108fn., 157, 164